Battlegroun

COCKLESHELL RAID

C000196760

JON WILKINSON

Battleground series:

Stamford Bridge & Hastings by Peter Marren
Wars of the Roses - Wakefield / Towton by Philip A. Haigh
Wars of the Roses - **Barnet** by David Clark
Wars of the Roses - **Tewkesbury** by Steven Goodchild
Wars of the Roses - **The Battles of St Albans** by
Peter Burley, Michael Elliott & Harvey Wilson
English Civil War - **Naseby** by Martin Marix Evans, Peter Burton
and Michael Westaway
English Civil War - **Marston Moor** by David Clark
War of the Spanish Succession - **Blenheim 1704** by James Falkner
War of the Spanish Succession - **Ramillies 1706** by James Falkner
Napoleonic - **Hougoumont** by Julian Paget and Derek Saunders
Napoleonic - **Waterloo** by Andrew Uffindell and Michael Corum
Zulu War - **Isandlwana** by Ian Knight and Ian Castle
Zulu War - **Rorkes Drift** by Ian Knight and Ian Castle
Boer War - **The Relief of Ladysmith** by Lewis Childs
Boer War - **The Siege of Ladysmith** by Lewis Childs
Boer War - **Kimberley** by Lewis Childs

Mons by Jack Horsfall and Nigel Cave
Néry by Patrick Tackle
Le Cateau by Nigel Cave and Jack Shelden
Walking the Salient by Paul Reed
Ypres - Sanctuary Wood and Hooge by Nigel Cave
Ypres - Hill 60 by Nigel Cave
Ypres - Messines Ridge by Peter Oldham
Ypres - Polygon Wood by Nigel Cave
Ypres - Passchendaele by Nigel Cave
Ypres - Airfields and Airmen by Mike O'Connor
Ypres - St Julien by Graham Keech
Ypres - Boesinghe by Stephen McGreal
Walking the Somme by Paul Reed
Somme - Gommecourt by Nigel Cave
Somme - Serre by Jack Horsfall & Nigel Cave
Somme - Beaumont Hamel by Nigel Cave
Somme - Thiepval by Michael Stedman
Somme - La Boiselle by Michael Stedman
Somme - Fricourt by Michael Stedman
Somme - Carnoy-Montauban by Graham Maddocks
Somme - Pozières by Graham Keech
Somme - Courcelette by Paul Reed
Somme - Boom Ravine by Trevor Pidgeon
Somme - Mametz Wood by Michael Renshaw
Somme - Delville Wood by Nigel Cave
Somme - Advance to Victory (North) 1918 by Michael Stedman
Somme - Flers by Trevor Pidgeon
Somme - Bazentin Ridge by Edward Hancock
Somme - Combles by Paul Reed
Somme - Beaucourt by Michael Renshaw
Somme - Redan Ridge by Michael Renshaw
Somme - Hamel by Peter Pedersen
Somme - Villers-Bretonneux by Peter Pedersen
Somme - Airfields and Airmen by Mike O'Connor
Airfields and Airmen of the Channel Coast by Mike O'Connor
In the Footsteps of the Red Baron by Mike O'Connor
Arras - Airfields and Airmen by Mike O'Connor
Arras - The Battle for Vimy Ridge by Jack Sheldon & Nigel Cave
Arras - Vimy Ridge by Nigel Cave
Arras - Gavrelle by Trevor Tasker and Kyle Tallett
Arras - Oppy Wood by David Bilton
Arras - Bullecourt by Graham Keech
Arras - Monchy le Preux by Colin Fox
Walking Arras by Paul Reed
Hindenburg Line by Peter Oldham
Hindenburg Line - Epehy by Bill Mitchinson
Hindenburg Line - Riqueval by Bill Mitchinson
Hindenburg Line - Villers-Plouich by Bill Mitchinson
Hindenburg Line - Cambrai Right Hook by Jack Horsfall & Nigel Cave
Hindenburg Line - Cambrai Flesquières by Jack Horsfall & Nigel Cave
Hindenburg Line - Saint Quentin by Helen McPhail and Philip Guest
Hindenburg Line - Bourlon Wood by Jack Horsfall & Nigel Cave
Cambrai - Airfields and Airmen by Mike O'Connor
Aubers Ridge by Edward Hancock

La Bassée - Neuve Chapelle by Geoffrey Bridger
Loos - Hohenzollern Redoubt by Andrew Rawson
Loos - Hill 70 by Andrew Rawson
Fromelles by Peter Pedersen
The Battle of the Lys 1918 by Phil Tomaselli
Accrington Pals Trail by William Turner
Poets at War: Wilfred Owen by Helen McPhail and Philip Guest
Poets at War: Edmund Blunden by Helen McPhail and Philip Guest
Poets at War: Graves & Sassoon by Helen McPhail and Philip Guest
Gallipoli by Nigel Steel
Gallipoli - Gully Ravine by Stephen Chambers
Gallipoli - Anzac Landing by Stephen Chambers
Gallipoli - Suvla August Offensive by Stephen Chambers
Gallipoli - Landings at Helles by Huw & Jill Rodge
Walking the Italian Front by Francis Mackay
Italy - Asiago by Francis Mackay
Verdun: Fort Douamont by Christina Holstein
Verdun: Fort Vaux by Christina Holstein
Walking Verdun by Christina Holstein
Zeebrugge & Ostend Raids 1918 by Stephen McGreal

Germans at Beaumont Hamel by Jack Sheldon
Germans at Thiepval by Jack Sheldon

SECOND WORLD WAR

Dunkirk by Patrick Wilson
Calais by Jon Cooksey
Boulogne by Jon Cooksey
Saint-Nazaire by James Dorrian
Walking D-Day by Paul Reed
Atlantic Wall - Pas de Calais by Paul Williams
Atlantic Wall - Normandy by Paul Williams
Normandy - Pegasus Bridge by Carl Shilleto
Normandy - Merville Battery by Carl Shilleto
Normandy - Utah Beach by Carl Shilleto
Normandy - Omaha Beach by Tim Kilvert-Jones
Normandy - Gold Beach by Christopher Dunphie & Garry Johnson
Normandy - Gold Beach Jig by Tim Saunders
Normandy - Juno Beach by Tim Saunders
Normandy - Sword Beach by Tim Kilvert-Jones
Normandy - Operation Bluecoat by Ian Daglish
Normandy - Operation Goodwood by Ian Daglish
Normandy - Epsom by Tim Saunders
Normandy - Hill 112 by Tim Saunders
Normandy - Mont Pinçon by Eric Hunt
Normandy - Cherbourg by Andrew Rawson
Normandy - Commandos & Rangers on D-Day by Tim Saunders
Das Reich – Drive to Normandy by Philip Vickers
Oradour by Philip Beck
Market Garden - Nijmegen by Tim Saunders
Market Garden - Hell's Highway by Tim Saunders
Market Garden - Arnhem, Oosterbeek by Frank Steer
Market Garden - Arnhem, The Bridge by Frank Steer
Market Garden - The Island by Tim Saunders
Rhine Crossing – US 9th Army & 17th US Airborne by Andrew Rawson
British Rhine Crossing – Operation Varsity by Tim Saunders
British Rhine Crossing – Operation Plunder by Tim Saunders
Battle of the Bulge – St Vith by Michael Tolhurst
Battle of the Bulge – Bastogne by Michael Tolhurst
Channel Islands by George Forty
Walcheren by Andrew Rawson
Remagen Bridge by Andrew Rawson
Cassino by Ian Blackwell
Anzio by Ian Blackwell
Dieppe by Tim Saunders
Fort Eben Emael by Tim Saunders
Crete – The Airborne Invasion by Tim Saunders
Malta by Paul Williams
Bruneval Raid by Paul Oldfield
Cockleshell Raid by Paul Oldfield

Battleground Europe

COCKLESHELL RAID

PAUL OLDFIELD

Pen & Sword
MILITARY

First published in Great Britain in 2012 by
Pen & Sword Military
an imprint of
Pen & Sword Books Ltd
47 Church Street
Barnsley
South Yorkshire
S70 2AS
Copyright © Paul Oldfield 2012
ISBN 9781781592557

The right of Paul Oldfield to be identified as Author of this
Work has been asserted by him in accordance with the
Copyright, Designs and Patents Act 1988.
A CIP catalogue record for this book is available from the
British Library

Typeset in 10 pt Palatino by
Factionpress
Printed and bound by
CPI Group (UK) Ltd., Croydon, CR0 4YY

Pen & Sword Books Ltd incorporates the Imprints of Pen &
Sword Aviation, Pen & Sword Maritime, Pen & Sword Military,
Wharncliffe Local History, Pen and Sword Select, Pen and
Sword Military Classics, Leo Cooper, Remember When,
Seaforth Publishing and Frontline Publishing.
For a complete list of Pen & Sword titles please contact
PEN & SWORD BOOKS LIMITED
47 Church Street, Barnsley, South Yorkshire, S70 2AS, England
E-mail: enquiries@pen-and-sword.co.uk
Website: www.pen-and-sword.co.uk

CONTENTS

Introduction

OPERATION 'FRANKTON' is a story of how a handful of determined and resourceful men achieved what thousands could not by conventional means. They were not supermen. In the main they had enlisted for 'Hostilities Only' and, except for their leader, none had been in a canoe before. However, with a few months training they carried out what one German officer described as, 'the outstanding commando raid of the war'.

They became known as the 'Cockleshell Heroes', having been immortalised in a film and a book of that name in the 1950s. It was a soubriquet their leader, Major 'Blondie' Haslar, hated, but it has stuck, as heroes they certainly were. They did not fight a battle in the traditional sense, indeed they did everything possible to avoid contact with the enemy. Despite this they demonstrated the very highest standards of courage, endurance and skill.

'Blondie' Haslar was an extraordinary man, who combined modesty and a caring attitude with strong personality and single-minded professionalism. He always had the interests of his men at heart and never let them down. In return they trusted him totally and would have followed him to the ends of the earth.

This book covers the whole of the 'Frankton' story including the development of the Royal Marines Boom Patrol Detachment, the planning and preparation for the raid, its aftermath and an account of the horrific war crimes inflicted on those who were captured. It also includes the epic escape by Haslar and Corporal Bill Sparks across occupied France into Spain. The modern Special Boat Service traces its origins back to the Royal Marines Boom Patrol Detachment is very proud of its predecessors' achievements.

The outcome of the raid was never going to affect the course of the war, but it was another nail in the coffin of the Axis blockade-runners to the Far East. It demonstrated what a small group of resolute canoeists could achieve. It also added to the other pinprick raids, each of limited significance, but collectively causing the Germans to retain masses of troops in occupied Europe that could have been used on the fighting fronts. When viewed through that prism, Haslar's team achieved a huge amount. In the harsh profit and loss account of war, for the cost of a few men they added considerably to the British cause and sent shivers through the entire Axis high command.

Numerous sources were consulted and there is a list at the end, which readers may find useful for further study, but this book does cover the events reasonably comprehensively. The 'Frankton' and other related files in the National Archives were particularly valuable. I would also commend Quentin Rees' various books for their meticulous research.

Paul Oldfield, *Wiltshire, January 2012*

Chapter One

DEVELOPMENT OF STEALTHY ATTACK TECHNIQUES ON SHIPPING

FROM THE EARLY DAYS of the war, Major 'Blondie' Haslar advocated using canoes to penetrate enemy harbours. The Admiralty regarded his idea as impracticable and even stated that the equipment did not exist, which annoyed Haslar as it patently did. His attempt to interest HQ Combined Operations in the spring of 1941 also failed, due in part to the existence of the canoe equipped Special Boat Sections within the Commandos.

As the First World War drew to a close on 1 November 1918, Italians Raffaele Paolucci and Raffaele Rossetti rode a torpedo into Pula harbour (now in northern Croatia) and sank the Austro-Hungarian battleship SMS *Viribus Unitis* and a freighter, using magnetic Limpet mines. In 1939, the Italians resurrected the concept. By 1941, Commander Vittorio Moccagatta had organised the unit into *Decima Flottiglia Mezzi d'Assalto* (10th Assault Vehicle Flotilla or 10th MAS). It operated fast explosive motorboats (EMB)

Major Herbert George 'Blondie' Haslar had a lifetime interest in small boats, designing and building his own canoes and yachts. In May 1940 he commanded two landing craft at Narvik and was awarded the OBE and Croix de Guerre for landing French troops and getting the wounded off a burning vessel before it blew up. He had an incredibly inventive mind, designing a floating boom, self steering gear for yachts, roller reefing sails and the windsurfer all well ahead of their time. He initiated the east to west single-handed Trans Atlantic yacht race in 1960 and set up the Round Britain Race in 1966. He was also a playwright, artist, farmer and writer.

and manned torpedoes as well as using assault swimmers.

On 25 March 1941, 10th MAS sank or severely damaged the cruiser HMS *York*, two tankers and a cargo ship at Suda Bay in Crete. The Italians had a base in the interned tanker *Olterra* which was moored at Algeciras, southern

The badge of *Decima Flottiglia Mezzi d'Assalto* **(10th MAS or Assault Vehicle Flotilla).**

SMS *Viribus Unitis* sinking in Pula harbour. She was commissioned on 5 December 1912, the first Austro-Hungarian dreadnought battleship.

Above: Raffaele Paolucci.

Left: Raffaele Rossetti.

Commander Vittorio Moccagatt

HMS *York* serious damaged at Suda Bay in 1941.

Italian manned torpedo, known officially as the Low Speed Torpedo, but mor commonly to its crews as Maiale (pig).

Olterra at Algeciras. A hatch in the hull allowed 10th MAS to commence its attacks against Gibraltar unseen.

Spain, from which they conducted operations against Gibraltar, including one on 10 September in which three ships were sunk. On 19 December, Lieutenant Luigi Durand de la Penne led an attack on Alexandria harbour resulting in the battleships HMS *Valiant* and *Queen Elizabeth* and a tanker being sunk and the destroyer HMS *Jervis* being damaged. In total 10th MAS sank or damaged five warships and 20 merchantmen during the war. However, there were also setbacks; on 26 July 1941 an attack on Valetta in Malta failed. Fifteen crewmen were killed, including Vittorio Moccagatta, and 18 captured.

Churchill agitated for a similar capability and on 26 January 1942, Hasler was posted to the Combined

Lieutenant Luigi Durand de la Penne.

HMS *Valiant*.

HMS *Queen Elizabeth*.

Valetta harbour, Malta.

Operations Development Centre (CODC) in Portsmouth, commanded by Captain TA Hussey RN. He was to study and develop all methods of attacking enemy ships in harbour by stealth. Several Italian EMBs were captured at Valetta and one was brought to the Royal Navy's torpedo school, HMS *Vernon*, at Gosport. Haslar inspected it on his first day with CODC, along with Hussey and Commander Peter Du Cane. Vospers began working on a British design, which for security purposes was designated 'Boom Patrol Boat' (BPB), ostensibly to patrol the boom

Commander Peter Du Cane, Managing Director of Vosper's and a member of Combined Operations' scientific staff. He designed high-speed boats, including *Bluebird K4*, the world speed record holder in 1939. He started the war as a Fleet Air Arm pilot.

HMS *Vernon* in the 1930s.

across the eastern entrance to the Solent.

Haslar threw himself into the project and within a day had written draft Terms of Reference and a plan for how to meet them. Next day he and Hussey went to London to meet the Chief of Combined Operations (CCO), Commodore Louis Mountbatten. Haslar was tasked to concentrate upon the development of an EMB and how to use it to attack ships in harbour. He wasted no time and on 31 January saw Rear Admiral Horan, Landing Craft and Bases, and Special Operations Executive (SOE) officers to discuss matters of mutual interest.

The Italian EMB was aimed at a target and the pilot then ejected himself backwards. In the water he boarded a small raft to avoid the underwater concussion of the charge exploding. He then had no option other than to give himself up. Haslar wanted to be able to get away and his idea was to use EMBs and canoes together – the former to press home the attack and the latter to find paths through surface obstacles and recover the pilot.

A new device was also developed, the Chariot, a British version of the Italian human torpedo, with two operators sitting astride the hull. The problem was how to get close enough to the target to attack, as the Chariot had very limited range. Air delivery was considered with the crew strapped to it and Haslar attended numerous parachute trials, but it wasn't until later in the war that Lieutenant David Cox carried out a live drop off Harwich – it was not for the faint hearted and he was awarded the MBE.

Despite having to concentrate on the BPB, Haslar pursued other developments. On 6 February he met with Commander

Mountbatten replaced Admiral of the Fleet Sir Roger Keyes as head of Combined Operations on 27 October 1941. Churchill instructed him to, 'Mount a programme of raids of ever increasing intensity with the invasion of France the main object'. By 18 March 1942 he had been promoted to Acting Vice Admiral, had a seat on the Chiefs of Staff Committee and could order resources controlled by Churchill as Minister of Defence. He was later Supreme Allied Commander South East Asia, the last Viceroy of India and its first Governor-General following independence. He was First Sea Lord 1954-59, followed by six years as Chief of the Defence Staff, during which he consolidated the single services into the Ministry of Defence. He was murdered by Irish republican terrorists in 1979.

Cromwell-Varley DSO, who had designed a diving suit and was also involved with the X-Craft midget submarines first launched in March 1942. Haslar worked with the Avro company to see if a BPB could be loaded into a Lancaster bomb bay and conducted tests to see how high it could be released onto water without breaking up. He was involved in a number of meetings about

the Rotachute, a parachute using free spinning rotor blades like an autogyro; an RAF officer brave enough to try it needed two hands to hold a glass afterwards.

On 10 February, Haslar met SOE officers for a second time and this meeting may have sparked the idea that led to the Motorised Submersible Canoe (MSC), known as the 'Sleeping Beauty'. This was a battery powered, single seat, submersible canoe with alternative paddle and sail propulsion. It weighed 280 kgs unladen, could dive to 15m and operate up to 64 kms

The British Chariot, based on the Italian Maiale.

at three knots. Haslar was proud of it, but admitted it was, 'the most dangerous vessel in which I ever ventured to sea'.

The staff requirement for the BPB was ready on 16 February and from then on Haslar had a close relationship with Vospers. However, without a means of delivering it close to the target it was useless. Delivering it by air was not possible in the foreseeable future and it would not fit into a submarine, all of which added weight to his view that canoes were the answer.

Rotachute.

Despite some limitations, canoes were small, silent and light. Other units, particularly in the Middle East, had used them offensively and Haslar sought out their commanders to see what he could learn. He met Lieutenant Commander Nigel Clogstoun Willmott (who formed Combined Operations Pilotage Parties (COPP) to

The Motorised Submersible Canoe or 'Sleeping Beauty'. 'A most dangerous vessel.'

Major Roger James Allen Courtney was the first to use two-man canoes. 'Jumbo' had been a gold prospector, big-game hunter in East Africa, sergeant in the Palestine Police and had paddled the length of the Nile and Danube. In July 1940 he proposed a canoe-borne raiding and reconnaissance force. To prove his point he boarded a ship undetected in the Clyde at night, stole a gun cover and presented it to the ship's captain still dripping at a conference ashore. As a result he recruited 11 men for the Folbot Troop attached to No.8 Commando at Arran. This was the beginning of the Special Boat Sections (SBS) of the Commandos. No.1 Section went to the Middle East in February 1941 and during the year carried out 15 submarine-launched missions. Courtney came home to set up No.2 SBS and the original No.1 SBS was absorbed into 1st Special Air Service Regiment in September 1942.

Early in 1941, Lieutenant Commander Herbert Nigel Clogstoun Willmott DSO DSC and Major Roger Courtney MC canoed off the coast of Rhodes and took it in turns to swim ashore and survey beaches for a proposed Commando landing. Clogstoun-Willmott raised teams for beach reconnaissance and assault force navigation, which became the COPPs. They played significant roles in the landings on Sicily and at Anzio. From summer 1943 they prepared for Normandy. On 6 June 1944, COPPs 1 and 9 marked the landing limits from X-Craft, while COPP 6 used assault boats to pilot the leading DD tanks onto the beaches. COPPs also operated in the Far East and assisted in the crossing of the Rhine and Elbe in Germany in 1945. After the war the functions transferred to RMBPD.

Captain Gerald Charles Stokes 'Monty' Montanaro, from a Maltese military family, was commissioned into the Royal Engineers. From 1940 he commanded 101 Special Canoe Troop in No.6 Commando. This was absorbed into No.2 SBS when it formed on 1 March 1942. Later in 1942 he received a special commission as a Lieutenant Commander in the Royal Navy for duty on submarines. He returned to the Army in 1945, serving in Hong Kong, Korea, Germany and Aden, retiring as a Brigadier in 1965. He went on to have a successful civilian career with Reed Paper Group, Reed Development Services, Reed Transport, Norton Villiers and Dolphin Construction in Malta.

conduct pre-invasion beach reconnaissance, Major Roger Courtney of the Folbot Troop in No.8 Commando and Captain Gerald Montanaro commanding 101 (Folbot) Troop in No.6 Commando.

The German designed Folbot.

In general they had used German designed Folbots with a rubberized skin stretched over a wooden frame. They could be dismantled into a couple of large kitbags, but there were limitations. Assembly took 30 minutes and they could not be dragged over a beach without the skin puncturing. They were not rigid enough to be lifted or slung when fully laden and could not be passed through a submarine torpedo hatch without being partly dismantled.

Haslar examined every other type of canoe available, but none had the characteristics he needed. He learned most from Gerald Montanaro, who combined an adventurous spirit with a technical mind. His group had mastered the Folbot in challenging Scottish waters, lying up by day and moving at night. They also developed a number of techniques of interest to Haslar, such as navigation in a canoe and camouflage. They attached Limpet mines below the water line using long placing rods and had magnetic holdfasts to keep their canoes in position alongside the target.

Montanaro's unit visited Portsmouth early in 1942 and Haslar visited it in Dover on 31 March, where he watched a Limpet attack demonstration as well as spending a few hours exercising with the Folbot in the dark. On the night of 11/12 April 1942, Montanaro and Trooper Preece were launched a mile off Boulogne from *Motor Launch 102* and sank a 5,500 tons iron ore carrier. They were back in Dover for breakfast and were awarded the Distinguished Service Order (DSO) and Distinguished Conduct Medal (DCM) respectively.

Previously, on 9 March, Haslar met with Courtney and Montanaro to set the staff requirement for a new canoe; this was an historic meeting as the design of all future military canoes stemmed from it. It also decided the name 'Cockle' should be adopted for small boats. The key characteristics required in the new canoe were:

Able to operate in up to Force 4 wind.

Carry two men plus 50 kgs of stores.

Capable of being propelled by two men at 3.5 knots fully loaded.

Fully decked.

Able to pass through a submarine torpedo hatch.

If collapsible, no loose parts and able to be assembled in 30 seconds.

Maximum weight 45 kgs and draft of 15 cms.

Able to withstand grounding and working alongside other vessels.

Watertight cockpit cover, releasable quickly in emergency.

Coincidentally the next day, Fred Goatley, former works manager of Saunders Roe (Saro) Laminated Woodwork Ltd, sent some drawings of a new canoe design to Commander ES Felton of HMS *Dolphin*, the Submarine School at Fort Blockhouse, Gosport. Goatley's design incorporated many of the features Haslar required; it was able to pass through a 24" diameter hatch, it was collapsible, easily assembled in the dark and had

Fred Goatley, a boat designer and builder from Oxford. Goatley went with SE Saunders when he moved his business from Oxford to West Cowes, to open Saunders Boat Building Syndicate (later Saunders-Roe, shortened to Saro). Goatley designed a collapsing boat, the Quest, for Shakleton's expedition. In 1937 he designed an assault boat and the War Office ordered 1,000, but during the latter stages of production he became seriously ill, sold his interest in the patent and retired after 43 years with the company. During the war he became a consultant for Saro working from home and designed 11 boats, including an unsinkable lifeboat and a collapsible pontoon for bridging. In addition to the Cockle Mk.2, he also designed the Cockle Mk.2** three seat canoe. Despite all his work for the war effort, a recommendation for the MBE was not successful. He died in October 1949.

The collapsible river assault boat designed by Fred Goatley in 1937. The War Office ordered 1,000.

no removable parts. It had buoyancy bags and an optional airbag around the canoe waterline gave it added stability and beam.

Haslar briefed Hussey on his ideas. The Folbot (Cockle Mk.I in HQ Combined Operations parlance) did not interest him, but Limpet attack did. Hussey suggested he discuss the problem with Fred Goatley, whose former company had won a War Office competition for a river assault boat. They met on 27 March and Haslar sent a copy of the staff requirement to Goatley's home (Tonalba, 157 York Avenue, East Cowes, Isle of Wight). The two formulated the more advanced Cockle Mk.II – see Appendix 1.

A pilot model was produced, which Haslar tested, making small improvements until they arrived at a production model. When CODC approved the design, an order for six Cockle Mk.IIs was placed with Saros on 14 April. They were to be distributed to a number of units for trials; CODC received two. On 22 April the term 'Cockle' was approved officially. Despite being at the meeting on 9 March that proposed the title, Haslar objected to the designation, which he thought derisory; he preferred 'Tadpole'.

As well as canoeing, Haslar began to develop operational swimming. Fins were a relatively new development and he also experimented with the Davis Submerged Escape Apparatus (DSEA) and its oxygen supply. In the summer he was often seen using it to catch flatfish off Southsea. However, DSEA was only designed for short periods and was of limited use for long distance swimming.

16

The Davis Submerged Escape Apparatus – an oxygen rebreather invented in 1910 by Sir Robert Davis. Intended as an escape apparatus for submarine crews, it was also used as an industrial breathing set and for diving. It comprised a rubber breathing/buoyancy bag, containing barium hydroxide to scrub carbon dioxide and a steel cylinder holding 56 litres of oxygen. The breathing bag was connected to a mouthpiece by a flexible tube and the nose was closed by a clip. On reaching the surface the air in the breathing/buoyancy bag served as a life preserver. It had a rubber apron held out by the wearer to reduce the speed of ascent. DSEA was adopted by the Royal Navy in 1929. A smaller version, the Amphibious Tank Escape Apparatus, was produced for crews of Duplex Drive swimming tanks.

Until 28 June he concentrated upon the development of small boat attack on enemy harbours. Two men from No.6 Commando were attached for the experimental work. Ten BPBs were laid down, powered by Lagonda V12s or Mercury V8s. In conjunction with Commander-in-Chief (CinC) Portsmouth, night exercises were combined with patrols of the eastern boom (Patrol Margate), using canoes equipped for counter-attacking human torpedoes and other small enemy craft. For this purpose Haslar got hold of two canoes, named Cranthorpe and Blondin, but their types are unknown.

Haslar's work was leading towards a new concept of attack by BPB supported by Cockles. The latter would gain access to enemy harbours for the BPBs by cutting through booms, preferably silently, but if not, explosively. Having established a gap the Cockles would mark it with screened lights. When the BPBs were inside the boom defences, the Cockles would follow to pick up the driver when he baled out and escape with him under the cover of smoke floats. However, before it could be tested operationally, Haslar's attention was diverted.

The eastern boom, a defensive barrage of concrete blocks about 2m below high water level. During the war it bristled with surface and underwater obstacles. It runs from Lumps Fort on Southsea seafront out to Horse Sands Fort (left background) in the Solent. A similar barrier ran from No Mans Land Fort (right) to Seaview on the Isle of Wight. The channel between the Forts was patrolled by boom defence vessels. Most of the Southsea end is still intact.

Chapter Two

THE ROYAL MARINES BOOM PATROL DETACHMENT

URING LATE APRIL 1942, Haslar proposed future lines of development for BPBs, including setting up a unit to conduct trials and operations. On 23 April, he and Hussey agreed they needed a cover story to explain why BPBs and canoes were operating in the Solent. Hussey also believed the unit should consist solely of Royal Marines. Next day Haslar visited HQ Combined Operations to present the case to the Chief of Staff (COS), Colonel GE Wildman-Lushington RM, a former Fleet Air Arm pilot. HQ Combined Operations and CinC Portsmouth were sceptical initially, until it was emphasised the unit would have a genuine defensive role.

Haslar realised they would need to gain experience with fast motorboats and planned to acquire suitable craft for trials and training. However, privately he reasoned that if the canoe could get through to assist the BPB, why did they need to bother with the BPB at all?

Colonel (later Major General CB CBE) GE Wildman-Lushington RM. He served in HMS *Swiftsure* during the Gallipoli campaign and transferred to the Royal Naval Air Service in January 1917, flying anti-submarine patrols. After a period ashore and afloat he joined the Fleet Air Arm when it formed in 1924, one of 19 RM officers who volunteered. After training he was a Flight Commander in 441 Flight aboard HMS *Eagle* and *Hermes* taking part in operations in Shanghai. Having returned to the Royal Marines he qualified at both RAF and RN Staff Colleges and was later on the Directing Staff of the RN Staff College. On outbreak of WW2 he took command of 1st RM Battalion until joining Mountbatten as COS HQ Combined Operations. When Mountbatten became Supreme Allied Commander South-East Asia, Wildman-Lushington went as his Assistant COS. In June 1945 he became GOC Commando Group and Chief of Combined Operations in 1947. He retired in 1950 and became Chairman of British Sulphur Corporation and President RM Association.

19

Haslar had instruction on the Italian EMB from Lieutenant Bill Ladbrooke RN at HMS *Northney*, a Combined Operations training establishment for landing craft. He removed the balsa wood float at the stern and left it on the jetty before setting off down Hayling Island's Mengham Rythe at full speed. After half an hour Ladbrooke found Haslar on a shallow mud bank. He had decided to see how quickly the EMB would stop, so shut the throttle at 25 knots. It stopped so quickly he was swept off by the wake catching up, because he had left the stern float behind.

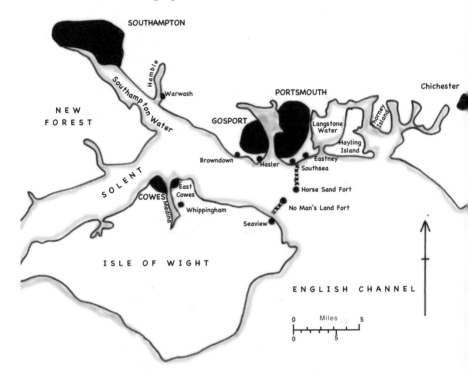

The area around Southsea used for the development and training of the RMBPD.

Haslar began practicing canoeing along the eastern boom in the Solent. He did this to study how the boom was affected by weather and tides, to learn how to handle canoes under realistic conditions and practice avoiding patrols. He did not tell the authorities what he was up to and on 25 April returning to

20

Southsea he was arrested, but was soon released.

On 12 May, the new Commandant CODC, Lieutenant Colonel HFG Langley RA, sent a written proposal to HQ Combined Operations for the formation of the Royal Marines Harbour Patrol Detachment. It envisaged BPB and Cockle crews in the same unit able to operate together or independently. The unit would be entirely composed of Royal Marines (except for the Royal Navy Maintenance Section), under the operational control of Combined Operations. It would be manned by volunteers, with Haslar as commander. To hide its offensive role, the cover story was to represent the unit as a form of harbour defence. The proposed strength was four officers and 34 other ranks – Officer Commanding (OC), Second-in-Command (2IC), four administrative staff and two sections each of an officer and 15 other ranks. As the men would be training at all hours and would have to change location frequently, it was recommended they be granted Commando subsistence of 6/8d per day (£0.33) to live on the local economy.

The proposal was approved in principle and Haslar was informed on 20 May on his way to Manchester. The meeting giving final authority was held at HQ Combined Operations on 26 June. Mountbatten personally approved the proposal and amended the title to Royal Marines Boom Patrol Detachment (RMBPD). The establishment was also amended; each section was reduced by two Marines and a Maintenance Section of a Sub Lieutenant and 11 Royal Navy ratings was added. The total strength was 46 all ranks.

Haslar threw himself into a programme of self-training. Night after night he went out in a canoe or dinghy and was arrested twice, but on 4 June he managed to get inside the harbour unchallenged after an all night patrol. He also had a myriad of details to contend with – varnish for the canoes, camouflage cream, fluorescent paint to find items in the dark, paddles showing the smallest silhouette but able to push a canoe off a beach, how to navigate and many others.

Volunteers for hazardous service were called for. They needed to be eager to engage the enemy, indifferent to personal safety, intelligent, nimble, free of strong family ties, able to swim and of good physique. A large number of suitable men had already volunteered for the Commandos and a number of undesirable types came forward. Haslar was looking for determined, resourceful, self-reliant and intelligent individuals, not 'taproom commandos'.

On 19 June, Haslar dined with Lieutenant 'Jock' Stewart, with whom he had served previously, and offered him the post of 2IC. Stewart jumped at it, much to Haslar's relief, as he needed someone to relieve him of the administrative and trials burden, while he trained and developed the new unit. HQ Royal Marines agreed the transfer.

Haslar interviewed ten volunteer second lieutenants on 25 June at the Royal Marines Small Arms School at Browndown. He selected two – JW MacKinnon and WHA Pritchard-Gordon. Similarly on 1 July he interviewed two sergeants, three corporals and twenty-eight Marines at Plymouth. At the end of each interview Haslar asked each man the same question, 'Do you realise that your expectation of a long life is very remote?' At this Marine Sparks' face cracked into a huge grin; he was in.

One sergeant, one corporal and four Marines were selected for training as instructors, while the remainder were formed into a training squad and underwent drill, swimming and PT. Those who dropped out were replaced by the Adjutant of Plymouth Division. None of those selected had any experience in boats.

Those who had were already in the Commandos and Haslar was not able to use men with such experience in the Army and RAF. Some could not swim at first. Others were good on the surface, but could not cope with claustrophobia underwater and vice versa.

On 3 July, Lieutenant Stewart reported as 2IC. The next day Second Lieutenants McKinnon and Pritchard-Gordon joined to command the two sections. Then an administrative team, consisting of Colour Sergeant WJ Edwards as Detachment Sergeant Major, and three Marines arrived on 6 July, the official formation date for RMBPD. At 2100 Haslar lectured all ranks on the rugby field on the vital need for security. They became known around Eastney as 'Hasler's Party', but generally kept to themselves. They lived in local billets and

Lieutenant JD 'Jock' Stewart became 2IC on 3 July. Known as the 'Old Man', he was a pre-war advertising agent, much admired for his administrative abilities and technical skill.

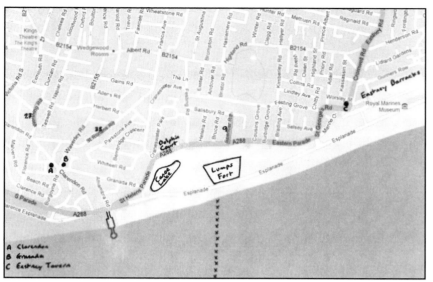

The area of Southsea in which the RMBPD lived and trained.

worked long hours day and night. Their only chance to relax was usually on Saturday evenings, when they frequented local pubs such as the Granada, Eastney Tavern and the Clarendon.

The period 7-23 July was spent training the trainers, or the 'Nucleus' as Haslar termed it. Their training consisted of:

The Granada.

Seamanship: handling canoes, assault boats and dinghies in all weather day and night.
Weapons: .455 Pistol, Sten, Thompson, signal pistol.
Explosives: preparation and firing of 5lbs (2.3 kgs) depth charges.
Swimming: freestyle, breaststroke, surface diving, life saving.
PT: muscle development, balancing and climbing.

Eastney Tavern, Cromwell Road, Southsea with the former Royal Marines barracks behind.

Haslar demonstrated the method, followed by emulation and critique. He also dictated notes, which became the instructor's handbooks, as most subjects were not in

The Clarendon undergoing renovation as the New Clarendon in 2011.

standard training manuals. Each week every man had a personal progress report.

On 20 July, Sub Lieutenant Bill Ladbrooke joined to head the Maintenance Section. He was a former RAF Lysander pilot until his eyesight failed and was a powerboat racer in the 1930s. While employed by 23rd Technical Training Group (Civilian) he went to Malta to recover and inspect an Italian EMB abandoned during the abortive raid, following which he was commissioned into the RNVR.

Next day Haslar went to HQ 3rd Submarine Flotilla, aboard HMS *Forth*, on the Clyde to discuss how to launch canoes from a submarine. He had a working model to show how he envisaged doing it, using the submarine's gun as an improvised crane. As a result of the meeting, HMS *Forth* was to develop a girder extension to the submarine's gun, while Haslar designed and produced the sling to fit around the canoe and allow it to be lifted fully laden into the water and floated off.

Haslar delivered a final talk to the 'Nucleus' on 23 July just before the main body of 23 Marines arrived from Plymouth. This made the unit four over the approved establishment, but it was expected the next phase of training would weed out the excess, which it did. Those assembled were:

Major Haslar

Lieutenant Stewart

Colour Sergeant Edwards

Marines Drew, Brown & Phelps – Storeman, Orderly & Driver respectively:

No.1 Section

Lieutenant MacKinnon)
Sergeant Wallace) Trainers
Lance Corporals Laver & Sheard)

Marines Moffatt, Mills, Colley, Ellery, Sparks, Ewart & Conway.

Marines Blaymire, Carroll, David & Hughes were soon returned to their former units.

No.2 Section

Lieutenant Pritchard-Gordon)
Corporal King) Trainers
Lance Corporals Johnston & Bick)

Marines Saunders, Ruff, Duncan, Turfrey, Stevens, Lambert, Martin, Cattrell, Watson, McCarroll, Ashton & O'Dell (joined 28 July).

One of the RMBPD Nissen huts at Lump's Fort.

Next day training started, beginning with Haslar addressing all ranks on the purpose of the unit and security. In a fresh breeze and moderate sea they started working with canoes. Three capsized, but all were salvaged. On 26 July they trained with the Cockle Mk.I, during which one sank, as did an assault boat crewed by Laver and Mills when it became held against the boom by a spring tide. On 27 July, Patrol Margate was exercised by the officers and NCOs for the first time on a calm sea and under a full moon.

Their training base was centred on two Nissen huts on the Southsea front beneath the grass ramparts of Lumps Fort. It was immediately at the end of the boom and next to the Canoe Lake,

Site of the two Nissen huts used by RMBPD with Lumps Fort ramparts behind. During the Napoleonic Wars the Fort was armed with three 32 Pdr guns. By 1822 it was a semaphore station on the line to London. In 1827 part of it fell into the sea and the semaphore closed in 1847. It was reconstructed as a Palmerston Fort in 1859-69, with two 6" breach-loading Mk.IV guns. The guns were removed in 1906, but the Fort was rearmed in 1914 with a 6 Pdr Hotchkiss. After WW1 a rose garden was created within the Fort, which also became the site of the Southsea Model Village.

Southsea Canoe Lake with Dolphin Court in the background.

where Haslar first learned to canoe as a boy. One Nissen hut was for stores and the other for training and lectures. The RMBPD

Haslar set up the RMBPD office in the nearest first floor flat at Dolphin Court, 24 St Helens Parade, Southsea.

offices were in a flat at Dolphin Court, taken over from CODC, which under Captain Hussey RN had transferred to HQ Combined Operations to become the Directorate of Experiments.

Haslar was determined to avoid the poor behaviour of some special units, but was not averse to taking advantage of other organisations knowing little about them. Most did not know CODC had moved, enabling Haslar to demand all sorts of stores. Ironically when he needed a boat he turned to the Army and for cars the Navy.

Colour Sergeant WJ 'Bungy' Edwards, a Regular pensioner recalled on the outbreak of war, stood no nonsense from the youngsters, but also did everything he could for them.

Haslar went to see Lieutenant Colonel Joseph Picton-Phillipps for advice. He was training the first Royal Marines Commando on the Isle of Wight at the time and was killed a few months later on the Dieppe Raid. They concluded that although the unit was special it still needed parade ground discipline. Drill took up little training time, but it was conducted with as much enthusiasm and perfection as everything else they did.

Getting to places in time for lessons was tight so Sergeant Wallace devised a special rapid march – the 'Southsea Stroll'.

They wore no unique badges, but were superbly fit, always immaculate and exuded an air of self-confident pride. Living on the economy also made them more independent. Haslar didn't care what they did off duty, within reason, provided they turned up fit for training each morning.

No.1 Section lived with Mrs Leonora Powell in the 'White Heather' guesthouse at 27 Worthing Road. Her husband was a long serving regular Royal Marine, at that time on HMS *Aurora*. Daughter Heather had a keen eye for dress and was quick to point out how proper Marines would do it if she sensed their standards were slipping. She helped darn and repair clothes

The former 'White Heather' guesthouse at 27 Worthing Road, Southsea.

and even made them write home when families had heard nothing for a while. When Colour Sergeant Edwards arranged the billet, he advised Mrs Powell to take up her carpets and put away her good blankets. Heather objected, 'Suppose one of them was Dad?' The carpets and blankets remained. Marine Robert Ewart very quickly formed a special relationship with Heather.

No.2 Section boarded with Mrs Montague at 35 St Ronan's Road. The officers lived in the mess at Eastney until they moved into 9 Spencer Road, where Haslar joined them having been living with his mother at Glyn Corrig

35 St Ronan's Road, where No.2 Section was billeted.

Eastney Barracks, Southsea with the sign of the Eastney Tavern on the left.

at Catherington, 12 miles from Portsmouth. The other officers then discovered that Haslar was partial to

27

9 Spencer Road, Southsea where the RMBPD officers lived.

a pint of beer with breakfast. He insisted they speak only French three evenings per week.

Haslar continued to be busy with other matters as well as training the new unit. Fortunately he was able to leave much of the day to day running to Stewart. On 28 July, having been out training most of the night, he visited Saros at Cowes to discuss modifications to the backrest and cockpit cover of the Cockle Mk.II with Goatley. The same day *Spider Boy*, an 18' Chris Craft, was collected from Dorset Yacht Co and brought by road to Warsash to act as a training motorboat. Two days later he was in London to follow up progress on various developments with HQ Combined Operations and SOE's technical department. This included a meeting with Douglas Fairbanks Jr about dummy boats. Fairbanks was on the staff of HQ Combined Operations dealing with landing craft and later camouflage and deception. Haslar also met Professor Newitt to discuss the 'Sleeping Beauty' before returning to Southsea to practice wire climbing and sinking mooring buoys.

Training for the unit was varied and relentless. They canoed day and

Douglas Fairbanks Jr, the famous actor, was attached to HQ Combined Operations in 1942. He witnessed and took part in some British training and operations and gained a deep understanding of military deception. He formed the Beach Jumpers in 1943, a unit simulating amphibious landings away from the actual landing beaches. The Beach Jumpers were first used in the invasion of Sicily and later throughout the Mediterranean. Fairbanks was awarded the US Legion of Merit, the Italian War Cross for Military Valour, the French Legion d'Honneur and Croix de Guerre and British Distinguished Service Cross. Fairbanks was also awarded the Silver Star for bravery while serving on PT Boats. He was made an Honorary KBE in 1949.

night in the Cockle Mk.I, including practicing navigation and learning about the effects of tides and wind. Working out compass deviation was a major issue, particularly when the Cockles were loaded with magnetic Limpet mines. With one, two or three men in a canoe, they practiced changing over and getting in and out at sea. When not on the water, they rehearsed building and dismantling their canoes and how to repair them. Eight men, including all the officers, were given basic training in handling *Spider Boy*, but it was suspended due to mechanical problems and difficulties in obtaining spares.

Swimming in open water over long distances was a regular activity, using breast stroke and back stroke without the limbs breaking the surface. There was also shallow water diving using DSEA. Weapon training was carried out with pistols and the Thompson, Sten and Lanchester sub-machine guns. They

carried out lots of extra physical activity and rope and wall climbing. Handling explosives became routine. In addition to the specialist training, there were the usual infantry battle drills, assault course and signals. At times roles were swapped to allow the junior NCOs to gain experience of being in charge.

Only one case of indiscipline occurred when a Marine went absent without leave. As their fitness improved and they became used to the hard physical work, they were less

Haslar and Stewart testing the Cockle Mk.II off Southsea.

Horse Sand Fort, built to protect the eastern entrance to the Solent. The boom ran out to it from Southsea.

No Man's Land Fort at the western end of the entrance to the Solent, supported Horse Sand Fort. The boom continued from it to the Isle of Wight.

likely to injure themselves and the numbers reporting sick fell.

On 1 August, Haslar and Stewart tested the Cockle Mk.II and practised hurdling it over part of the tubular boom. The same day the trainees paddled out to Horse Sand Fort and practiced changing from double to single paddles. On 4 August they conducted a long trip up the Solent and next day visited the boom and sea-gates in their canoes. Three days later they visited No Man's Land Fort and began learning how to stow stores and carry out the attack drills for Patrol Margate.

Haslar's punishing schedule showed no signs of relenting. On 8 August, he and Stewart tested the Foldflat canoe produced by Cavendar and Clark, builders of the Cockle Mk.I. On 13 August, Haslar attended a demonstration of fast motor boating at HMS *Tormentor*, a Combined Operations naval training centre for landing craft and small boats on the Hamble, by Sub Lieutenant Ladbrooke. During it they crossed to Cowes to see Goatley about the Cockle Mk.II and then Vospers about the BPB. Next day he was in London to see Professor Newitt about underwater propulsion and was back there on the 17th to discuss the role of the RMBPD with HQ Combined Operations and liaise with the Special Service Brigade. Two days later he was off to Ringway by air to see a demonstration of the Rotachute, picking up Commander du Cane at Farnborough on the way.

On the way back they were diverted due to low cloud and Haslar got back early next day and immediately set off with Stewart to test the new wider Cockle Mk.II. On 22 August the two of them took the Mk.II to visit a stranded steamer on the East Winner bank off Hayling Island; it behaved well. They also tried out the Lanchester sub-machine gun. Two days later at Bursledon, Haslar embarked on HMS *Camperdown* to witness a demonstration drop of the Uffa Fox rescue dinghy from a Hudson. The dinghy was destined for the RAF, but if the drop

The Uffa Fox rescue dinghy rigged for sailing alongside a Vickers Warwick, the aircraft he designed it to be dropped from. 600 aircrew were rescued thanks to the rescue dinghy during the war.

Uffa Fox grew up in Cowes and aged 21 set up a boat building business on an old floating bridge. He was a somewhat unorthodox character; on one occasion he led a group of Sea Scouts in a 7.6m open boat across the Channel to within a few miles of Paris, when their parents thought they were sailing around the Solent. He designed the planing dinghy, which in 57 starts in the International 14 Avenger class in 1928 gained 52 first, two second and three third places, including winning the Prince of Wales Cup. He also designed and built two sailing canoes which Roger De Quincy and himself took across the Atlantic and brought back the International Canoe Trophy. After the war he raced with the Duke of Edinburgh and designed a range of planing keelboats and cruiser/racer yachts.

was successful, Haslar thought the BPD might be similarly delivered. Although HMS *Camperdown* is the name given for the ship involved in the demonstration, the latest ship of that name was not launched until February 1944 and its predecessor was sold in 1911.

On 26 August, officers from the Small Scale Raiding Force (SSRF) and SBS visited to compare the performance of different canoes. They tried the Foldflat, Camper and Nicholson rigid canoe and Cockles Mk.I and II in turn over long distances.

As the basic skills were learned, training became more ambitious. On 10 August, No.1 Section attempted to reach the Isle of Wight in canoes in rough seas, but three were swamped and the attempt had to be abandoned. The crews hung onto the boom and were rescued by a

Probably taken on 26 August 1942 when officers from the SSRF and SBS visited RMBPD to compare the performance of various canoes. Major Roger Courtney is standing centrally on the seawall with hands in pockets.

The same scene today, but the shingle is much higher up the seawall than in 1942.

patrol boat. Once all the canoes had been salvaged, they rather aptly had a lecture on the effect of tides. On 14 August the junior NCOs were given experience of taking charge by running the swimming and signals training. Next day both Sections made the trip to the Isle of Wight successfully and returned in the afternoon.

Patrol Margate took place again on the night of 17 August, but had to be called off at 2300 when a smoke screen was released to mask Portsmouth during an air raid. Stewart and Laver were lost in the smoke without a compass and had no way of knowing which way they faced. To continue paddling risked being swept out to sea, so they just had to ride it out and eventually drifted onto a dummy barge, which they crawled onto to spend a wet and uncomfortable night.

Patrol Margate was repeated the next night, but called off at midnight due to wind and rain. 25 August saw another Patrol Margate and on the 28th the Cockle Mk.II was tested for capsizing. The cockpit cover was difficult to open underwater; not something the crew would wish to have to deal with in an emergency.

It wasn't all work. When Haslar got the chance he relaxed sailing his dinghy *Mandy* in the Solent. To overcome wartime restrictions he kept some items of uniform on board to make it look official and was usually ignored by patrols; they got used to him. He even kept a Wren's hat on board for when he took female company along.

Haslar constantly had to balance his time between training the unit, trialling equipment and attending meetings with other organisations. On 17 August he attended a meeting about amalgamating RMBPD with SSRF, COPP, SOE, SBS and others. All these units believed they were unique and for the time being the status quo continued, but Haslar was always concerned his unit would be taken over.

Relations between officers and men in RMBPD were close, as they lived hand in glove in their canoes sharing duties equally, but the formal differences remained. Haslar was somewhat disturbed to hear the young officers occasionally went to the Eastney Tavern in Cromwell Road, Southsea with their men for drinking and singing, but did not forbid it. He did not wish to damage the excellent spirit and morale they had developed. Haslar only appeared when specially invited and did not stay long. He found his own entertainment with an occasional 'run ashore' and overcame it with exercise next morning. He discovered that pure oxygen breathed under pressure through the DSEA was a great hangover cure; underwater swimming training following a night out was not always coincidental. The men looked forward to an occasional scrap with the Navy.

Although navigation training was tedious, it was essential if they were to find their targets at night. Haslar originally allowed two weeks in which to teach basic seamanship and navigation, but progress was slow and he eventually had to seek help. Lieutenant Charles Symonds Leaf RM was brought in solely for this training. Leaf was a noted archaeologist and had served in the Buffs in the First World War. He owned *Lalage*, which he and three others crewed in the 1936 Olympics at Kiel to take the 6m Class Gold Medal. In WW2 he served in Balloon Command before transferring to the Royal Marines aged 47.

At the beginning of September longer exercises commenced with a three-day overland trip covering Havant – Compton - Brook Bridge - Fareham. During it they practiced with grenades, stalking and attacking sentries, ambushing, night work, climbing trees with ropes, prisoner drill, living in the field, memorising routes and producing reconnaissance reports. On the 4th they carried out their first diving exercise in the sea and then wrote a report from memory of the three-day exercise before conducting physical, swimming and canoe training. The rest of the month continued much the same – canoeing in all weathers, diving from canoes and getting back inboard, long distance swimming, climbing, weapon training and firing, drill, navigation, signals, boat repair and the obstacle course with weapons.

Early in September, MacKinnon bought the unit a 12-week old Cocker Spaniel named 'Tich' and billeted it at Spencer Road. There is mention in some sources of the unit also having a Saint Bernard; if true it must have proved something of a challenge to feed in wartime.

On the night of 10 September, No.2 Section left Southsea to attack

'Tich'.

Thorney Island in canoes, but none reached the objective. Next day Haslar was in London for a conference about the Rotachute, but returned in the afternoon to meet Lieutenant Colonel Goldsworthy at RAF Thorney Island to review the previous night's exercise. That day, No.1 Section was out with assault boats and outboards. The Thorney Island exercise was repeated by No.1 Section on 13 September. This time five of the seven canoes reached the target. They returned next day via Langstone Harbour and on 16 September went on seven days leave. Corporal Laver appears to have injured his foot during the exercise as he had to rest it while on leave.

That afternoon a new exercise was introduced named 'Grundy', designed to improve endurance and trial drugs to keep them awake and enhance their night vision. Professor Solly Zuckerman of HQ Combined Operations conducted night vision tests with Paradrene, a drug that dilates the pupils and improves adaption to night vision, and Dipthal. The night vision tests did not work very well, but they learned to allow time for their eyes to adapt to night conditions and only used red light. Afterwards Haslar and Corporal EST Bick marched all night in an endurance test. On return they joined the rest for a full day's training starting with swimming, followed by canoeing to the Isle of Wight and back. They were tested before and after with Dipthal and found it fairly convincing. Haslar then worked in the office until 1830 and unsurprisingly went to bed early.

No.2 Section took their leave

Solly Zuckerman was born in Cape Town to Jewish immigrants. Educated at the University of Cape Town and Yale, he came to London in 1926 to complete studies at University College Hospital and taught at Oxford University 1934-45. The RAF loaned him to the Combined Operations scientific staff to test methods of improving night vision, using RMBPD as guinea pigs. As Scientific Director of the British Bombing Survey Unit he helped persuade Eisenhower to disrupt the French transportation system by bombing the railways and marshalling yards prior to the invasion. Post-war he taught at Birmingham and East Anglia Universities until 1974. He became Chief Scientific Adviser to the MOD 1960-66 and the British Government 1964-71. President London Zoological Society 1977-84. He wrote a number of books, including two autobiographies: *From Apes to Warlords* and *Monkeys Men and Missiles*. Zuckerman was knighted in 1956, made KCB 1964, OM 1968 and Baron 1971.

on 24 September when No.1 Section returned. On 27 September working hours were changed to allow training to be carried out more frequently at night. Both sections worked until 1330 daily and one section on alternate nights 1900-0500. Patrol Margate was carried out on 30 September.

Paddling the canoes all night was extremely arduous. The arms and shoulders did the work and the legs often became senseless. There was a tendency to hallucinate and imagine lighthouses or large ships. The No.1 was apt to believe the No.2 behind was not pulling his weight. At times Haslar made the crews sit in their canoes, crouched and motionless for hours.

Some men could not get along with their crewmate and had to be swapped with others. For example, Sparks and Fisher were best of mates ashore, but could not get on in the canoe. According to Sparks, Fisher was also accident-prone. On one canoe exercise they were to drop a 5 lbs charge overboard. Fisher crimped the fuse to initiate it, dropped the pliers overboard and the charge into the bottom of the canoe; a mad scramble followed to jettison it before it exploded. Sparks was pleased to join Haslar while Fisher teamed up with Ellery. After these initial teething problems, the crews settled down fairly quickly.

Gradually they became fitter; Stewart and Laver paddled 34 miles in a single night. Training also involved feet hardening by running along the shingle beach. The ability to move stealthily was paramount both on land and on the water. Even when local shore defences had been notified of their exercises, some sentries did not get the message. Corporal Johnston and his No.2 were pinned down by rifle fire on the beach at Hayling Island and Haslar was held at gunpoint for half an hour at Seaview by two Home Guards, while their officer phoned to confirm his identity.

They regularly practiced getting aboard the Boom Gate and Solent Patrol vessels unseen and occasionally tied up and went on board for a well-deserved drink. Some boats were manned by WRNS and when well offshore during quiet periods in the summer, they were apt to strip off to sunbath. These boats made very tempting targets for a stealthy approach. They learned to avoid being silhouetted by the moon and training in escape techniques was also given.

Haslar continued to be busy with other tasks. On 3 September he went to see Professor Newitt and Major Reeve at SOE Welwyn about submerged propulsion and underwater charges.

On 7 September he was at the Admiralty Experimental Works at Haslar (a location in Gosport unconnected with Blondie), for Cockle tank tests. The same day he saw Lieutenant Commander Shelford at HMS *Dolphin* to discuss shallow water diving. Next day he was taken by Royal Army Service Corps boat to Cowes with No.1 Section to test assault boats with outboard engines. On 9 September, Mr McGruer of the Department of Naval Construction came to discuss paddles and Commander May of the Admiralty Compass Observatory visited to discuss the use of compasses in canoes. The following day, Fred Goatley visited to discuss Cockles Mk.II and IV. On 12 September, Major Wills of SOE Welwyn came to discuss camouflaging canoes. It is surprising Haslar found the time to carry out any training at all.

Although Haslar was on seven days leave from 22 September, on the 23rd he went to Rochester to inspect a motor barge for suitability as parent vessel to the BPBs. On 24 September he visited the Superintendent of Mine Design at Havant to inspect a countermining switch for Limpets. On 26 September he and Stewart went to the Ashley Walk bombing range in the New

Lieutenant Commander (later Captain) WO 'Bill' Shelford, a submariner and shallow water diving expert who became the first Superintendent of Diving at HMS *Dolphin*. He formed the Admiralty Experimental Diving Unit in 1942, developing diving equipment for Chariots, X-Craft, mine recovery parties and port clearance parties. An exhaustive programme of human experiments was conducted on the physiological problems associated with diving with Professor JSB Haldane acting as adviser. Shelford is pictured here at a 1959 Divers' Reunion Dinner

Ashley Walk was used by the Aeronautical & Armaments Experimental Establishment at Boscombe Down to test airborne bombs, rockets and guns during the war. It had a variety of simulated targets including a dam wall, railway lines and a submarine pen. Pictured is the water filled crater created by the first live Grand Slam (10,000 kgs) bomb dropped from a Lancaster on 13 March 1945 and used next day to destroy the Bielefeld Viaduct in Germany. Behind is the overgrown simulated U-boat pen.

Forest to watch large parachute trials. They witnessed a 180 kgs iron weight, representing a loaded canoe, plummet to the ground followed sometime later by its parachutes.

Training in October continued much the same as in September, except there was more night work, including silent approach and night landing, stripping and assembling weapons in the dark and night marches. Nautical terms were covered in some detail, plus lectures on dockyards and unarmed combat in the dark.

In early October they were practising climbing a 10m wall above some rocks. While Moffatt was climbing, another man started behind him, which was too much for the stake holding the rope and they fell into the shallow water. Both sprained their ankles, but Moffatt's was not too serious and he was on light duties for only seven days.

Professor Zuckerman returned on 1 October to carry out endurance tests and administer various treatments for recovering energy. They got used to rowing the assault boat and on 14 October carried out comparative testing with it and the Strausler Assault Boat. On 16 October the whole unit proceeded to Langstone Harbour in assault boats and carried out mud exercises. On 20 October they canoed to Hayling Island and practised launching into heavy seas. The next day No.1 Section continued this training while No.2 Section constructed a tubular arrangement simulating a submarine casing from which to practice launching Cockles Mk.II. On 24 October they constructed vertical iron plating representing the side of a ship on which to practice placing Limpets. On 26/27 October, assisted by all ranks, Haslar experimented with a quick release hook for launching Cockles Mk.II from ship or submarine.

One Saturday, Sergeant Wallace announced there would be no run ashore that night; they were going on an exercise. There was a deal of grumbling as the men looked forward to their weekly night off. After dark they launched the canoes with a grinning Sergeant Wallace and couldn't understand why he was so happy. They followed him until they were off the end of Southsea pier, where (the dance band could be heard. Rafting up Wallace explained the band kept their beer for the interval in a room at the back of the stage. Their mission was to enter the room, remove the beer and disappear without being seen. Suddenly they were enthusiastic. The No.1 in each canoe held it

Southsea Pier from the beach below Lump's Fort.

firmly against one of the pier stanchions while the No.2 climbed up. They found the door unlocked and there was the beer as Wallace had predicted. Bottles were stuffed inside battledress tunics and they slipped down into the canoes. Back at the canoe sheds they drank their ill-gotten gains and wondered what the band would make of it at the interval.

Haslar continued to be pulled in all directions. On 1 October

The Cockle Mk.II was extremely adaptable and could also be propelled by sail as demonstrated here by Haslar and Stewart off Southsea.

he was at HMS *Dolphin* to see Lieutenant Commander Shelford about shallow water diving dress. Next day he and Stewart witnessed trials of the original BPB. On 5 October the Small Boat Development Sub-Committee met at the RMBPD offices in Southsea and Haslar attended. Next day Haslar and Stewart conducted trials sailing the Cockle Mk.II. On 7 October, Haslar witnessed a Cockle Mk.II tank test at the Admiralty Experimental Works at Haslar and then visited the SBS and Special Service Brigade to inspect waterproof clothing, before proceeding to the Isle of Wight to see Saros about the development of the Cockle Mk.II. He went to Saros again on the 10th about equipment for the Cockle Mk.II.

On 15 October, Haslar tested a water telescope and later in the day he and Stewart visited HMS *Tormentor* to inspect training speedboats and then on to Vospers about abandon boat trials for the BPB. They returned on the 17th and tested the drills, which proved successful. On 20 October he and Stewart went to Fareham to inspect firing gear for BPBs. That afternoon Haslar visited Saros with Majors Salter and Badger of HQ Combined Operations. Next day Stewart joined Haslar there for a conference on BPBs. On the 23rd the pair went to Horsea Island in Portsmouth Harbour to try out Chariot diving suits. On 26 October, Stewart was back at the bombing range at Ashley Walk to watch a heavy load dropped by parachute. Next day, Commander RED Ryder VC, of St Nazaire fame, visited RMBPD and with Haslar inspected Cockles Mk.II and BPBs at Vospers and speedboats at HMS *Tormentor*. On 27 October, Haslar went to West Meon to discuss stores with Paymaster Lieutenant Commander GS Mowll and then continued to London and HQ Combined Operations.

Despite all the development work, getting canoes within striking distance of a target was still a tricky problem. Trials of parachuting straight into water were not going well. Parachuting onto land first was viable, but would cause a long delay while the canoes were constructed, stores loaded and then launched. Approaching in a submarine seemed to offer the best chance of success and the SBS had already used this method in the Mediterranean.

Chapter Three

GENESIS OF THE RAID

IN THE 1930s, the Nazi German government resolved to be self-sufficient by the time war came, in order to reduce the effect of naval blockade. By 1939 Germany produced 83% of its food with another 14.5% being imported over the borders from her immediate neighbours. Only 2.5% had to be delivered by sea. Although food security was just about guaranteed, vital war supplies were a different matter.

German scientists had developed substitute (ersatz) natural resources or alternatives. For example, they extracted nitrates essential for explosives and fertilisers from air rather than relying on Chilean imports. Other commodities were more difficult to substitute or could not be produced locally in sufficient quantities, including oil, tin, wolfram, bauxite, whale oil, wood pulp and steel, of which Germany imported 22M tons per year.

The Germans deliberately stockpiled resources for war and these proved sufficient for the short campaigns in 1939-40, but could not sustain military effort during prolonged and intense campaigns, such as in Russia. Ensuring a steady flow of imported material by beating the blockade was essential.

On 27 August 1939, the 2,466 German registered merchant ships were ordered to make for home, friendly or neutral ports. Some evaded detection, but others were taken as prizes and pressed into Allied service. To increase problems for the Germans, the British Ministry of Economic Warfare bought up stocks of commodities in neutral countries, whether Britain needed them or not.

By April 1940, 246 German merchant ships were confined to neutral or friendly ports worldwide, 58 others had been sunk or captured, but 82 vessels had run the gauntlet and reached Germany. Provided the others remained in remote sections of ocean, the overstretched Royal Navy could do little about them. It was only when the ships ventured into narrow sea-lanes or tried to approach homeports that the Royal Navy had an opportunity to intercept them.

The campaigns of 1940 changed the situation completely.

Suddenly Germany had access to the resources of conquered countries and ports on the Atlantic and Mediterranean. The Royal Navy was able to blockade the North Sea and English Channel, but not the entire coast from the North Cape to the south of France. The Soviet Union also cooperated, providing Germany with 4.5M tons of material; the Trans-Siberian railway alone delivered almost 29,000 tons of rubber and 460,000 tons of other products from the Far East.

In these early years of the war the German merchant marine had a relatively easy time and its blockade-runners got through regularly. The German High Command knew war with Russia was coming and on 14 November 1940 Oberkommando der Kriegmarine began preparations for regular merchant traffic with the Far East to ensure vital war supplies continued to arrive.

The French Atlantic ports became the focal point for this trade. Bordeaux was particularly well placed due to its extensive dock facilities, excellent rail communications, the natural protection of being 62 miles inland and formidable defences. However, the blockade-runners needed very close coordination to ensure they were not accidentally intercepted by U-boats and, when close to shore, received destroyer and U-boat escorts, particularly in the Bay of Biscay. This necessitated large amounts of signal traffic, which was eventually their undoing.

The first ship to make a home run was *Ermland*. She left Kobe

Ermland, the first blockade-runner to make it back from the Far East

The port of Bordeaux.

U-boats could be as deadly to Axis blockade-runners as Allied naval and air forces, unless strictly controlled.

on 28 December 1940 and arrived at Bordeaux on 4 April 1941. However, some neutral countries began to seize German merchantmen sitting in their ports. The Americans did so on 30 March 1941 and this prompted the Germans to order to France all ships stuck in other neutral ports. The result was numerous interceptions by the Allies in the middle of 1941.

On 9 May 1941, U-110 was rammed, but did not sink immediately and its Enigma cipher machine and codebooks were captured. This allowed the British to read U-boat signal traffic, but not that to blockade-runners. However, when U-boats were ordered to escort blockade-

The Enigma cipher machine, considered by the Germans to be unbreakable, was cracked at Bletchley Park.

runners that was usually sufficient for the Royal Navy to intercept.

The German invasion of Russia in July 1941 cut off supplies of vital war material from the Soviet Union and Japan via the Trans-Siberian railway. Trade with the Far East was restricted to sea-borne traffic and there was a limited number of ships capable of carrying it out. They had to be able to carry a worthwhile cargo half way around the world without stopping to refuel.

For the rest of 1941 and most of 1942 the Royal Navy and US Navy were overwhelmed with commitments and the blockade-runners were largely ignored. 75,000 tons of goods reached Europe and 32,500 tons went to Japan. In transit, blockade-runners maintained radio silence and passed pre-arranged points at specific times during which U-boats were forbidden from engaging ships within 200 miles.

Ships arriving in Bordeaux for the first time were modified, often armed, their decks strengthened, extra crew taken on and scuttling charges secreted in case capture was inevitable. Most blockade running took place in the winter months when the longer nights in the northern hemisphere helped to cover the movement of ships in and out of the Atlantic ports. Prior to late 1942 the Germans lost only a few ships.

Churchill was alerted on 9 May 1942 in a memo from the Minister of Economic Warfare, Lord Selborne. It was apparent

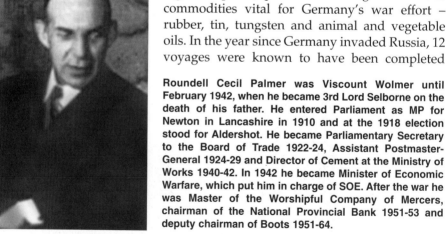

that German blockade-runners were making regular trips to Japan and returning with various commodities vital for Germany's war effort – rubber, tin, tungsten and animal and vegetable oils. In the year since Germany invaded Russia, 12 voyages were known to have been completed

Roundell Cecil Palmer was Viscount Wolmer until February 1942, when he became 3rd Lord Selborne on the death of his father. He entered Parliament as MP for Newton in Lancashire in 1910 and at the 1918 election stood for Aldershot. He became Parliamentary Secretary to the Board of Trade 1922-24, Assistant Postmaster-General 1924-29 and Director of Cement at the Ministry of Works 1940-42. In 1942 he became Minister of Economic Warfare, which put him in charge of SOE. After the war he was Master of the Worshipful Company of Mercers, chairman of the National Provincial Bank 1951-53 and deputy chairman of Boots 1951-64.

bringing about 25,000 tons of rubber. That level of traffic was sufficient to satisfy Germany's needs indefinitely and the ships had sufficient spare tonnage for other supplies. The nature of the traffic the other way was less clear, but Japan needed specialised equipment for manufacturing and prototypes of various weapons and special component parts. Intelligence estimated only 26 Axis ships remained that could make the journey via the Cape of Good Hope or Cape Horn. Once the USA entered the war the Cape of Good Hope was used more often than not to avoid the Pacific.

The Admiralty, Air Ministry and HQ Combined Operations were tasked to look at the problem. In the spring of 1942 the Admiralty had looked at the problem independently and a plan had been formulated around the Mobile Flotation Unit (MFU). This combined a submersible motorboat with storage for Limpets in pressurised chambers and two canoes on the deck. The concept was for the MFU to be positioned close to its target and sunk onto the bottom, while the crew hid ashore. On a timer it would rise to the surface, the canoeists would retrieve a number of Limpets and launch their attacks. Using various delayed action fuses, attacks could be spread over a number of nights, with the Limpets set to explode simultaneously well after the crew had made their escape. The intention had been to attack Bordeaux in November 1942, but due to technical difficulties the MFU was never used operationally.

A conventional naval attack was not feasible, because Bordeaux was too far inside enemy territory. RAF bombers

The massive U-boat pens constructed at Bacalan in Bordeaux.

could reach Bordeaux, but they could not destroy pinpoint targets such as moored ships without causing destruction to the city and its largely friendly population. Raids against the Bacalan submarine base in Bordeaux in 1941 and March 1942 had caused many French casualties, with little impact on the U-boats. The Foreign Office did not wish to create further adverse French reaction.

Intercepting blockade-runners at sea by naval or air forces was considered, but resources were heavily committed and the effort to find a single ship sailing on an unknown date by an unknown route in the vastness of the oceans was inordinate. At that time intelligence on sailings was poor, but it improved when

A U-boat crew bring their vessel into one of the pens on the Atlantic coast.

Ultra was able to reveal the names of ships, their cargoes and sailing dates, although not before the 'Frankton' raid. Even when a blockade-runner was identified it was not always possible to intercept and sink it. On one occasion the Allies committed a carrier, three destroyers, eight bombers and 53 fighter-bombers against a single ship, which was escorted by 11 German surface vessels and 13 U-boats. The ship reached Bordeaux despite the Allies having diverted enormous resources to destroy it.

Some preventative submarine patrolling and mining of the Gironde entrance was carried out and RAF Coastal Command's ability to patrol the Bay of Biscay was increasing and aircraft were being fitted with radar to increase their effectiveness.

However, the battle against the blockade-runners had to compete with the fight against the U-boats, escorting convoys, standing by to tackle surface raiders such as *Tirpitz* and participating in combined operations. During the summer of 1942 all enemy held ports were photographed and the RAF Medmenham Central Interpretation Unit set up a card index of every ship over 2,500 tons to identify potential enemy blockade-runners. Recognition cards were prepared for patrol aircraft. When blockade-runners were expected to run, Bordeaux was photographed twice weekly and sometimes daily, but it was sometimes not possible to be sure if movements were real or just repositioning within the port as decoys.

The Central Interpretation Unit was based at RAF Medmenham (Danesfield House), a few miles from the photographic reconnaissance aircraft based at RAF Benson.

HQ Combined Operations was at Richmond Terrace in Westminster. The white building to the right is the Foreign Office on Whitehall.

HQ Combined Operations concluded there were only two generic solutions; destroy the ships in harbour or render the harbour unusable. Bordeaux was 62 miles up the Gironde, an equivalent distance of Margate to the Tower of London. In addition to the natural defence distance from the sea gave, the enemy had strong naval and air forces in the area and on land there were coastal defence batteries and patrols; the difficulties spoke for themselves.

Lord Selborne raised the issue again on 22 June, this time to Deputy Prime Minister Attlee, while Churchill was in Washington. The Chiefs of Staff (COS) were asked to look into the issue and provide advice. In mid-1942 British and US air patrols were about to commence between West Africa and Brazil, but both countries struggled to provide sufficient aircraft to support the small number of surface vessels. In any case the war against the U-boat was still a higher priority.

The HQ Combined Operations Search Committee, under Commander JH Unwin, met on 27 July to consider options for

Bordeaux during the German occupation.

attacking the blockade-runners. It had already been decided on 1 July that landing a substantial military force was not viable; three divisions plus naval and air forces would be required and such forces were not available. They concluded that a number of options or a combination were possible:

Bombing, but a strong force would be required.

Mining the entrance to the Gironde.

Continuous submarine patrol off the Gironde.

Canoe saboteurs landed by submarine.

Much of this was old ground and no further action followed, but on 5 August, Lord Selborne spelled out the problem again to the War Cabinet, warning that the traffic was set to increase in the following three months. Three ships were on their way from the Far East, three were expected to sail before the end of August and 15 more were awaiting cargoes in French Atlantic ports. Intercepted communications indicated shipments were planned in both directions. The matter was once again passed to the COS.

These developments came at a bad time as the Allies suffered setback after setback; Singapore had fallen on 14 February, U-boats sank the largest tonnage of ships in 1942, Rommel was sweeping across the Western Desert and the Germans were advancing in Russia. But there had also been glimmers of hope such as the St Nazaire raid on 28 March and in May the seizure of Madagascar and the American victory in the Coral Sea.

On 18 September, Haslar was at HQ Combined Operations to discuss the prospect of conducting an operation with Colonel Robert Neville RM, the chief planner. He wanted something relatively simple to test their training and see if their tactics and equipment were correct. Neville called for some target files and Haslar looked them over, but found nothing suitable. Disappointed he returned to Southsea, but a few days later was contacted by Lieutenant Colonel (later Major General CB OBE) Cyril Horton RM, a senior planner at HQ Combined Operations; they might have found something worthwhile.

Haslar went straight back to London on 21 September. He spent all day examining the 'Frankton' file and the charts. Having discussed it at length with Neville, he slept on it at the Royal Ocean Racing Club in St James Place and next day wrote an outline plan. He proposed launching three 'Cockles' from a submarine five miles from the mouth of the Gironde estuary during a dark moon period. From there they would paddle to the target, attack eight ships on the fourth night and return downstream to the mother ship or escape overland.

Submarines had been used to deliver canoes before, but usually in and out on the same night. This operation would require great endurance and skill to cover the distance and remain undetected before making the attack. Escape was going to be very tricky and Mountbatten thought none would get back. Having done his work, Haslar attended a meeting on small boat development and was sitting on the 1745 train just about to leave Waterloo when he was dragged off to discuss the parent craft for 'Frankton'. Clearly his outline plan was gathering pace. Haslar caught a later train and by 2145 was working in his own office at Southsea. Two days later he went on seven days leave, spending much of it in his mother's garden sleeping in the autumn sun.

On 22 September, the HQ Combined Operations planners submitted the outline proposal to the Search Committee, charged with selecting potential targets for attack; it passed their scrutiny. The Examination Committee, chaired by the COS, considered the viability of such proposals before they went forward for detailed planning work; on 13 October it approved the plan. The revised outline was completed on 18 October, having been provisionally accepted by Flag Officer Submarines, whose cooperation was essential. On 30 October, Mountbatten wrote to the COS Committee:

> *Operation Frankton has been planned to meet Lord Selborne's requirement, referred to in COS (42) 223 (O) and subsequent papers, that steps should be taken to attack Axis ships which are known to be running the blockade between France and the Far East.*
>
> *Both seaborne and airborne methods of attacking the ships have been carefully examined, and the plan now proposed is the only one which offers a good chance of success.*
>
> *On an average, between six and ten blockade runners are usually found alongside the quays at Bordeaux, in addition to other shipping. It is hoped to deal with at least six blockade runners.*
>
> *Briefly, the plan is for one officer and five other ranks of the Royal Marine Boom Patrol Detachment to paddle up the River Gironde in 'cockles', moving during the hours of darkness only, and to place 'limpets' on the water-line of the ships they find at Bordeaux. The 'cockles' will be carried to within nine miles of the mouth of the river in a submarine which will be on passage to normal patrol duty and thus will not require to be specially detailed.*

At their meeting on 3 November, the COS approved the plan for Operation 'Frankton'.

Chapter Four

INTELLIGENCE

THE PLANNERS learned the Gironde estuary was flanked by low-lying muddy or sandy shores. Lower down there were long narrow wooded and generally uninhabited islands. The east bank was largely unbroken by creeks and the sandy beach was about 500m wide at low water, backed by sand dunes in places. To the south, sand gave way to mud up to 1200m wide at low water. At Blaye and beyond was a steep bank. Numerous inlets and creeks in this area could be used for concealment at high water, but were often used by fishermen. The west bank was protected by a sea wall at first before giving way to flat marshy low-lying fields with drainage ditches and creeks. In many places the bank was covered in reeds, which would provide excellent cover during the day. At low water the mud extended as far as 1200m from the shore, reducing to 100m at Pauillac. The reed beds were considerably thicker at St Estephe. South of Pauillac there was a bank, but reeds extended as far as Lamaroque, south of which the population density increased towards Bordeaux. From November the low-lying fields behind the shore tended to flood and thick fog was likely

A typical stretch of the Gironde eastern bank near Blaye.

Sand dunes close to Pointe de Grave.

In many places the banks of the Gironde are covered by almost impenetrable reeds and thick mud

One of the many creeks used by fishermen.

Royan across the entrance to the Gironde from Pointe de Grave lighthouse.

to occur after a sunny day. Areas for hides were limited due to agriculture down to the shoreline in places.

The entrance to the estuary was protected by batteries and minefields. There was a six-gun medium battery at Royan and another of four guns near Pointe de Grave lighthouse. Other coastal batteries were located at Arcachon. An old French battleship was berthed near Royan. There was a radar station (W310) just north of Point de Negade at Soulac-sur-Mer and flak batteries around Bordeaux.

Two armed trawlers patrolled the entrance and there were minesweepers in the area. It was assumed the river was patrolled, but details of the craft involved were not known. Quays capable of handling ocean-going ships were located at Bordeaux, Bassens on the east bank four miles below Bordeaux and Pauillac 25 miles downriver.

The Gironde entrance was shallow except for two channels, Passe de l'Ouest and Passe Sud. A submarine could not approach safely closer than 11 miles to the south of Pointe de Grave. The channels in the Gironde were well marked by buoys. The tidal range was 3-5.6m with a current of up to 5 knots depending on the state of the tide. The estuary was subject to a tidal bore at spring tides. No booms or nets were expected.

In addition to the blockade-runners, there were other significant targets in the area; two large dredgers kept the port and approach channels from silting up and massive concrete U-Boat pens were being constructed in Bordeaux's No.3 Basin on the west bank at Bacalan. The U-Boat pens were beyond a series of parallel locks, which ruled them out as a target because of the difficulty of blocking them simultaneously.

It was concluded that any approach by sea would have to be carried out in stages, lying up in hides during the day. The longest section covered by defences was at the entrance to the estuary where a small craft would have to pass 15 miles of defended area. A favourable flood tide was essential at night to make progress against the strong flow, which limited the days when the operation could be carried out.

To be really effective the canoes would need to deliver attacks over a number of nights, with the Limpets timed to explode after the last attack. However, the MFU was still experimental. Chariots could pack a bigger punch than Limpets, but they did not have the endurance to make the journey. The attack would therefore have to be made within the capacity of the canoes.

There were six minesweepers and three escort vessels in the Gironde. Another six M-Class minesweepers were based at Royan or Le Verdon and 12 E-boats and 12 R-Boats were believed to operate from the northern Biscay ports. Coastal routes used by these forces were well known and were to be avoided. U-boats transited the Gironde regularly and there were searchlights at Pointe de la Negade and other places.

708 Infanterie Division, a static formation consisting of two regiments (*728* and *748*), was in the area. The Germans had airfields at Bordeaux, Hourtin and Royan, but the number and types of aircraft were unclear.

The HQ Combined Operations planners had a very comprehensive intelligence picture to guide them.

A German sentry keeps watch over the River Gironde and the approaches to Bordeaux.

Chapter Five

PLANNING

HASLAR HAD TO TAKE STEWART into his confidence about the raid immediately. The two of them worked around the clock at times, sometimes being forced to use Benzedrine, a form of amphetamine used by servicemen of all nations to remain alert, to keep going. The plan had to be revised, improved and amplified before gaining approval by numerous authorities. There were also modifications to be made to the Cockles and food, stores and clothing to be procured.

Haslar met with Captain Raw RN, Chief Staff Officer to

Captain (later Vice-Admiral) Sidney Moffat Raw was very well educated at RN Colleges Osborne and Dartmouth, Trinity College Cambridge, Naval Staff College and Army Staff College Camberley. He entered the Royal Navy in 1914 and saw action at the Battles of Heligoland Bight, Dogger Bank and Jutland. Raw gained extensive experience on battleships, battlecruisers, light cruisers and submarines. In 1939 he was involved in raising the submarine HMS *Thetis*. He commanded the submarine depot ship HMS *Medway* from August 1940 until March 1942, during which he had experience landing SBS canoe units in North Africa. He commanded the light cruiser, HMS *Phoebe* from June 1944. In 1950 he was appointed Flag Officer (Submarines) at HMS *Dolphin*. He is pictured here in 1952 as Vice Admiral and Fourth Sea Lord (Chief of Supplies and Transport). Raw retired in August 1954 having been awarded the KBE and CB.

Admiral Sir Max Kennedy Horton GCB DSO, Flag Officer Submarines, was overall commander of Operation 'Frankton'. He entered the Royal Navy in 1898 and went into submarines in 1904. On returning to port in Submarine *E9*, having sunk the German cruiser SMS *Hela* on 13 September 1914, he initiated the tradition of British submarines hoisting the Jolly Roger. He also sank the cruiser SMS *Prinz Adalbert* in the Baltic in July 1915, three German destroyers, two transports and several merchant ships. He commanded the battleship HMS *Resolution* 1930-32, 2nd Battle Squadron 1933-35 from HMS *Malaya* and later HMS *Barham* as a Rear Admiral and 1st Cruiser Squadron from HMS *London* as a Vice-Admiral 1935-36. In 1940 he took command of home-based submarines and moved his HQ from Aberdour to Northway in London, officially to gain a freer hand in running his command, but purportedly to be near his favourite golf courses; he played a round almost every day during the war. He became CinC Western Approaches in November 1942 until the end of the war.

HMS *Forth* – 9,043 tons, length 151m, beam 22m, maximum speed 17 knots, armament eight 4.5" and eight 2 Pdr AA guns. Launched by John Brown on Clydebank 11 August 1938 and commissioned 14 May 1939 as a Maidstone Class Submarine Depot Ship (A187). She could accommodate up to 1,167 men and was based in home waters during the war apart from a brief period at Halifax, Nova Scotia in 1941. Renamed HMS *Defiance* in 1972, she was scrapped in 1985.

Admiral Sir Max Kennedy Horton, Flag Officer Submarines (FOS), also known as Admiral (Submarines), at Northway, London, to persuade him of the importance of allocating a submarine. Raw agreed, but they would have to leave from the Clyde where the 3rd Submarine Flotilla was based on the depot ship HMS *Forth* anchored in Holy Loch off Kilmun. Captain Hugh Meynell Cyril 'Tinsides' Ionides commanded 3rd Submarine Flotilla and HMS *Forth* simultaneously from December 1941 to April 1943.

In addition, Raw told Haslar the submarine could not return for them eight nights later, as the enemy would be looking for it after the attack. In any case the canoeists would be unable to navigate accurately enough to find a submarine at night many miles off shore. The escape would therefore have to be overland through enemy territory into Spain.

Haslar was not deterred. Leaving from the Clyde would help with their cover story; they would announce that the section going up there was to conduct advanced training, which was partly correct. On 12 October, Haslar and Stewart went to HQ Combined Operations and spoke to Lieutenant Commander GP L'Estrange about submarines. L'Estrange was responsible for coordinating all the operational planning for 'Frankton' and acting as the link between Haslar and Whitehall. He would also prepare reference cards for each canoe setting out details of tide, moon and morning and evening twilight. Before the war he had been a rubber planter in Malaya. Haslar visited HQ FOS again to tie up final details of the submarine with Captain Raw.

Authority for the raid was granted by Mountbatten on 13 October, but he ordered Hasler not to take part because of his experience as a canoe specialist. Haslar was distraught. On 18 October he went to HQ Combined Operations again to discuss the operation with Lieutenant Commander L'Estrange. Whilst there he saw Colonel Neville with tears in his eyes. He said it was impossible for him not to take part in the raid, "If they go without me sir, and don't return, I shall never be able to face the others in my party again."

Neville agreed to intercede with Mountbatten and Hasler also submitted his reasons in writing through Horton and Neville. He argued that the operation stood a good chance, but seamanship and navigation were paramount. His 2IC had only a few months experience and, if he commanded, the chance of success would be reduced and failure could prejudice future operations. The unit was new, so the commander had to show the way or lose respect and credibility. In addition he was no longer a member of the Combined Operations development organisation. His final point was - if not allowed on this mission, then what mission would he be able to undertake? He cited the case of Major David Stirling who formed the Special Air Service in Egypt.

On 21 October, Haslar went to Chatham with Captain Selby RN and Lieutenant Commander L'Estrange. They discussed a rehearsal for the raid, Exercise Blanket, with Captain (later Commodore CB CBE) Robert Gordon Hood Linzee, Staff Officer (Convoys) at Nore Command. Haslar was at HQ Combined Operations on the afternoon of 28 October to talk about the operation and Exercise Blanket. Next day he and L'Estrange went to Chatham again to attend a conference with Nore Command, before returning to HQ Combined Operations at 1700 for a meeting chaired by Mountbatten. In attendance were Brigadier Joseph Haydon, Mountbatten's Vice Chief, plus Hussey, Selby and Neville. The plan was considered in detail. When it came to command, Mountbatten looked at Haslar.

Mountbatten:
I understand you want to lead this raid yourself?
Haslar:
Yes Sir.

Mountbatten:

Why?

Haslar:

Because it is an important mission sir and I think we should put our best team into it. MacKinnon and his men have been doing intensive boat training for a few months, but I have been using small boats all my life, and it is only natural that I'm better at it than they are."

Mountbatten:

What about the other half of your unit, which you would be leaving behind?

Haslar:

Capt Stewart is fully capable of carrying on the training and development work with No.2 Section sir.

Mountbatten:

The fact remains that this is a risky operation, with an unusually difficult withdrawal plan. If you go, there is a strong possibility that you won't come back. We originally got you into Combined Ops because you were well qualified to develop new ideas for us, and all that side of things will be prejudiced if you go.

Haslar:

Sir, I don't see how I can develop raiding techniques and equipment properly if I've never been on a raid myself. And I don't see how I could go on commanding the unit if I sent No.1 Section away in its present inexperienced condition without my guidance; and if the operation were a complete failure, and they didn't come back, I simply shouldn't be able to face the others Sir.

Mountbatten went round the table asking others for their views. All were against him going and Haslar's heart sank until Neville said, 'I think he should go sir. He's mad keen to. I know Blondie and I'm pretty confident he'll get back all right.' Mountbatten smiled and said, 'Well much against my better judgement, I'm going to let you go.' Haslar was delighted.

Following the meeting, HQ Combined Operations produced a summary of the outline plan for consideration by the COS. At that time only three Cockles were envisaged. They were to leave the Clyde on 25 November, with the first possible night for leaving the submarine nine miles off the Cordouan Lighthouse being 3/4 December and the last 12/13 December. Because it was likely some of the canoes would not reach the target, Mountbatten doubled the number to six.

At 2115 on 29 October, Haslar boarded the train for Glasgow

The Cordouan Lighthouse with waves breaking over the surrounding shoals. It was designed by Louis de Foix, completed in 1611 and is a Renaissance masterpiece still in use today. Standing 68m tall it is visible for 41 kms.

and arrived at HMS *Forth* next day. He met up with No.1 Section, which had travelled independently from Portsmouth. The COS were expected to approve the raid any day (they did on 3 November), so Haslar met with Captain Ionides to work out the final details. Feeling very content with progress, Haslar spent the night drinking with Tommy Lambert (Lieutenant CWSC Lambert DSC was lost commanding HM Submarine *P615* when she was torpedoed by U-*123*, 100 miles southwest of Freetown, Sierra Leone on 18 April 1943; he is commemorated on the Portsmouth Naval Memorial).

On 7 November, Haslar and Stewart went to London for meetings next day about Exercise Blanket with Colonel Neville, Lieutenant Commander L'Estrange and Paymaster Lieutenant Mowll. On the 9th, Haslar went to Chatham to tie up final details for the exercise, booked accommodation at the Royal Marines Barracks and met with Captain Linzee. Later that day, MacKinnon and No.1 Section arrived. Next day Lieutenant Commander L'Estrange arrived to discuss 'Frankton' and returned on the 13th with Paymaster Lieutenant Mowll to visit No.1 Section on the exercise, details of which are covered in Chapter 6. The day after the exercise ended, Haslar left Chatham for HQ Combined Operations to discuss 'Frankton' again.

On 16 November, Lieutenant Commander Boyle of the Landing Craft Obstruction Clearance Unit (also known as Boom Commandos), visited RMBPD to discuss explosives. Boom Commandos were first ashore on D-Day, destroying over 2,500 obstacles for the loss of two frogmen killed. The 17th found Haslar at SOE Welwyn again to discuss Limpet mine time delays and explosive chain and wire cutters, before returning to HQ Combined Operations. Next day, Stewart and Ladbrooke joined Haslar and Lieutenant Commander Allen at Badger's Yard, Tower Bridge to inspect the motor barge *Larry* as a potential parent vessel for the motor boats. That afternoon MacKinnon joined Haslar at HQ Combined Operations to meet with Major Ronnie Sillars about the No.3 Code, by which simple messages could be sent back if taken prisoner. MacKinnon still knew nothing about the raid and it is not known what he thought about all the mystery and intrigue.

On 24 November, the COS Committee approved an amendment to the 'Frankton' plan – the cessation of mine laying in the Gironde estuary by the RAF over the period 5-12 December. This would make it safer for the delivery submarine, HMS *Tuna*. In addition, with no aircraft flying in the area, it was hoped the defenders would be less alert. In any case it was a no-moon period, during which air operations were usually curtailed, so there was little chance of the defenders being suspicious of the reduced activity.

The final plan was for six Cockles Mk.II to be transported to the mouth of the Gironde by submarine. From there they would paddle upstream to Bordeaux to carry out a Limpet attack before escaping through Spain. 3rd Submarine Flotilla was responsible for launching the Cockles successfully. The raid was not to be launched until the Flotilla Commander, Captain Ionides, was satisfied this could be done. The submarine was to sail around 30 November, carrying out day and night launching drills en route. The submarine was to launch the canoes 9.5 miles southwest of Pointe de la Negade, south of the estuary.

Weather and tidal conditions were critical. It had to be a no-moon period with the tide in flood at night or at least slack to allow the canoes to make headway. A Force 3 wind with a slight swell was the maximum tolerable for launching the canoes. The first night possible for launching was 5/6 December and the last 12/13 December.

Because so many magnetic mines had been sown off the Gironde, HMS *Tuna* was degaussed a number of times prior to 'Frankton'. This was not lost on her crew; they knew something was on. The mines were plotted with an accuracy of only one mile, so *Tuna* was not to approach these areas or shallow waters.

Overall command was vested in FOS who could cancel the operation for any reason. The naval force commander was Lieutenant Commander Dick Raikes and the landing force commander was Major Haslar. Raikes could cancel the operation if he believed the weather or enemy risked the submarine and Haslar if he believed the enemy seriously prejudiced the safety

A Limpet mine of the type used on the raid attached to a keeper plate. In July 1939, the head of the technical section of Military Intelligence (Research), Major MR Jefferis (later General Sir Millis Jefferis KBE MC), read in Armchair Science about a powerful magnet developed by GEC in America. He contacted the editor, Stuart Macrae, who with Cecil Vandepeer Clarke, designed a mine of 4.5 kgs, including 4 kgs of explosive, to attach directly to a ship by six magnets. Placed below the water line the pressure accentuated the blast and blew a 1m diameter hole in a ship. A liquid ampoule broken inside the fuse dissolved a washer to release the striker pin and detonate the charge, but the delay was affected by temperature and was not accurate. Three Limpets was the minimum considered necessary to sink a ship, with one normally placed on the engine room to immobilise it if the others failed. Experimental sympathetic fuses were fitted to detonate when concussed by the explosion of another. Military Intelligence (Research), otherwise known as 'Winston Churchill's Toyshop', worked on devices for Auxiliary Units and cooperated closely with SOE. By the end of the war it had developed 26 new weapons.

of his force making success unlikely. The action to be taken in various emergencies was thought through in some detail:

If the submarine was surprised on the surface, the forward hatch was to be closed, those on deck would inflate life jackets, load their canoes and get in with covers fastened. If the submarine dived they would float off and proceed with the mission.

If there was no time, everyone on deck was to get below via the conning tower hatch, having destroyed the canoe buoyancy bags to ensure they sank and did not fall into enemy hands. Any canoe losing the main formation was to proceed independently.

Boats were to be avoided and canoeists were to freeze in the low position and hope to avoid detection.

If a patrol boat came alongside, the canoeists were to use hand grenades and attempt to seize the boat, allowing the other canoes to get away.

If challenged from the shore they were to adopt the low position and let the current take them away without paddling or firing back.

Lieutenant Richard Prendergast Raikes, one of five children of an Indian Army officer, entered Dartmouth in 1925 aged 13 and was presented with the King's Dirk by King George V. In 1933 the 'bullshit' of the gunnery course at HMS *Excellent* on Whale Island made him determined to serve only in small ships without guns. Later that year he attended submarine training at HMS *Dolphin* and served on *L22*, HMS *Clyde*, *H32* and HMS *Severn* before the war. He trialed conning a submerged submarine while holding onto the periscope - Maltese fishermen believed he was walking on water like Paul of Tarsus in the same place in AD30. His first command, *L26*, was used as a target for destroyers working up anti-submarine dills at Scapa Flow. In September 1941 he took command of HMS *Seawolf* and made a sighting of *Tirpitz* in March 1942. On 26 August 1942 he took command of HMS *Tuna*, coming out of refit at Blythe. By March 1943 he was exhausted and posted to the officer training establishment at King Alfred, Hove. Soon after he was diverted to Coastal Command as the anti-U-boat adviser. At the end of the war he commanded U-*3514* and a number of others during Operation 'Deadlight', the scuttling of over 100 U-boats off the north coast of Ireland. Invalided out of the Navy in July 1946, he worked in the hotel business, Royal British Legion and Marconi's publicity department until 1972. Haslar regarded him as, "the very best type of British naval officer."

If seen by French people while lying up, they were to say they were British and ask them not to tell anyone else.

If approached by a few enemy they were to kill them as silently as possible, conceal the bodies below the high water line and get away as soon as possible after dark regardless of the tide.

A canoe in distress was to be helped by its division. They should try to get a damaged canoe and crew ashore. If not the escape bags were to be retrieved, the canoe scuttled and the crew left to make their way ashore.

Any crews unable to make the target were to scuttle their canoes, lie up for at least four days after leaving the submarine and then escape.

If the alarm was raised during the attack individual canoes were to press on using their own initiative.

After launching the canoes, HMS *Tuna* was to withdraw 200 miles west into the Bay of Biscay before reporting the situation. Initially the canoes would travel in two divisions each of three canoes in arrowhead. When they were one mile north of Pointe de Grave, Haslar would decide which bank they would follow to the first lying up point. He would also give final instructions to B Division, as it would travel independently thereafter under MacKinnon. This would ensure that if one Division was intercepted, the other had a chance of getting through. While moving they were to avoid the buoyed channel and keep well clear of the shore. There was to be no move in daylight, even in thick fog.

They would paddle by night on the flood tide and hide by day. Haslar had sectional charts of the estuary made up, colour coded with their suitability for concealment during the day - red impossible, yellow difficult, blue likely and green good. Notes were provided for each stretch detailing what the area might provide. While lying up they had to stay low and avoid movement, as undetected enemy positions may be close by. Each division would have one sentry on duty. As each chart was finished with, it was to be destroyed to preserve security.

The advanced base for the attack was to be within 10 miles of the target. There the air photos were to be destroyed or concealed. They would fuse the Limpets, restow their kit ready for the get away, fold the breakwaters and stow compasses below.

Haslar's intention was to sink 12 merchantmen in Bordeaux harbour; two per canoe. The attack was to be made at high water slack. Canoes were to attack the following targets independently:

TARGET AREA	A DIVISION	B DIVISION
Bordeaux west bank	*Catfish* (Haslar/Sparks)	*Cuttlefish* (Mackinnon/Conway)
Bordeaux east bank	*Crayfish* (Laver/Mills)	*Coalfish* (Wallace/Ewart)
Bassens north and south	*Conger* (Sheard/Moffatt)	*Cachalot* (Ellery/Fisher)

Each canoe was to place two Limpets about 1.5m below the water line on the four largest merchantmen in their target area. To avoid duplication, A Division was to place theirs on the upstream end of each target and B Division on the downstream, thus ensuring an even spread. *Catfish* and *Cuttlefish* also carried explosive cutters to be placed on any vessel during the withdrawal, having noted a suitable target on the way in.

Secondary target areas were designated in case they could not penetrate into the main target area. Tankers were secondary targets, because extra bulkheads made them more difficult to sink, followed by any smaller vessels. A list of equipment carried in the canoes and what the canoeists wore, is at Appendix 2.

Following the attack they would paddle downstream with the ebb tide, avoiding the channels and shoreline until low water. They would then destroy remaining charts and papers, retrieve their escape equipment, destroy all buoyancy and scuttle the canoes before making their escape from the east bank. On arrival in Spain they were to find the nearest British Consul and report they were part of a Combined Operations mission, but give no other details.

Chapter Six

TRAINING AND PREPARATIONS

TRAINING FOR THE RAID started in earnest on 20 October, although the participants were unaware. Haslar arrived at Glasgow Central at 0745 on 30 October following the crucial meeting with Mountbatten the previous day. He bathed in the gents lavatory and had breakfast before catching another train to Gourock, then a steamer to Dunoon and a bus to Ardanadam, eventually reaching HMS *Forth* in Loch Long at 1230. That afternoon he sorted out the purpose of the visit with Captain Ionides and discussed how to fix the hoisting out apparatus for the canoes.

No.1 Section left Southsea for HMS *Forth* the same day for advanced training on the Cockle Mk.II, accompanied by

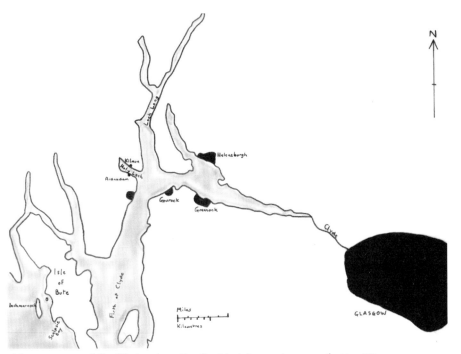

The area around the Clyde where the final training and preparations were carried out prior to the raid.

Storeman 'Dickie' Drew and Marine Todd to act as orderly to the officers. They were met by Haslar at Gourock on 31 October and the stores arrived by lorry at 1500. This was the first time No.1 Section saw the latest Cockles Mk.II, the ones they would soon use for real. While they were away, No.2 Section continued training around Portsmouth under Captain Stewart, concentrating on the Cockle Mk.I, motor boating and shallow water diving.

Lightly loaded canoes had been launched from submarines in the comparative calm of the Mediterranean. The empty canoes had been lowered onto the forward hydroplanes where the crew climbed aboard and their kit was passed to them. The submarine then trimmed down and the canoes floated free. Haslar knew their heavily laden canoes would be swamped in the Atlantic swell before they could be launched. His solution was to hoist them out fully loaded with the crew aboard and the cockpit covers done up. The Mk.II's base was strong enough to accept this treatment, but the launch was still difficult and required practice.

HMS *Tuna*, a T-class submarine built by Scotts of Greenock and commissioned on 1 August 1940. She was adopted by Aldershot. Her two diesels, ironically German MANs, could move her at 14 knots on the surface. Underwater her electric motors moved her at 8 knots flat out for 90 minutes or 2 knots for 20 hours. Her armament was six torpedo tubes forward with six reload torpedoes, a 4" gun and a 20mm Oerlikon AA gun. She sank the 7,230 ton Norwegian *Tirranna* off the Gironde on 22 September 1940, which had been captured by the Germans; unfortunately most of those who died were captured Allied sailors. *Tuna* also sank the German *Ostmark*, the French tug *Chassiron* and U-*644*. Other attacks on U-*302*, the Italian submarine *Brin*, two unidentified submarine contacts and the German tanker *Benno* failed. *Tuna* was broken for scrap at Briton Ferry, Wales in June 1946.

The first few days were spent practicing hoisting out from a submarine and Limpet attacks. The procedure for the attack was to approach with a favourable tide, single paddle, assessing the ship from a distance, as alongside it was impossible to distinguish the type. On a signal from No.1 the No.2 attached them to the ship with the magnetic holdfast at shoulder level. No.1 separated one of a pair of Limpets from the keeper plate and hooked it on the end of a placing rod. Reaching down he lowered the Limpet to the full depth and gradually moved it towards the ship's side until it took hold. The placing rod was released by pushing down. At a signal from No.1 the No.2 released the holdfast and they drifted or paddled carefully to place the next.

Haslar's drawing illustrating how to place a Limpet; it appeared in *Cockleshell Heroes* by CR Lucas Phillips in 1956.

HMS *Tuna* had been allocated for the operation, but was not immediately available, so Ionides allocated two other submarines for training; HMS *Sea Nymph P223* under Lieutenant GDN Milner DSC RN and HMS *Taurus P339* under Lieutenant Mervyn RG Wingfield RN. Before the canoeists progressed to launching from a submarine, they first practiced from the Dutch minesweeper *Jan van Gelder*.

3 November saw them conduct an exhausting trip up Loch Long with fully laden canoes. The Loch was normally used for testing torpedoes. Next day they practiced hoisting out fully loaded from *Jan van Gelder*. She then steamed at two knots while the Cockles practiced Limpet attacks in a simulated tidal stream, first of all in daylight and then after dark. They

Jan Van Gelder, a Jan van Amstel class minesweeper of the Royal Netherlands Navy, commissioned on 13 September 1937. Damaged by her own mines in October 1939, she returned to service in April 1940. When the Netherlands was overrun she served with the Royal Navy at Milford Haven, Portland, Harwich and the Isle of Wight in various Minesweeping Flotillas, before going to Scotland as escort ship to 3rd Submarine Flotilla. She returned to the Royal Netherlands Navy in 1946 and served in the Dutch East Indies until 1950. She was converted to a boom defence vessel and from 1961 she was a Zeekadetkorps vessel until being scrapped.

Lieutenant (later Captain) Mervyn Robert George Wingfield DSO DSC was a submariner on active service throughout WW2. He had tours on battleships HMS *Benbow*, *Valiant* and *Warspite* before opting for submarine service in 1934. He commanded submarines H*28*, HMS *Umpire* and HMS *Sturgeon*. On 19 July 1941, *Umpire* was sunk in collision with an armed trawler off Great Yarmouth. *Sturgeon* was involved in Arctic convoy protection and was the navigation marker for the St Nazaire assault force during Operation Chariot on the night of 27/28 March 1942. On one occasion Wingfield's submarine was part of a convoy when he signalled an escorting destroyer, "If attacked at night I intend to remain surfaced." He received back, "So do I." *Taurus* sank the Spanish merchant ship *Barolo*, which because it was neutral, caused some anxiety, but the British Ambassador to Spain signaled, "Since your sinking all trade to Occupied

France has ceased. Well Done." After the collapse of Italy, *Taurus* went to the Indian Ocean and was the first British submarine to sink a Japanese submarine, *I34*. When the Germans surrendered, Wingfield was put in charge of twenty-five U-boats in Norway. He had a variety of appointments after the war in the Admiralty, on the cruiser *Euryalus* (Mountbatten's flagship), Washington, Brussels, Virginia, Athens and Tel Aviv. His final tour was commanding the naval air station at Abbotsinch in Scotland and he retired in 1962. In civilian life he worked in a charitable organization, was chairman of two companies, a marine manager and worked as second mate on several merchant vessels.

returned to HMS *Forth* at 2330. Despite it being November they also resumed open water swimming training.

On 5 November, No.1 Section camouflage painted their Cockles while Haslar and Stewart, who arrived that day, cut up charts, drafted orders and planned Exercise Blanket. Even if they said nothing, the camouflage paint must have had No.1 Section thinking that something was afoot. Stewart was there to observe from *Jan van Gelder* the hoisting out trials from HMS *Taurus*.

With No.1 Section aboard, HMS *Taurus* set off at 0740 next morning into a fresh southeasterly. The weather at Rothsay meant *Jan van Gelder* was unable to make contact with the submarine, but the hoisting out trial went ahead in the lee of the Isle of Arran during heavy squalls. They gained much valuable experience before returning to HMS *Forth*. Having packed all stores, they proceeded to Glasgow and on 9 November arrived at Chatham to meet up with Haslar, who had gone ahead, while Stewart returned to Portsmouth.

Before conducting the operation they needed a rehearsal in conditions as close to the Gironde as possible. The only river estuary in Britain that came close was the Thames. On arrival at Chatham, No.1 Section was briefed on Exercise Blanket. The aim was to penetrate the 70 miles from Margate to Deptford and back unobserved by defenders or inhabitants. From Margate they would move along the north Kent coast to the Swale estuary keeping within three miles of the shore. After crossing the Swale Boom they would pass through the East and West Swale to the Medway and then past Garrison Point into the Thames, keeping inside the Thames Boom to Deptford. The return would be the reverse except in the Medway they would finish at Boatship Wharf in Chatham Dockyard.

Local defences and police forces were told the exercise was to test the possibility of small boats penetrating the Thames defences. The canoes would move by night and lie up during the day. If seen the canoes were to be challenged with, "Boat Ahoy" and the crew response was 'Blanket', following which they would be allowed to proceed. If sighted on land they had special exercise passes to prove their identity and would be allowed to proceed without their canoes being searched. Sightings were to be reported to Nore Command.

The crews were briefed the evening before the exercise commenced and Haslar and MacKinnon had to work until midnight to prepare the tide tables. Meanwhile the men, lodged in a pub, took advantage of the local hospitality. Next night, 10 December, they set out at 2015 in ideal conditions, paddling out to sea from Margate jetty. Things began to go wrong early on,

The route for Exercise 'Blanket' from Margate to Deptford.

The P8 Compass used from 1937 in the Spitfire, Hurricane and other aircraft.

starting with Haslar becoming separated from the rest; he did not see them again until the end of the exercise.

Proceeding north out of the Swale in fog, MacKinnon grounded in mud flats and marsh grass. By the time he had twisted and turned in the dark to get clear he was completely disorientated. The P8 compass they were using had a grid that could easily be read 180° out. MacKinnon headed north, or so he thought, for 30 minutes until returning to a railway bridge he had already passed and then realised he was going south. MacKinnon thereby joined what Haslar's Party called the 'Reciprocal Club'.

Many other problems were encountered. Corporal Sheard thought he was following the stern of Haslar's canoe, until it took off; it was a gull. He was also heading the wrong way along the estuary. One canoe was holed on the East Swale boom on the first night. Three canoes lost formation on the second night, but regained it by moving in daylight. On the third night rough weather dispersed the whole force. Only two canoes penetrated the Scar's Elbow boom in darkness, one got within two miles of Deptford before withdrawing to Erith and the remainder failed to make the distance mainly due to poor navigation and lack of stamina.

It took them five nights to reach Blackwall, utterly exhausted and short of the target. All canoes were challenged at least twice, not least because the defences were alert, but also due to the clear conditions. It was concluded that six canoes moving together was too large a formation.

Blackwall Point, occupied by a power station in 1942 and now

Blackwall Point, the furthest point reached by any canoe on Exercise Blanket, now occupied by the O2 Arena.

by the O2 Arena, was reached by Haslar at 0600 on the 14th; the only canoe unseen throughout the exercise. He went back to collect MacKinnon and three canoes at Greenhithe before they all returned to Chatham later in the day. No.1 Section returned to Portsmouth next day and spent a few days preparing stores, while Haslar went to HQ Combined Operations for the exercise post-mortem. At lunchtime in the all-ranks canteen Mountbatten saw him:

Mountbatten:

Well, how did the rehearsal go?

Haslar:

I'm afraid it was a complete failure sir."

Mountbatten:

Splendid! In that case you must have learned a great deal and you'll be able to avoid making the same mistakes on the operation.

Buoyed up by the unexpected response, Haslar did not feel quite so exhausted and spent that evening with MacKinnon at a Wrens' party. They had indeed learned a lot and the lessons were not lost. Haslar used them to focus the final period of training.

A Bedford lorry driven by Marine Phelps arrived at 'White Heather' on 18 November to pick up No.1 Section. Ewart did not appear particularly perturbed at leaving Heather and joined in the high-spirited fun with the others. As they left they called out, "Heather, look after our things; we'll be back soon." She must have sensed something despite knowing nothing about the forthcoming mission. As they turned back into the empty and silent house she broke down on her mother's shoulder crying, 'Oh Mother! They'll never come back. I know they'll never come back.'

Heather was not the only one to have had a premonition. As MacKinnon took leave of Pritchard-Gordon he said, 'Well goodbye Bill. I shan't see you again.' Pritchard-Gordon told him that was nonsense, but MacKinnon was adamant, 'No, I don't think I shall Bill.'

They travelled to London by train, joining Haslar and MacKinnon who were already there to attend a meeting at HQ Combined Operations about the No.3 Code. All were taken in three blacked out taxis to a studio where they were photographed before being taken back to HQ Combined Operations. Together they travelled by train to Glasgow, arriving at HMS *Forth* at 1230 on the 19th. The stores arriving at

Al Rawdah with a submarine alongside. She was built in 1911 as the *Chenab* for the Nourse Line of London. Sold in 1930 to the Khedivial Mail Steamship and Graving Dock and renamed *Ville de Beyrouth*. In 1939 she was sold again and renamed *Al Rawdah*. Requisitioned by the Ministry of Shipping, for six months she was a prison for Irish republican internees moored off Killyleagh in Strangford Lough, before becoming an accommodation ship for the Royal Navy. After the war she returned to her owners and was scrapped in 1953.

Gourock by lorry and in the afternoon were transferred to HMS *Forth*. However, all the cabins were occupied and they were accommodated on a hotel ship, the *Al Rawdah*, a former merchant ship, moored close by.

On 20 November they unpacked the stores and built their canoes before landing at Ardanadam for a short forced march over the hills and instruction on the .45 Colt pistol and Silent Sten. That evening there were lectures on the Cockle Suit and their escape equipment, followed by a small party for Moffat's 21st birthday on *Al Rawdah*. Next day they landed for a cross-country march and in the afternoon there were lectures on fitting the .45 Colt holster, the Fairburn-Sykes fighting knife and fusing Limpets. On 22 November they fused Limpets and dropped them on the seabed. In the afternoon they practiced single paddle drill, approaching ships and hull work. That evening there was another small celebration, this time for Colley's 21st.

The same day, Lieutenant Commander Dick Raikes finished six days leave and reported to HQ FOS at Swiss Cottage. He was briefed about a forthcoming special patrol involving launching canoes close to the Gironde estuary.

The 23rd was a long day for No.1 Section. In the morning was navigational training, assisted by HMS *Forth's* navigation officer. In the afternoon they embarked on *Jan Van Gelder* and in upper Loch Long carried out dummy Limpet

Colt .45 Pistol.

Sten Gun fitted with a silencer.

attacks in a 1 – 2.5 knot current. They repeated the procedures in darkness starting at 1930 and returned to HMS *Forth* at 2330. The 24th and 25th were spent on board carrying out navigational training, preparing stores, speed building and collapsing their canoes and fusing Limpets until they could do it in the dark. They also loaded their canoes and learned how to find any item of equipment by touch.

The transit submarine, HMS *Tuna*, arrived at HMS *Forth*. She had returned from a series of abortive patrols in appalling weather in the north having been refitted at Swan Hunters on the Tyne during the summer. Haslar went aboard on 25 November to meet the 1st Lieutenant, John Raymond Henry 'Johnny' Bull, to discuss stowing and launching the canoes. Bull suggested they use the floating off method, unaware of the developments that had taken place, but was receptive to Haslar's alternative and agreed to fit the girder to the submarine's Mk.12, 4" gun and accepted the slings Haslar provided. He was assisted by 2nd Cox'n Fright and the casing crew to fit the hoisting out girder. To fit in the canoes, stores and 13 Marines, Bull had a great deal of reorganization to carry out within *Tuna* before they sailed, including the removal of a number of spare torpedoes. Bull was later promoted to Commander, commanded HMS *Severn* and HMS *Clyde* and was involved in special operations in the Far East; he was awarded the MBE, DSC & Bar and US Bronze Star.

The quickening of the training pace made No.1 Section realise something was afoot and there was some speculation. The general consensus seemed to be it would be Norway. Captain Stewart arrived on the 25th with more stores and Lieutenant Commander L'Estrange next day. Together with Haslar they met with 3rd Submarine Flotilla officers on HMS *Forth* on the 27th.

Carrying eight magnetic Limpets and a holdfast in each canoe caused enormous compass deviation. To reduce the effect they were kept well to the stern of the canoe, away from the compass on the foredeck. They were also kept in pairs face to face with a keeper plate between, which helped to reduce the magnetic field. Before departing on a mission or exercise, each canoe had to be fully loaded and the compass swung to take account of the deviation. The navigating officer of HMS *Forth* assisted with swinging their compasses in fully loaded canoes on 26 November.

Haslar realized everyone was getting stale with the unrelenting pressure of training and decided they needed a 'run ashore' on the night of the 27th. Mackinnon and Ewart took the opportunity to visit their families in Glasgow. On previous leaves Ewart had taken Conway and Sparks, but on this occasion went alone. His 11 year-old brother, George, remembered Ewart telling his mother he would be away for a while. Mackinnon didn't even mention to his family that he was only a few miles away.

Haslar and Stewart took the opportunity to climb a hill on Bute, with the intention of getting an early night after dinner, but Haslar's diary records he spent that evening drinking with Poles on *Al Rawdah* with disastrous results. The Poles insisted Haslar and Stewart join them in a glass of 'port' before bed. They produced a bottle of homemade grain spirit, which had a most peculiar effect. Next morning as Sergeant Wallace reported the parade correct he remarked to Captain Stewart he thought his face was covered in chalk he was that pale.

The men selected to go on the raid were divided into two divisions each of three canoes (see Appendix 3 for biographical details):

A Division

Catfish	- Major Hasler and Marine Sparks.
Crayfish	- Corporal Laver and Marine Mills.
Conger	- Corporal Sheard and Marine Moffat.

B Division

Cuttlefish	- Lieutenant Mackinnon and Marine Conway.
Coalfish	- Sergeant Wallace and Marine Ewart.
Cachalot	- Marine Ellery and Marine Fisher.
Reserve	- Marine N Colley.

Colley suffered a metatarsal injury in training, which put him in hospital for a while. He was replaced by Conway, who completed Exercise Blanket. MacKinnon ensured Colley went along on Frankton as the reserve, but his injury almost certainly saved his life.

Final preparations included painting their canoes and Cockle suits with special flexible paint for use on rubberized material. Each canoe's name on the bow in white, was painted over. Rank badges, Royal Marines shoulder flashes and Combined Operations insignia were sown on their uniforms.

The men were told they would be away on a long exercise for some time and should tell their families not to expect word for a while. Mills wrote home that he was in a ship, "… but cannot tell you anymore and if I don't come back for some time, don't worry". He later wrote he did not expect to come home at all, but this letter was one of those written aboard *Tuna* and not posted until after she returned from patrol. Conway who was expecting to go home, wrote to say leave was temporarily stopped but he didn't know where he was going. With a premonition Ewart wrote a final letter to his parents and brothers:

I'm enjoying every minute of it. I hope that what we have done helps to end the mess we are in and make a decent and better world… I've a feeling I'll be like a bad penny, so please don't upset yourself about my safety.…I can't thank you enough for all you have done for me but will take it with me wherever I go, so trusting we meet again I'll say goodbye to you all, thanking God for a Mother and Dad giving me the courage as you have done.…'

Ewart also wrote to Heather, saying nothing about his fears. The letter was full of his feelings for her and his hopes for the return. She had even stronger premonitions than when he left Southsea. She bought a cigarette case for his approaching 21st birthday, but an NCO advised her not to send it and wait until he came back.

Corporal Laver wrote home about missing his elder brother's, Jack Laver, wedding to Phyllis Page at Barnet on 20 November. He was sure he'd get leave afterwards. Laver should have been the best man.

With a monumental hangover, Haslar met Dick Raikes for the first time on 28 November, only a few days before they set sail. They immediately bonded and had similar outlooks on their tasks. They formed a life long friendship. Both were calm cool perfectionists, setting an excellent example and able to make their command presence felt down to the lowest level. Both were capable of going long periods without sleep. Raikes dominated every inch of *Tuna* by sheer personality, but rarely had to raise his voice. He was the ideal submarine commander, always where his presence was required, quick to rectify what was wrong and by sleeping on the wardroom settee was always ready to react.

Raikes had his sailing orders and aboard *Tuna* was the only one who knew about the operation. He and Haslar discussed in detail how it would proceed. While serving as 1st Lieutenant on HMS *Talisman*, Raikes had been involved in offloading a canoe and two agents (one French, one British) off the Gironde estuary, using the floating off method, so he had some experience of these types of operation. Sub Lieutenant Rowe, the navigation officer, was told the Marines would be accompanying them on an exercise in a few days time.

At 1100 on 29 November, the principal officers (Haslar, Ionides, Raikes, L'Estrange and Rowe, but not Stewart) met for a final planning conference on board HMS *Forth*. L'Estrange produced the latest air photographs, hydrographic, topographic and intelligence information, together with a full set of sectional charts for each canoe showing the areas thought safe and unsafe for lying up. Haslar was still the only one in the know. L'Estrange briefed him on the escape instructions; where to make for, how to dress, how to behave etc and provided French money for them all.

On that last afternoon before sailing Haslar and Sparks took all bags for the canoes to HMS *Forth* in readiness for loading HMS *Tuna*. That night Haslar packed his papers and effects and gave them to Stewart, together with an extensive list of tasks to be completed while he was away. He was to continue developing underwater attack by swimmers and submersibles, a suitable underwater suit and progress delivery of the BPBs and canoes. Stewart would not get much rest while Haslar was away.

Fairburn-Sykes Fighting Knife – a double-edged knife with a foil grip developed by William Ewart Fairbairn and Eric Anthony Sykes in Shanghai before the war and made famous by British Commandos. The first batch of 50 were produced in January 1941 by Wilkinson Sword.

Chapter Seven

THE INSERTION

A FTER DARK on the evening of 29 November the folded canoes were carefully lowered through HMS *Tuna's* forward torpedo hatch, followed by the cargo bags. Next morning No.1 Section embarked, expecting another exercise until, as Sparks recalled, they lined up on the rear casing and were addressed by Captain Ionides. He told them that the day they had been training for had arrived, but he did not know what they were going to do and where. At 1030 watched by L'Estrange and Stewart, HMS *Tuna* moved slowly away from HMS *Forth* with the ship's company lining the deck; as was

Folded Cockles stacked on a jetty.

Passing a canoe through the torpedo hatch on the forward deck of a submarine.

traditional the Marines were on the after casing at attention. Once below, apart from a few hours that night they wouldn't see the sky again until they launched off the French coast.

With no watches to keep and able to relax and smoke below while they were on the surface, they were quite content at first despite the cramped conditions. It was a new experience and the Navy looked after them very well, giving up some bunks and mess spaces.

An hour into the journey Haslar gathered them in the forward torpedo space amongst the canoes and equipment. "This time it is the real thing. I haven't been able to tell you before, but we have now started to carry out an actual operation against the enemy." He told them the outline of the plan, with the details to be briefed over the coming days. They were excited, apprehensive and surprised. Until then Sparks thought they were going after the *Tirpitz* in Norway.

Wallace asked the inevitable question, "How do we get back sir?" Making their way through an alien and partly hostile country was startling and unexpected, but they soon recovered. When Haslar offered a way out if they felt the operation was too much for them, they looked at each other, grinned and thought, "Not likely".

Haslar lightened the tension by telling them he would be at the greatest disadvantage; what little French he spoke was with a German accent. Jokingly Wallace said if captured he would declare himself neutral as he was born in Ireland. Mackinnon said nothing, but may have been smiling inwardly as he realised what the French speaking evenings at Spencer Road had been all about. When the initial briefing was over, Fisher described their feelings:

The morale was really something and had to be seen to be believed. We all had tremendous faith in the Major and would have followed him anywhere. Of course, occasionally, someone might raise a query about the escape plan, but old 'Stripey' Wallace at once had a few words to say, as he always did on such occasions, and everything was all right again. We were going to have a smack at Jerry and he wouldn't know what had hit him. Everyone was in fine shape and rarin' to go.

Trials showed it was unlikely launching six canoes could be completed in less than an hour. Raikes and Haslar planned to surface 20 miles off the French coast, assemble the canoes on deck, load them and then trim down and continue the approach to 12 miles offshore southwest of the Gironde estuary. This meant the submarine would be stopped on the surface for only 45 minutes. The launch point was a compromise; the closest Raikes was prepared to go to the coast and the furthest acceptable to Haslar to enable him to get well inside the Gironde before the end of the flood tide.

While the Marines were being briefed by Haslar, HMS *Tuna* underwent trials including diving for a period and cruising at periscope depth. At 1519 she stopped in Scalpsie Bay on the Isle of Bute (in the Inchmarnock South exercise area) for final practice of hoisting out for the Marines, but the only opportunity for *Tuna's* crew. The best time for five canoes was 31 minutes, which was very satisfying. *Coalfish* was not launched as she was damaged coming out of the torpedo hatch; a foretaste of what was to come. The damage was not serious and it was repaired before the mission was launched. *Cuttlefish's* compass was damaged as she was being recovered over the ballast tanks. The number of rehearsals is unclear, but they were at it from 1530 until 2000, suggesting quite a few were conducted. Raikes recalled practicing everything about three times, the first run taking one hour and 40 minutes. At 2235, HMS *Tuna* was joined by HMS *White Bear* as escort and fighter cover was also provided.

Two days into the voyage Haslar gave them the full orders for the attack. Over the next days they studied the air photos

HMS *White Bear* – a motor yacht of 1,647 tons built as *Iolande* in 1908. She was registered in New York in the 1930s and hired by the Royal Navy in 1939 as a submarine training target and inshore escort with 3rd Submarine Flotilla. She later became the survey ship *Lexamine*. Her figurehead was removed during the war and is reputed to be mounted outside a restaurant in Seattle.

looking for likely lying up places and making themselves familiar with the tide tables. They went over and over the orders, every man being quizzed to ensure he knew every detail. They all had to be able to complete the mission alone if necessary. MacKinnon exercised them in the No.3 Code and they learned a few French phrases.

The journey was not very comfortable. They were crammed into a small space and for the first two days were on the surface in the Irish Sea and Bristol Channel in a Force 4, which rolled the submarine; many were seasick. The smell of oil and diesel did not help those feeling nauseous.

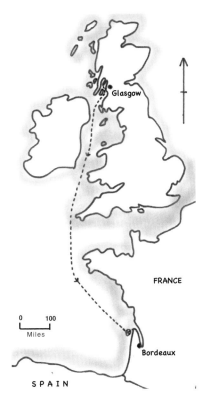

Haslar and MacKinnon were allocated bunks given up by Raikes and another officer. Wallace was looked after in the Petty Officers' Mess and the rest slept on the deck between the stores in the forward

Route taken by HMS *Tuna* from the Clyde to the launching point off the Gironde estuary.

torpedo space. Conditions were very trying for fit young men used to being in the fresh air. In quiet periods some men wrote letters home. Mackinnon wrote on 30 November, saying nothing of the mission and told his family not to worry if they heard nothing for a few weeks. He finished tongue in cheek, "I will carry on watching crossing the road."

HMS *Tuna* averaged nine knots and at 1700 on 2 December was 7 miles off Wolf Rock Lighthouse, (eight miles southwest of Land's End). She transferred all charts no longer needed to HMS *White Bear* before she headed for Falmouth at 1710. They were now within enemy surface ship and

Wolf Rock Lighthouse off Land's End – the last sight of Britain as *Tuna* set out for the Gironde.

aircraft range and had to dive during the day, surfacing at night to charge batteries and freshen the air. At 1800 HMS *Tuna* dived for an hour and spent the rest of the night on the surface zig-zagging. At 0740 on 3 December she dived and remained below all day until 1900. The Marines settled into the routine – heavy activity took place at night when the boat was surfaced, once submerged everyone was encouraged to get as much rest as possible and conserve energy and air. On the 4th, Ewart celebrated his 21st birthday. That day HMS *Tuna* was submerged from 0735 until 1847.

Some accounts state that during the journey a U-boat fired a couple of torpedoes, which missed and HMS *Tuna* retaliated, also without hitting. There is no evidence for this incident in HMS *Tuna's* log or patrol report.

The first night possible to launch the mission was 5/6 December, but during the passage Haslar carried out further work on the tide tables and asked Raikes to delay launching for a day. Having heard aircraft overhead at 0135 and avoided fishing vessels most of the night, HMS *Tuna* dived just before 0726 on 5 December. Going down the conning tower ladder Raikes dropped an Aldis lamp and it landed on Signaller Smart's head causing a nasty gash. Raikes was most apologetic. To add insult to injury, Smart was thereafter known as 'Ivory Dome' by the crew.

At 0905 two trawlers were spotted with white hulls and black superstructure flying yellow flags. Most of the day was spent avoiding fishing boats and the submarine had to go deep at one time. Visibility was poor and getting an accurate fix was difficult. They could see plenty of houses and churches but none was distinctive enough to be identified positively. During the day the Marines continued with briefings on lying up positions and Haslar and MacKinnon continued working on the attack timetable, following which Haslar wrote up a fair copy of the orders and studied possible advance bases.

On surfacing at 1850, HMS *Tuna* had to avoid more fishing boats, but fortunately they had lights and were easy to spot. The high concentrations of plankton caused heavy phosphorescence, which was a concern. Aircraft were heard again and HMS *Tuna* dived at 0720.

The Marines started the 6th in high spirits, cracking jokes as they expected to launch that night. Setting the force off from an accurate position was vital if they were to make the crucial turn into the Gironde estuary. Mist prevented accurate land and astro fixes to be made. Fishing boats appeared again at 0800 and at 0929 an Arado floatplane flew past. It was four hours before the submarine was clear of the fishing boats and made landfall. They had to be very careful that the periscope was not seen and reported. Indeed it was believed that some boats carried Germans with radios to report such sightings. HMS *Tuna* suffered from inexplicable changes in the density of the water causing her to be perfectly trimmed one moment and hitting the bottom the next. It made periscope work very difficult.

Rowe and Raikes spent the day trying to fix their position accurately, but late in the afternoon Raikes had to admit to Haslar the situation. The men had already commenced their four-hour prior to launch preparations. Their disappointment was clear until some wag cracked, "Oh well decent breakfast tomorrow instead of compo rations."

HMS *Tuna* surfaced at 1900. Haslar joined Raikes on deck and saw that conditions would have been perfect for the launch with a mist for cover. In order to get an accurate sun or star sight, Raikes decided to head 20 miles south of the Gironde estuary. Having dived at 0700, HMS *Tuna* spent the day of the 7th slowly working north along the coast.

Air activity was intense: Bf 109, Bf 110, Ar 196, Ju 88 and

Bf 109G with drop tank for extra range during patrols over the sea.

Bf 110 E-2 fitted with bomb racks under the fuselage and wings.

Ar 196A.

Ju 88A.

Above: Do 18 V4. Airspace over the approaches to the River Gironde estuary was busy with German maritime patrol aircraft.

Dornier 18s were identified.

The sea surface was oily calm with a long swell. At 1345 a positive fix was made and further fixes every 30 minutes until Raikes spotted the distinctive Cordouan Lighthouse. Knowing its height, they were able to calculate an accurate range through the high-powered periscope. Haslar was also allowed some time at the periscope in preparation for the night ahead.

At 1800 a patrol trawler was observed running a line 130°-310°, almost through the area planned for the launch. Raikes had no option but to get closer inshore, much to Haslar's delight. However, it took the submarine closer to the minefields. It also meant the whole operation would have to be carried out in one, coming to full buoyancy only four miles offshore and 10 miles from the radar station. On the plus side it meant Haslar's men would have an extra hour with a favourable tide and they would be launched accurately. The position chosen for launching was 45° 22′N by 1° 14′W. Once he knew it was on for that night Haslar went to sleep.

At 1515, four hours before launch, the raiders began their final preparations. One by one the canoes were constructed with breakwaters down, buoyancy bags inflated and fitted and other bags loaded and stowed ready to pass up on deck. They greased the hatches allowing access to the buoyancy bags, fitted their compasses and partly dressed. At 1700 Haslar gave the men a final talk and at 1745 they had a meal. One of the final tasks was to smear their faces with camouflage cream. Haslar gave Raikes his papers and diary for safekeeping.

HMS *Tuna* surfaced at 1917 onto a flat calm sea at 45° 21′.8N by 1° 14′.1W. Raikes was first up with the officer of the watch and two seamen lookouts, all fully adapted to night vision having worn red goggles for the previous hour. Raikes was troubled by the clear night and could see the patrol trawler to seaward no more than 4,500m away. However, he knew they were unlikely to be visible to the trawler with the dark eastern sky and land behind them. Rowe was positioned on the periscope standards about 4m higher than the rest for a longer-range view. At 1919 Raikes ordered engines stopped.

"Major Haslar on the bridge", Raikes called down the voice tube. Seconds later he arrived breathless with excitement. Raikes told him the situation and asked if he wanted to start. Haslar paused, moved across to look towards France and said, "Yes." Raikes called down the tube, "Canoes up"; there were no wasted words on a submarine.

The operation commenced at 1920 according to HMS *Tuna's* log, but 1937 in other accounts. The forward hatch was opened in a few seconds and the casing party swarmed out, followed by the hoisting gear, then the canoes manhandled by their crews. The canoes were laid out in reverse launching order forward of the hatch, leaving room for the two officers' canoes immediately aft. They would be launched first to control the others in the water. If the launch had to be aborted when only half completed, the two officers would continue with the mission alone.

MacKinnon supervised below. The drill was well practiced and went well until Ellery lost his footing when the submarine rolled slightly and *Cachalot* knocked against the hatch clamp tearing an 18" gap in its canvas side. Haslar checked it, "I'm afraid you can't go. Strike the boat below again. You will have to go back in the submarine". Despite their pleadings, Ellery and Fisher had to be left behind. Fisher burst into tears.

Haslar returned to take leave of Raikes and thank him for everything before going off to prepare his own canoe. They initially agreed to meet for lunch at the Savoy on 1st April, but Raikes thought All Fool's Day was inappropriate and they decided upon the 2nd instead. Raikes gave Haslar the latest estimate of the magnetic bearing and distance to Pointe de la Negade (259°, 9.5 miles), which was set on the canoe compass grids. Below, Haslar joined Sparks to pass their canoe up and had a momentary flash of anger when he noticed the ratings had loaded his men with chocolates and other treats. He didn't blame them for their generosity, but was angry they had added

Pointe de la Negade looking towards the distant launch point.

extra weight to the already laden canoes. He said nothing.

By 1945 five canoes were ready on the fore deck with their bags stowed. HMS *Tuna* trimmed down and began launching them using the slings and extended gun. As the first canoe (Haslar and Sparks) was put in the slings and swung out, searchlights suddenly swept the sea from Pointe de la Negade and all down the coast. There were no searchlights directly opposite the submarine and in any case she was out of range. The last canoe was swung out at 2003 according to HMS *Tuna's* log (2020 in other accounts), a remarkably fast time and entirely due to the sterling work of Lieutenant Bull and his deck hands.

Raikes believed the searchlight activity was the result of the radar station picking them up, and this was confirmed as the patrol trawler began to close. Radar station W310 had indeed detected

Radar and searchlight installations covering the approaches to the Gironde estuary.

87

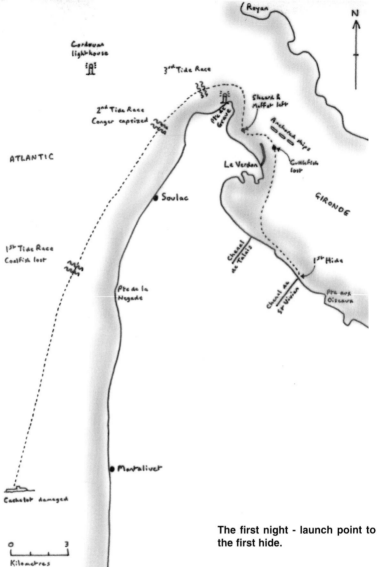

Royan

N

Cordouan
lighthouse

3rd Tide Race

2nd Tide Race
Conger capsized

Shoard &
Muffot left

Anchored ships

Pte de
Grave

ATLANTIC

Le Verdon

Cuttlefish
lost

GIRONDE

Soulac

1st Tide Race
Coalfish lost

Pte de la
Negade

Chenal de Talais

1st Hide

Chenal de St Vivien

Pte aux
Oiseaux

Montalivet

**The first night - launch point to
the first hide.**

Cachalot damaged

0   3

Kilometres

an object four kilometres to the southeast of Pointe de Negade
according to German accounts. They probably meant southwest,
as four kilometres southeast would have been inland. Major
Beyer of *Leichte Flak Abteilung 999* (Light Flak Battalion 999)
reported this to the Operations Officer at HQ 708 Infanterie
Division. Local units were ordered to increase vigilance and the
contact was reported to *Marine Artillerie Abteilung 284* (Naval
Artillery Battalion 284) based at Royan, which was responsible
for engaging enemy ships and the defence of ports and sensitive
defence sectors.

Kapitän zur See Max Gebauer, who commanded *Marine Flak Schule II* (Naval Anti-Aircraft School II) at Dax, Landes, was deputizing for *Seekommandantur* Gascogne (Senior Naval Officer Gascony) at the time. He was at his HQ at Royan having dinner with *Admiral* Johannes Bachmann, *Marinebefehlshaber Westfrankreich* (Naval Commander West France), who was there to attend practice firing of the batteries on the Gironde on 8 and 9 December. At 2200 a report reached Gebauer about the radar contact. He ordered the searchlights to make a sweep, but nothing was picked up and it was concluded that a fishing boat had lost its way.

As Wallace was being lowered into the sea he noticed the submarine's number on the conning tower, 'See that boys, nine and four make 13….we'll need all the luck that's going on this spree.' Fisher wished his mate Moffatt good luck and told him, 'Hurry up back and I'll have a pint waiting for you at the Granada.' The reserve was not needed so Colley remained aboard with *Cachalot's* crew.

At 2010 Raikes waved goodbye to, "A magnificent bunch of black faced villains with whom it has been a real pleasure to work". He then withdrew to the southwest, while Lieutenant Bull's deck team dismantled the hoisting gear. At 2112 on 8 December, HMS *Tuna* signaled FOS the canoes had been launched at 2100 the previous day. Some accounts state the signal was sent the same night as the launch and FOS received it late the following afternoon and passed it to Mountbatten immediately. The plan was certainly not to make contact until the day following the launch.

Admiral Johannes Bachmann joined the Imperial Navy in 1909 and served on torpedo boats in WW1. He remained in the Navy between the wars serving as a gunnery officer, instructor at the Naval Academy and in 1928 became navigating officer on a light cruiser. In 1929 he became first officer on a cruiser and in 1935 took command of the light cruiser *Emden*. From August 1936 he was COS to the Second Admiral of the North Sea and on 21 August 1940 became Commander of the East Friesland Coast. On 8 August 1942 he was appointed Naval Commander West France, controlling the Atlantic coast from St Malo in Brittany to the Spanish border. Following dismissal from this post in March 1943 he was retired from active service on 31 May 1943. He died fighting US forces on 2 April 1945.

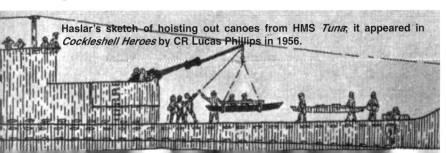

Haslar's sketch of hoisting out canoes from HMS *Tuna*; it appeared in *Cockleshell Heroes* by CR Lucas Phillips in 1956.

A Division led by Haslar set off in arrowhead with the two remaining canoes of B Division behind. They steered 35° to pass two miles west of Pointe de la Negade. It was calm, with a low swell, no cloud and slight haze over the land, but otherwise very clear and bitterly cold. The canoes rode low in the water due to their weight. Out of the submarine's fetid atmosphere, they sucked in the cold pure air, which made them feel a little lightheaded and euphoric.

Haslar quickly realised his compass was about 20 degrees out, despite all the care taken to swing them. Fortunately he could see the North Star and used it to correct his heading. His canoe had a slight leak and Sparks had to bale out every hour. Haslar heard Sergeant Wallace being sick, but otherwise progress was good and the passage was event free. After an hour Haslar made the signal to raft up (hand on top of head). All crews reported they were fine and after a short rest they set off again.

The swell began to build and Haslar took soundings. About 2350 they passed over Banc des Olives with the swell building into steep rollers. The flood tide could be felt and they altered course a little to eastwards to follow the coast visible one and a half miles away. They then heard the roar of water ahead (45° 31'N by 1° 10' W), which came as a shock to Haslar as nothing was apparent from charts or sailing directories. Haslar was impressed with the intelligence he received, but was angry that three tide races they encountered that night were missed. He was also concerned about the amount of freshwater in the Gironde as it made the canoes less buoyant and required greater effort to paddle, all of which affected his careful calculations.

Haslar could see the white breakers of a tide race ahead and the tidal stream was too strong to avoid it. They rafted up while he explained what it was and told them to adopt their normal rough water drill. He had experienced tide races, the rest had not and he was under no illusion how terrifying it would be for them in the dark. They secured their cockpit covers tightly, braced themselves and put their canoes head to the waves. They were soon battling through. The Cockle was able to weather it provided it remained head to wave and the cockpit covers were secured.

After 10 minutes Haslar came through on the other side and turned to watch the others, all soaked, chilled and buffeted, but ready and willing to continue. The party reformed, except for Sergeant Wallace and Marine Ewart in *Coalfish*. Hasler ordered them about to search and Sparks used the gull call. They would have been unable to avoid coming through even if they had capsized, but no trace was found. After 10 minutes, and having baled out, with the force of the tide and the imperatives of the mission they had to press on. From six canoes they were already down to four.

The remaining canoes passed around Pointe de Grave, with the lighthouse clearly visible and thankfully extinguished. They then heard a second tide race (45° 33'.30N by 1° 6'.30W), worse than the first with five foot waves and running at a slight angle to their intended course. While passing through it a cry was heard from *Conger* with Corporal Sheard and Marine Moffatt aboard. They capsized, but managed to cling to the hull and came through the race. The rest rafted up around *Conger*, but with waves crashing over, it was impossible to bale her out sufficiently for them to get back on board.

They were being swept on at great speed by the tide and it was already 0200, with half the night already gone. Just then the Pointe de Grave lighthouse was switched on, illuminating the group of bunched canoes. Haslar knew the only way to bale out *Conger* was to beach her first, but that was not an option on the

Pointe de Grave with the lighthouse nestling in the dunes on the left.

defended beach under the lighthouse. He ordered MacKinnon and Sparks to scuttle *Conger* as best they could with their clasp knifes. Sheard hung on to the back of Haslar's canoe and Moffatt to the back of MacKinnon's, as the tide swept them round Pointe de Grave about 400m offshore. Haslar intended dropping the two as close to the shore as possible, allowing them to swim the rest of the way with a chance of survival. He knew they would be half dead with cold and in no condition to avoid capture, but he had little choice; he was taking a huge risk.

They entered the estuary, brilliantly illuminated and with the dead weight of two men in the water reducing their speed to only one knot. It seemed impossible they would not be seen. Then came the noise of a third but lesser tide race (600m northwest of Pointe de Grave). Fortunately this one only had three-foot waves, but it was still an ordeal for the frozen men in the water. They came through it and the tide took them round the Pointe and into the Gironde at around 0300. They had been paddling for six and a half hours and were tiring. Haslar had wanted to make the eastern bank because the wind direction made it less likely to be detected by dogs on land and there was less danger of being silhouetted against the rising sun as they came ashore. However, there were no safe landing areas before St Seurin and they could not get that far before daylight. It had to be the western bank and time was running out.

They were making laboured progress and uvre in the tidal stream. Haslar saw a mile ahead the outline of the pier at Le Verdon and the tide was taking them straight for it. He had no choice other than to abandon Sheard and Moffat immediately, otherwise they would not get round the pier. Getting as close to

The third tide race off Pointe de Grave on a calm morning, with the Cordouan Lighthouse beyond.

The pier and ferry terminal at Le Verdon in 1942. The raiders were swept towards it by the tide from the left, but managed to swing round the end.

the shore as he dared, Haslar had them raft up again and leaned over the side to whisper to Sheard, "I am sorry, but we have to leave you here. You must swim for it. It is no distance. I am terribly sorry". Sheard replied, "That's all right sir, I understand. Thanks for bringing us so far". They all shook hands and Haslar was surprised when Laver stuffed a small rum flask inside Sheard's life jacket; another gift from the submarine's crew.

Plage de la Chambrette looking north – it was in the middle of this bay, where the X is, that Haslar was forced to abandon Sheard and Moffatt. In the left background is the entrance to Port Medoc, Le Verdon and Pointe de Grave, while on the right on the other side of the Gironde is Royan.

93

Plage de la Chambrette looking south towards the derelict ferry terminal pier.

Haslar said, "God bless you both", and tight lipped set off sharply to the east paddling hard to avoid the pier. Sparks heard Haslar sobbing in front of him.

Sheard and Moffat were left one and a half miles southeast of Pointe de Grave. The tide would take them close to the pier. Although they wore life jackets they were very cold and tired and unable to swim effectively.

Haslar immediately ran into another problem. They were much closer inshore than intended and the tide forced them to pass between the pier (a blue light on the end was visible three to five miles away) and a line of three or four anchored patrol or escort vessels of the Chasseur type about three quarters of a mile to the east. Although not known to Haslar, they were there for inspection by Admiral Bachmann next morning.

Haslar rafted up and whispered to the two remaining crews,

A patrol or escort vessel of the Chasseur type.

We shall have to go through one at a time, single paddle, lowest position. I shall go first. Corporal you will follow when you see I have passed the line of ships. Mac you will follow when Crayfish is through. I shall wait for you both in the clear water beyond".

They changed to single paddle and Haslar slipped through cautiously, allowing the current to take them and making only minor adjustments with the paddles. Halfway through, the signal lamp on one of the ships began flashing towards the pier. It felt like a searchlight, but they were not seen and were soon through into the darkness beyond. They turned and watched the dark shape of *Crayfish* come through safely.

Waiting for *Cuttlefish* with MacKinnon and Conway, they heard a faint shout repeated a few times, then silence. They had no way of knowing if it was MacKinnon, a sentry or Sheard and Moffat. There was no reason to suspect any mishap. Sparks tried the gull call, but there was no sign of *Cuttlefish*. The four remaining raiders were bitterly cold. Haslar had to trust MacKinnon to continue as best he could; he was the type of man who would do just that. Haslar reluctantly turned away.

They continued on a course of 196° and picked up the west bank near Chenal de Talais before turning southeast. Around 0630 they attempted to land, but the way was blocked 200m from the shore by a line of half submerged stakes with a swell

The west bank south of Chenal de Talais with Le Verdon in the far distance right. Semi-submerged stakes, similar to those encountered by the raiders, are evident all along this stretch of the Gironde.

Site of the first hide near Pointe aux Oiseaux. The sandy promontory has been eroded away since 1942, but traces of it can still be seen just offshore.

breaking over them. Landing was too risky and they continued. As day was breaking Haslar managed to get ashore on a small sandy promontory near Pointe aux Oiseaux. He carried out a quick reconnaissance 100m either side, found some low scrub above the high water mark and the canoes were carried up and camouflaged with the nets.

The two remaining canoe crews were exhausted after paddling 26 miles in 11 hours. They had lost three canoes and six of their comrades, yet they felt they had done well, withstanding three terrifying tide races and evading detection by radar, searchlight, lighthouse and enemy ships. They were ashore in occupied France.

Chapter Eight

APPROACH TO THE TARGET

HASLAR AND HIS THREE remaining companions had some compo rations and a hot brew before settling into the canoes to sleep. Haslar took first watch and spotted Sparks having a crafty swig from a rum flask. Sparks expected a rebuke, but Haslar just held out his hand and said, "After you".

Soon after about thirty 5-9m long fishing boats (known locally as calups) emerged from Chenal de St Vivien on the first of the ebb tide. Ten of the smaller boats landed on the same beach and were met by women walking along the shore. The creek was drying out with the ebb tide and the men had collected their boats early and the women had come to meet them to prepare breakfast. They lit a fire only 15m from the raiders. There were about 12 men, the same number of women and a few children.

The French chatted away and laughed for a little while and then became quiet and began casting furtive glances towards the raiders. Con-

Chenal de St Vivien looking downstream towards the beach where the meeting with the French fishermen took place on the morning of 8 December 1942.

cealment was impossible and it was evident they had been seen. Haslar decided to speak to them or they would probably make a report to the police of suspicious activity. If he told them they were British there was a chance they would say nothing, but it was a risk either way.

Covered by the others, he unbuckled his pistol belt and emerged from cover. He said they were British and asked them

97

not to talk about their presence. The French were alarmed, concerned and sceptical and some said they were Germans; indeed Haslar's accent indicated he was. They were frightened and their first instinct was to avoid trouble. One of the men eventually took the lead. He told Haslar they would be better hiding 200m upstream in a small river mouth. They would not be disturbed there by other fishermen or Germans who were

Yves Ardouin.

working nearby. He promised they would say nothing, but made no commitments beyond that. The man was Yves Ardouin, who was there with his family and members of the Chaussat family to work on the oyster beds.

Haslar returned to his men. Quentin Rees in 'Cockleshell Heroes' says that Haslar took Yves Ardouin's advice and moved position before it became too light, but all other accounts, even Haslar's, do not mention this. The French finished their meal and drifted off to their boats or searched the sands for shellfish. Yves Ardouin handed over some bread. The women left and Haslar took first watch, telling Sparks he would wake him in an hour, but left him to sleep for four. During this time Haslar thought about their predicament; he reasoned it didn't matter whether the French believed they were British or German, if they reported the suspicious characters they would come to no harm. Added to that some of the missing men were likely to have been captured, which would cause a full-scale alert by land, sea and air. He was correct; the radar contact and the capture of Wallace and Ewart had caused alarm, prompting HQ *708 Infanterie Division* to launch a search for more Commandos along the coast and in the land behind. No German patrols came anywhere near Haslar's party though.

Around 1600 two women returned and stopped about 20m away, afraid to come closer. Haslar went out and chatted with them. One was young and attractive and the older one told him her husband was a prisoner in Germany. Haslar fell for the oldest trick in the book; she said something casually in German and Haslar answered, "Ja". When she told him he was obviously

German he laughed, telling her he had learned German at school and it was better than his French. She was not entirely convinced but carried on chatting. She told him the voices heard on the other side of the dyke were German soldiers working on new defences. Haslar was concerned and after a while the women left, still apparently unconvinced.

Jeanne Baudray recalled giving them a baguette and chocolate:

Fishermen came to fetch my father because he was the maire. They had seen English soldiers near the port of St Vivien and did not know what action to take. But my father was ill so he sent me in his place, even though I was only 18. I made the fishermen promise not to talk about this to anyone and took the food to the Marines. I saw them very close and I was moved. Moved to see for real that someone was helping France.

Jeanne Baudray was awarded the Legion d'Honneur and later became mayor of St Vivien de Médoc

Haslar rejoined the others and they tried to sleep to the sound of pick and shovel from behind the dyke. A few aircraft flew over and a few ships moved in the Gironde. During the afternoon flood tide the fishing boats returned to the Chenal de St Vivian. Similar behaviour was observed from boats emerging from the Chenal de Talais.

They slept with their feet either in the bow or stern of the canoes having unloaded the equipment bags. They had no blankets and slept fitfully in the wind and rain. Although able to wash and shave, movement was very restricted and going to the toilet was difficult. During the day they cleaned their weapons, destroyed used air photos and repaired the small rent in Haslar's canoe. Over a brew of tea Haslar briefed them on the night ahead. They needed to make up for the delays of the previous night, so it would be a long flog of 20-25 miles. Haslar also wanted to get over to the eastern bank, but there were only six hours of favourable tide in which to achieve this.

As the sun set one of them cried, "Look Jerries". Looking up there was a line of about 50 men advancing towards them. They drew pistols and Haslar readied the Silent Sten waiting for the fight. As the light faded the line came on slowly until Haslar had a look through his binoculars and laughed. It was a row of stakes

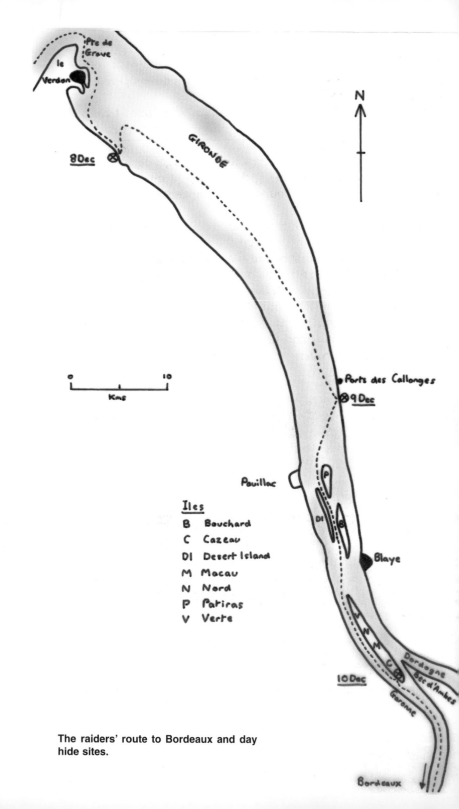

The raiders' route to Bordeaux and day
hide sites.

they had seen all day, but because they were tired they had been deceived by a hallucinatory effect most military men experience at some time.

They could not set off until the tide began to flood at 2330. This coincided with low water springs, which meant they had to drag their heavy canoes over 1,200m of sandy mud, but the Cockle Mk.II had been designed with this rough treatment in mind. Sparks remembered being thigh deep in mud in places and of course much of it ended up in the canoes when they eventually got on board.

Once on the water they had to negotiate a number of sandbanks over which quite large waves broke. This forced them to travel north at first before eventually making it out into the channel. Navigation was easy as the marker buoys showed a dim flashing blue light, which they kept about 200m to the east in order not to run into any ships. It was flat calm with no cloud and a haze over both shores, but bitterly cold. The icy water dripped on their hands and flicked onto their faces. The spray froze on the cockpit covers.

Haslar set a fast pace and they were glad of it to keep warm,

The double hedge site used for the second hide on 9 December 1942 and the farm have since disappeared under the nuclear power station at Le Blayais.

but they all had to take Benzedrine at some time. At each hour's break when they rafted up, Haslar and Laver would study the chart with a dim red torch, while Sparks and Mills cracked jokes with each other and nibbled on biscuits or chocolate.

The night was uneventful until they crossed the shipping channel and were almost run down by a convoy of six or seven large ships from astern. They got clear by paddling harder, but were rocked by the passage of the first ship. Sparks remarked, "More targets for us sir!".

They picked up the east bank just north of Portes de Calonge (Port des Callonges on modern maps) and followed it a mile offshore until daylight approached. Haslar could see hedges running down to the water's edge and kept going until seeing a double hedge running almost to the water. They were lucky in finding a suitable hide at the first attempt. Haslar stepped ashore, carried out a quick reconnaissance and called them in. The canoes were camouflaged in a dry ditch between the two hedges. They had covered 25 miles in six hours compared to 26 miles in 11 hours the previous night.

As soon as it was daylight they brewed tea and tried to sleep. A plane flew overhead so low they could see the pilot's face. A farmhouse 200m away did not disturb them, but a herd of cows came to examine the curious shapes. During the day they sorted their kit and buried stores no longer needed, to lighten their load. Haslar also ditched the Silent Sten. Upriver they could see the floating dock at Pauillac with a ship in it; a suitable target if only they had the means to attack it.

The next night there would only be three hours of flood, followed by six hours of ebb and another three hours of flood before daybreak. Haslar decided to adopt an intermediate lying up place on what he called 'Desert Island' to sit out the ebb tide. At twilight it was flat calm with no cloud and excellent visibility. Haslar took a risk to make the best of the limited flood tide by setting off earlier than was really prudent.

Silhouetted against the western sky they were seen by Alibert Decombes from the nearby farm (La Presidente at Braud et St Louis), who came to investigate. He kept his distance, obviously curious what the strange men were up to. Haslar went over and repeated the story of the previous day. Unlike the fishermen he grinned as he invited them to the house for a drink. Haslar refused politely despite being pressed. The man was obviously disappointed, even a little hurt that they did not want to share a drink on such a cold night. To make him feel better Haslar said, "Perhaps after the war". The farmer replied, "Well then the next time you are passing don't forget to come in. Good luck. I will say nothing you may be sure".

They were glad to get away and concerned despite Alibert's apparent good nature; he had actually seen them canoeing, whereas the fisher folk had not been close enough to see their equipment. Sparks remembered the incident a little differently. He recalled the man stumbled on them during the day when his dog found them. Haslar kept his promise, making several visits after the war, but after Alibert died in 1949.

They made good progress at first. Later their course lay between the islands of Patiras to starboard and Bouchaud to port. As the channel became more restricted they were uncomfortable about the noise they made at cruising speed. It was still early evening and onshore they were aware of people still going about their normal business. As they came up to the first island they were startled by a motorboat starting up. They hid in a clump of reeds until the boat passed about 100m away. The boat carried no lights and they wondered if it was a patrol lying in wait. However, one account says they could hear the crew talking in French.

They reached Desert Island as the ebb tide began to be felt and they could make little headway against it. The shore was lined with almost impenetrable reeds 2m tall and occasional trees. Behind were vertical banks of thick mud. During the first attempt to get in they were startled by a tremendous rustle and clatter, but never discovered the source. After many attempts at 2045 they found an opening to get ashore into a small clearing where they could leave the canoes to dry out as the tide fell and grab some sleep.

At 0200 next morning they set off again to catch the first of the flood. Clambering down the 2m deep bank and across 15m of thigh deep mud was exhausting and also alarmingly noisy. They found they were too early and had to wait 45 minutes for the ebb to stop. When the tide changed they set off, re-crossed the shipping channel and entered the narrow passage between the west bank of Ile de Verte and the mainland. They tried to be as inconspicuous as possible using single paddles and kept in close to the island reed beds, but they saw no sign of other life.

Ile de Cazeau – the raiders managed to g
ashore on the bottom left side of the isla
just as day was breaking.

By 0630 they were approaching the southern tip of Ile de Cazeau and looked for a lying up place. Rather confusingly this island is known as Ile de Verte to the north, Ile de Nord in the middle, Ile de Macau on the middle west bank and Ile de Cazeau in the south. The mainland bank was heavily populated and ruled out. The island banks were steep and the reeds were again all but impenetrable. Only with considerable difficulty did they get ashore near a small pier about 400m from the southern tip. Haslar went ashore. He followed a path through the thick wood and after 50m there was a clearing within which he saw a sandbagged rectangle. Intelligence believed there were anti-aircraft guns on the island. He crept back, re-embarked and continued moving south. With daylight approaching rapidly they went on a few hundred metres where the island began to peter out into a sharp point. They finally got ashore at 0730 with the dawn sky already bright and the sounds of movement on the mainland increasing as the working day commenced. There was very little cover and they had to place the canoes in the middle of a marshy field in long grass with camouflage nets over them.

It was a miserable day. They sat in their canoes, only able to nod off for a few moments at a time. They couldn't cook, smoke or even relieve themselves. They were covered in mud from the launch on 'Desert Island' and a thin rain fell all day. In addition they were still close to the possible anti-aircraft gun site and had to keep absolutely silent.

They were not observed, although a man with a dog passed 100m away. Again a herd of cows took interest in them, at one time standing in a circle all round the canoes, which was disconcerting as an aircraft flew over at the same time. The cows repeated the performance in the evening on their way back from the tip of the island. Sparks recalled this incident differently; he says two Germans some distance away became interested in the cows' behaviour, but did not approach and eventually seemed satisfied nothing was amiss. Unknown to them MacKinnon and Conway were lying up a few miles away on the east side of the island.

After dark they were able to move a little, but were stiff, soaked and frost had formed on their clothing. Haslar had wanted to attack on the night of 10/11 December, but they were not high enough up the river, so he decided to set up an advanced base that night close to the target area and attack early on the night of 11/12 December.

At 1845 on 10 December they launched the boats with considerable difficulty down the vertical slippery banks. By then they were on the Garonne, having passed the point where that river and the Dordogne combine to form the Gironde.

It was cloudy with occasional rain and a southerly breeze to cover their noise. For two miles they stayed mid-channel and then changed to single paddles and hugged the west bank, which was lined with thick reeds. Rounding a corner they saw two large ships moored at Bassens South being unloaded under floodlights. They hugged the west bank even more closely and saw a pontoon pier with a coaling lighter moored to the end. They ceased paddling, allowing the tide to sweep them on and ducked as they slipped under the pontoon. Directly opposite Bassens South and 30m south of the pontoon, they found a small

The raider's view from their last hide through the reeds over the river to Bassens South.

gap in the reeds and managed to force the canoes in at about 2300. When the tide ebbed, the boats dried out and they made themselves as comfortable as they could in their canoes for the rest of the night and the following day.

Unknown to the raiders a German High Command communiqué issued earlier on 10 December stated that a sabotage squad (Wallace and Ewart) had been caught near the mouth of the Gironde and eliminated. Lieutenant Colonel Cyril Horton saw it in the stop press of his evening paper in London; the story also appeared in *La Petite Gironde*, the local paper around Bordeaux. At HQ Combined Operations hearts sank at the news, but it was hoped that some of the force had managed to slip through.

Daylight revealed they were well concealed in 3m high reeds in an inaccessible location. However, behind them the reeds were only about 5m thick and the normal noises of daily life could be heard, but it gave them cover and they were able to chat

quietly and enjoy an occasional smoke. By standing up they could see traffic on the river and two good-sized ships, *Alabama* and *Portland*, opposite only a few hundred metres away.

During the day they quietly rearranged the stowage to have the escape gear handy in two bags. As evening drew on they prepared the Limpet fuses. Small tin boxes contained various coloured ampoules of acetone about the size of a finger end. Haslar decided to use the orange ampoules, which gave nine hours delay, but in the cold would last a few more hours before setting off the charges.

Each man took a pair of Limpets, slipped an orange ampoule into the fuse cavity of each and screwed the caps on. The caps were scored with a clasp knife to show they were fused. When both had been fused the pair was turned over and a soluble plug inserted into each sympathetic fuse. Finally they checked the placing rod fitted. To ensure nothing was missed the four worked together with Haslar ordering each stage and checking it was carried out correctly before proceeding to the next stage. It took an hour to complete this.

All the equipment was stowed, the compasses put away so the luminous face would not give them away and they blackened their faces again. Haslar planned to reach the start of the target area an hour before high water so they could drift along through the docks on the last of the flood. Having reached the far end they would turn at high water around midnight and drift back on the ebb. Working back he calculated they should leave the hiding place at 2040, but the new moon did not set until 2132 and with a clear sky it was too risky to cross its path. He decided to delay leaving until 2110.

Limpet mine fuse box with various time delay ampoules.

Chapter Nine

THE ATTACK

AT 2100 HASLAR ordered them to start the fuses. The thumb-screw on each one was turned until a faint click was heard indicating the ampoule had broken to release the acetone, which began to eat away at the soluble plug. They shook hands, wished each other good luck and left the lying up place at 2115.

The attack plan was for the canoes to separate. *Catfish* was to proceed three miles along the west bank to the docks in Bordeaux, while *Crayfish* went along the east bank. If no suitable targets were found in Bordeaux, Laver was to return to attack

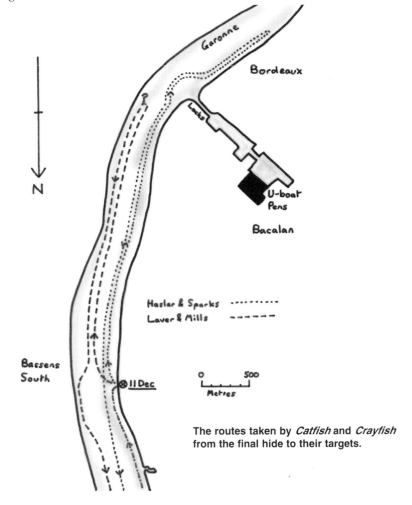

The routes taken by *Catfish* and *Crayfish* from the final hide to their targets.

the two ships at Bassens South. As each canoe finished its attack it was to continue downstream until the ebb tide ran out or daylight approached, land on the east bank, scuttle the canoes and escape as best they could.

It was absolutely clear with no wind, cloud or rain and the water surface was calm; conditions they could have done without. Haslar was surprised that unlike blacked-out Britain, the docks in Bordeaux were well lit. When they saw the target ships ahead all their fatigue evaporated. This is what they had come for, but how to close with such well-lit targets? The lights were switched on and off several times around 2230 before being extinguished. They came on again at 2300, but half an hour later were switched off using the same procedure.

Haslar kept *Catfish* 200m from the bank, outside the pools of

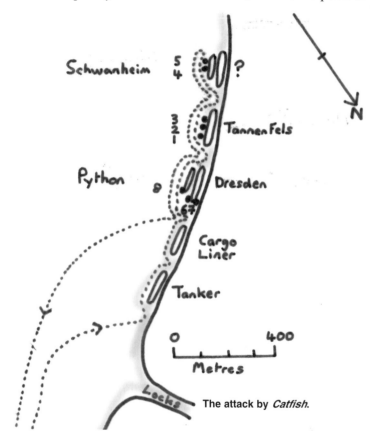

The attack by *Catfish*.

The section of Quai Carnot in Bordeaux where Haslar's and Spark's targets were moored.

light, particularly around the lock gate entrance to the basins and around a factory 700m south of the pontoon pier. In mid-stream he was well placed to observe the ships and work out which were worth attacking. Once alongside it would not be possible to work out what they were. He saw seven ships at Quai Carnot, five moored and two tied alongside two of them. There were many more ships further upstream, but the tide would turn before they could reach them, so Haslar concentrated upon this first group of seven.

They came back into the quay having passed the basins entrance. With hoods up and in single paddle they kept well into the wall or on the dark side of the ships to hug the shadows. The first ship was a tanker, which they ignored. The second was a cargo liner, which was worth a Limpet or two if they had any left on the return. The third was a large cargo ship, but it had a tanker moored alongside making it difficult to get at. The fourth on its own was a large cargo ship, *Tannenfels*; a perfect target, but already the tide was beginning to ebb. Haslar stowed his paddle and signaled Sparks to hang on with the holdfast.

The first Limpet was lowered down on the placing rod and

MS *Tannenfels* a Fels class Deutsche Dampfschiffahrtsgesellschaft Hansa ship from Bremen. At the outbreak of war she was at Kismayu in Italian Somalia, where she was used by the Kriegsmarine as a supply ship. She departed Kismayu on 31 January 1941, just 10 days before the Royal Navy cordoned off the port ahead of the invasion by 12th Division from Kenya. *Tannenfels* arrived at Bordeaux in mid-April and was used as a submarine supply ship until departing on 2 February 1942 with military equipment and machine tools for Yokohama. She commenced the return journey on 8 August carrying rubber, tungsten, titanium, copper, opium, quinine, edible oils and fats. On 27 September in the South Atlantic the German armed raider *Stier* became embroiled in a fight with the Liberty Ship SS *Stephen Hopkins,* which was sunk with heavy losses; only 15 of her crew reached Brazil, but *Stier* was so badly damaged she had to be scuttled. The survivors were taken aboard *Tannenfels*, reaching Bordeaux on 2 November. *Tannenfels* was scuttled as a block ship at Bordeaux Bassens on 25 August 1944 and the wreck recovered for scrap in 1956.

gradually moved towards the ship's side. There was a satisfying clunk. Moving amidships Haslar realized the increasing force of the ebb tide would swing the bow of the canoe out into the stream. He therefore took the holdfast and let Sparks place the next Limpet and another at the stern.

They occasionally had to move away from the ships to avoid flushing sewage or condenser outfalls. Moving on they reached a large cargo ship, but with a *Sperrbrecher*, the *Schwanheim*, moored alongside. *Sperrbrecher* (pathfinder) were minesweepers, often converted merchantmen of about 5,000 tons. They were equipped with magnetic field generators to explode magnetic mines at a safe distance while escorting other ships, including submarines into and out of port.

Haslar and Sparks had five Limpets left. With one ideal target behind them in a difficult location, Haslar decided to leave two Limpets on the *Sperrbrecher* a few metres apart on the engine room. It was time to swing round and head back on the ebb tide. This meant turning in a wide arc away from the side of the ship.

Halfway through the manoeuvre they heard a clang above and a torch shone down on them. A sentry could be seen clearly against the night sky looking over the rail 5m above. With a cautious thrust of the paddles they slid into the side of the ship and froze. As they drifted along the sentry followed them, his boots audible on the deck, but he seemed unable to decide what they were, possibly due to the camouflage paint.

Eventually they slipped under the bows where the sentry could no longer see them. Haslar signaled Sparks to hang on with the holdfast. Sparks rolled it onto the hull almost soundlessly. The sentry stopped above them and they could hear

Sperrbrecher 5 (ex-*Schwanheim*), was built in 1936 by Bremer Vulkan and owned by Unterweser Reederei AG, until taken over by the *Kriegsmarine*. She is seen here in the process of being sunk by RAF Beaufighters of 236 and 404 (RCAF) Squadrons off Royan on 13 August 1944.

his feet shifting occasionally. They waited five minutes; it was quiet, but the sentry was still there. Despite the risk they had to get on and Haslar instructed Sparks to let go. After two nerve-racking minutes drifting away from the *Sperrbrecher* they were out of sight and breathed again. They carried on, ignoring the first ship they had attacked.

Haslar wanted to attack the large merchant ship next, *Dresden*, distributing the remaining three Limpets along its whole length, but the tanker alongside blocked access to most of the hull. They could attack bow and stern, but not amidships. He set *Catfish* to drift in between the two bows until they were almost wedged. Sparks was about to stow his paddle and get out the holdfast when suddenly Haslar spread-eagled his arms between the two hulls. The two ships were slightly yawing in the tide and closing together, about to crush the Cockle. Sparks followed Haslar and they strained to push the canoe backwards out of the closing jaws. They backpaddled furiously, rounded the bow of the tanker and drifted towards the stern. Haslar said he felt like Atlas holding up the World.

At the stern they placed two Limpets as well spaced as they could and slapped the last one on the stern of the tanker, *Python*. Haslar swung round and shook Sparks' hand; they had done what they came for. With big grins on their faces and the canoe now surprisingly light, they set off downriver. Haslar positioned them midstream where the tidal flow was strongest and they paddled hard with single paddles, visible to both shores, but no-one saw them and they didn't seem to care anyway.

Laver's and Mills' attack route.

114

On 8 December 1940, RAF bombers attacked Italian submarines at Bacalan, Bordeaux. During the raid *Cap Hadid* caught fire and the French liner *De Grasse* was damaged, but the submarines received minimal damage. *Cap Hadid* was renamed *Python*, the original ship of that name having been scuttled in December 1941 when attacked by HMS *Devonshire*. The *Python* attacked by Haslar and Sparks is often described as a tanker, indeed Haslar mistook her for one, but at the time of the raid she was a supply ship, equipped to transfer fuel and other stores at sea to U-boats. *Python* was converted to *Sperrbrecher 122* in February 1943. She was scuttled on 25 August 1944 at St Nazaire, repaired in 1946 and renamed *Cape Hahid*. She was renamed again in 1953, *Cap Bon*. She is seen here as *Cap Hadid*.

Crayfish meanwhile had proceeded some way upriver along the east bank, but did not find any worthwhile targets. As the tide began to turn against them, Laver decided to go with the flow and attack the two ships seen during the day. They placed five Limpets on the large cargo ship and three on a smaller cargo liner. They saw no sentries.

Haslar and Sparks were well ahead of Laver and Mills and once clear of Bassens switched to double paddles and really began to move. As they stopped for a rest midstream near the southern end of Ile de Cazeau, they heard what sounded like a Mississippi stern-wheeler coming towards them. They knew instantly what it was. Turning round they saw *Crayfish* approaching fast under double paddles. Suddenly the canoe froze as its crew spotted *Catfish*. Haslar was impressed by their reactions. When he heard a cautious gull call he laughed aloud. *Crayfish* unfroze and paddled up to them. They had met by pure chance and chatted for a while. Laver told Haslar what he had done. Haslar told them they had all done very well and he was proud of them.

Haslar wanted to separate, but Laver persuaded him to stay together until just before they beached to start the overland escape. They wanted to put as much distance between Bordeaux and where they landed, but could only travel while the tide was favourable. They made best speed with double paddles, intending to reach the Blaye area by low water. Mills was disappointed he wouldn't be able to hear the explosions to celebrate his birthday.

Having passed the north end of Ile de Verte they crossed the shipping channel and passed between Ile de Petit Pagnard and Ile du Pate. They passed the French liner, *De Grasse*, anchored opposite Blaye, where she passed the war. Just north of Blaye they stopped and looked back to see a searchlight sweeping the area where the Dordogne and Garonne met. They continued a mile beyond Blaye and found open country before the tide turned.

At 0600 they rafted up for the last time. Haslar told Laver

Catfish and *Crayfish* passed between these islands towards the camera position to approach the shore north of Blaye.

De Grasse – a Trans-Atlantic liner laid down as *Suffren* in 1924, but renamed during building at Cammell, Laird & Co, Birkenhead. She operated on the Compagnie Générale Transatlantique (CGT), Le Havre – New York service until 1940 when seized by the Germans having been scuttled at Bordeaux. The Germans used her as an accommodation ship until 1941 when she became a depot ship for Italian submarines. In June 1942, *De Grasse* was returned to the Vichy Government for use as a seaman's training ship. She was sunk by gunfire at Bordeaux in August 1944, raised and re-entered service with CGT in 1947; the first French merchant ship to recommence the North Atlantic service. She was transferred to the Caribbean service in 1952 and sold to Canadian Pacific as the *Empress of Australia* in 1953. Bought by Grimaldi-SIOSA in 1956 and renamed *Venezuela* on the Italy-West Indies-Venezuela service, she was lost in 1962 off Cannes.

where he was and to land there, while he went on another 400m before he beached. Laver looked at him, 'Very good sir. Best of luck to you'. The two crews shook hands and promised to see each other in 'Pompey' (Navy slang for Portsmouth) in a few weeks time. Sparks had the last word, 'See you in the Granada. We'll keep a couple of pints for you!' They paddled off, Haslar looking back at *Crayfish* once with a heavy heart. Laver faced landing in a strange land knowing little of the language and having to guide his companion over hundreds of miles to safety; a daunting task for a well educated officer, never mind a young Corporal of only 22 years.

RODS, COLLAPSIBLE, PLACING, LIMPET
(PLACING RODS)

Catalogue No. D 198.

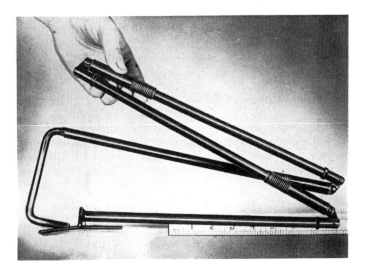

DESCRIPTION. This device consists of a rod which folds into four sections and is provided with a hooked handle at one end and a two-way bracket at the other; this bracket fits into a slot provided on the Limpet body.

METHOD OF USE. To open—pull the rod out into the extended position when it will automatically lock.

To fold—press the locking tube of each joint towards the handle of the rod when the link joint will be exposed and each of the four sections folded.

DIMENSIONS. Width 4¾". Length 15¼" folded.   **WEIGHT.** 2 lbs.

PACKING AND SPECIAL NOTES.
As required.

Chapter Ten

RETURN

THE RAIDERS had been given escape instructions with two aims – to contact the Resistance escape network and, if captured, to ensure they would be treated as POWs and not as saboteurs. Escape networks had been set up at great risk by Frenchmen and others opposed to the Vichy government and the Nazis, to help Allied personnel on the run from prison camps or shot down on missions over Europe. The Anglo-American landings in North Africa caused the Germans to occupy the whole of France, but they were not yet effective everywhere in the Vichy area and the Demarcation Line was still in force. Once over this Line an escaper stood a better chance, but still had to beware collaborators and Vichy/Nazi sympathizers.

The escapers had to behave in such a way that if captured they would be treated as escaping servicemen. In uniform there should be no dispute and it was generally accepted that soldiers escaping would attempt to disguise themselves as civilians provided they did not bear arms.

Their instructions were to move cross-country in pairs, supplementing their rations with food, drink and rest in barns provided by local people with whom they made contact. These encounters were risky for both. The escapers found it difficult to determine where the locals' loyalties lay, but there were no alternative food sources in winter and they had to take the risk. The population was about equally divided between those supporting the Allies and the Nazis. French citizens who sheltered, fed and guided these men risked arrest and execution; at best it meant a labour camp.

Their instructions were to find civilian clothes as soon as possible by legitimate means, paying if necessary. They were to discard uniforms and weapons, but retain their ID disks. Until they found civilian clothes they had to move by night and avoid roads and other public places. Once they had civilian clothes they should behave normally by using roads openly in daylight and avoid furtive behaviour. When they needed food they should ask and pay for it.

Having canoed 91 sea miles (105 miles) in enemy waters over

five nights, they now faced a long and arduous walk in mid-winter to reach Ruffec, where it was known they could contact the escape network. Although Ruffec had a German HQ, it was well placed for the start of an escape chain, sitting astride the N10 road and Paris-Bordeaux railway only 10 kms from the Demarcation Line. The Germans were also more likely to be looking for them on a direct route from Bordeaux towards Spain. Ruffec was about 70 miles northeast of Blaye, in Cognac and foie gras country. They were told the escape organisation would be looking for them on the outskirts of the town.

Catfish landed in a deserted area near St Genes de Blaye, close to Chateau de Segonzac. Haslar and Sparks recovered their escape gear, boots, a can of water and the remaining rations. They slashed the buoyancy bags and canoe sides before Haslar waded out waist deep and held Catfish until she was swamped. He pushed her into the stream and watched sadly as Catfish disappeared upstream on the tide with its bow just visible.

It took them 30 minutes to scale the 2m high bank and fight

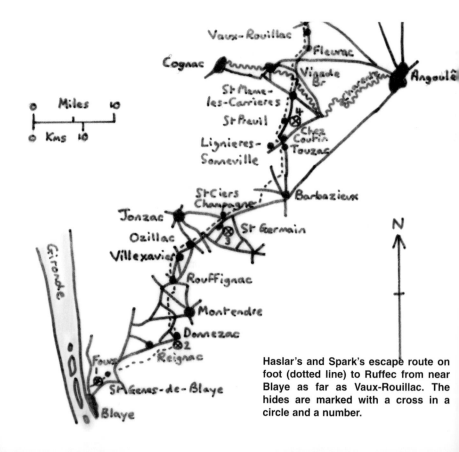

Haslar's and Spark's escape route on foot (dotted line) to Ruffec from near Blaye as far as Vaux-Rouillac. The hides are marked with a cross in a circle and a number.

Haslar and Sparks came ashore here near Chateau de Segonzac.

Chateau de Segonzac from the Gironde. Below the chateau are some of the many vineyard fences encountered by Haslar and Sparks.

The Gironde from Chateau de Segonzac.

their way through a dense forest of reeds, making far too much noise. It was about an hour before dawn and still dark when they emerged into a field. After a few yards they ran into a fence running through a line of bushes. They climbed it, but a few metres on had to cross another. Haslar thought they had just crossed a fenced track, but very quickly a third and fourth fence followed. Sparks was complaining about the number of fences in France, when Haslar burst out laughing as he realised they were in a vineyard. They decided to walk along the fences instead, but were plagued by them for days as they never seemed to run in the direction they wished to travel and added distance to their journey. Farms had to be avoided because of dogs.

By dawn they had covered one and a half miles. They enjoyed

walking after days stuck in the canoe and it helped to dry them. Dry mud formed an effective insulation layer and they soon warmed up. In a wood between St Genes-de-Blaye and Fours they found sufficient undergrowth to cover them. About 20m from a stream they gathered grass and bracken to make mattresses, brewed tea and ate some compo rations. One slept while the other kept watch and they passed a peaceful day.

On his watch, Haslar memorized every detail of the raid so he could report accurately on his return as they retained no notebooks or documents in case of capture. In the afternoon they washed and shaved in the stream so they would not appear to be too scruffy if they knocked on a door.

They set off again at 1900 on the 12th and managed to cover eight miles cross-country during the night. It may have been that night that just after crossing a road a gendarme cycled past. If he had seen them, he made no attempt to turn and investigate, but he showed up on the next lane they crossed. They waited for him on the third, knives at the ready, but he turned back at the last moment.

They were a mile south of Reignac at dawn and Haslar thought it was time to try obtaining some civilian clothing. They selected an isolated farm and approached across the fields. A wiry elderly farmer working with his hoe looked up, checked over the strange looking pair and ignored them. Haslar went up to him, 'Good morning monsieur. We are two English soldiers escaping from the Boches. Can you give us some old clothes?' He looked at them without a trace of expression, gave a classic Gallic shrug and indicated the house; they would have to ask Madame. He returned to his hoeing as if being approached by escaping soldiers was a routine event. His wife was evidently busy. She refused to accept they were British and said she could not help, but disappeared into the house and left the door open. The smells of cooking must have been torture. She returned looking worried and pushed an old beret and flat cap into their hands, then told them to go away and not to mention their visit. They thanked her and left. The old man ignored them.

The next farmer's wife refused to help and suggested they try the farm over the hill. This woman provided two pairs of worn trousers, a jacket and a sack in which to carry their belongings. As they left she even wished them luck; things appeared to be improving thought Haslar.

Moving into a nearby wood they transformed themselves into civilians and buried their weapons and uniforms, although Sparks says they were invited into the house and left their uniforms for the family to burn. Sparks wore the cap, jacket, blue naval sweater, trousers and felt soled issue boots. Haslar wore the beret and much the same as Sparks, but did not have a jacket. Haslar had deliberately allowed his moustache to grow long in the French peasant walrus fashion.

They pressed on all day despite having had no sleep the previous night and arrived at the village of Brignac. Some backdoor enquiries gained them another sack and a jacket large enough for Haslar, but it was getting dark and they didn't want to push their luck asking for shelter. They spent the night in a wood just south of Donnezac, having travelled only four miles towards Ruffec. Despite the bracken and sacks they spent a very cold night and were up and moving again by 0630 on 14 December.

Their maps and button compasses were good enough to keep a general direction using country roads. They kept away from the main Routes Nationales and large towns to avoid encountering Germans. They passed through Donnezac while it was dark, skirted round Montendre and were in Rouffignac before they could avoid it.

There were no signs within towns and they could not stop to check the compass without arousing suspicion, so they adopted a procedure. Before entering they studied the map and memorised every road leaving it and the bearing. Then sacks on backs they trudged along, not taking any interest as if they had lived there all their lives. Occasionally Haslar would say something in French and Sparks would play up with what he hoped looked like a suitable Gallic gesture, leaving out his usual Cockney humour to stop Haslar bursting out laughing. When they were uncertain which way to go, Haslar would get a cigarette off Sparks and while looking for matches in his pocket would retrieve the compass. With it in the palm of his hand he could check it while lighting the cigarette and not draw any attention.

They passed through Villexavier and Ozillac using this technique and covered 18 miles on 14 December. Despite being increasingly cold, tired and hungry, Haslar thought one more night out was necessary. It was miserably cold, wet and uncomfortable that night in a wood near St Germain-de-Vibrac. They slept little and next morning, reached their lowest ebb. Having eaten the last of the compo they set off, knowing they had to find food and shelter after eight nights in the open.

They passed through St Ciers-Champagne and four miles later detoured around Barnezieux as it would have too many police eyes. In the afternoon having passed through Barret, a mile south of Touzac, they saw a fat man outside a garage and asked him for help. He shrugged and gave the familiar answer, 'Ask madame!' At the back door she was unhelpful and sent

The road leading into St Preuil from the south, the direction from which Haslar and Sparks approached.

them away. Leaving the garage they were annoyed with themselves for going to a house with a telephone line.

Beyond the village were some small houses at Chez Coutin, where a woman in her 30s was feeding chickens in the garden. They asked her for help and she asked if they really were British. Sparks speaking no French, rubbed his stomach and said very slowly, 'Very hungry'. She understood, smiled, went inside and returned with a chicken leg and a half loaf of stale bread. While they ate she advised them to avoid Lignieres-Sonneville as there

Chez Coutin.

Nâpres Farm from the St Preuil road.

The rear of Nâpres Farm – the door through which Haslar and Sparks entered is behind the arched wall, which was added later.

were Germans there. Having eaten everything, they thanked her and left.

Having covered another 18 miles, they came to the village of St Preuil as it grew dark. It had rained all day and one of the compasses was no longer working due to the dampness. They knocked at the first house, a farm named Maine-Laurier. Madame Malichier was sympathetic but frightened. She called a tall gangly youth of about 17 named Cadillon and said, 'Go with him he will find you a place'. Some accounts say he was her son, others the son of a local vineyard worker. Haslar thought him half witted.

Cadillon led them into the woods and after a kilometre came to a tiny thatched house on its own, Nâpres Farm. An aggressive dog was barking and the whole scenario did little to improve morale. Cadillon knocked and spoke to a fierce looking woodman, Clodomir Pasqueraud,

Clodomir and Irene Pasqueraud.

125

aged about 40. His wife, Irene, and children Yves, Marc, Robert, two young girls and a baby were lined up behind him. They were taken inside quickly and the door bolted.

Inside was one large room with earthen floor, rough furniture, a large bed and a roaring kitchen range. It smelled of bodies, garlic, dogs, smoke and food. Clodomir fired off a string of aggressive questions, demanding proof they were English and what they were up to. Haslar showed him their ID disks and escape equipment. Clodomir was not sure, particularly about Haslar who could have been taken for a German, but Sparks came to the rescue when he grinned, pointed at himself and said, 'English – savvy?' It could not have come from a German.

Clodomir unbolted the door, shoved Cadillon outside and rebolted it. Having accepted who they were, Clodomir was suddenly friendly and generous. Irene prepared food having learned that Sparks, 'could eat a horse'.

Sparks made friends with the children while Haslar chatted with Clodomir. He had been alarmed that he was regarded as the local resistance centre, hence the hostile reception. He was a communist and happy to fight the Germans if the RAF would drop him weapons. He became quite animated, showing Halsar how he would do it, when there was a knock at the door. Clodomir grabbed a pistol and within a second had dragged in the visitor and had the gun to his head. He was Robert Patient, the baker's boy from Segonzac, who occasionally delivered a few free rolls to the Pasquerauds. Clodomir took the bread and sent Robert on his way with a look that would ensure his silence.

Yves and Marc Pasqueraud. Unconnected with Haslar and Sparks, in 1944 the two boys were arrested, deported to Germany and were never seen again.

Irene's meal was the best they ever tasted and the first hot food since leaving the submarine; vegetable soup followed by roast chicken and vegetables. Clodomir insisted when they returned to England they send a BBC message, 'Le poulet est bon – the chicken is good'; Haslar agreed. Having eaten and drunk some rough red wine they felt very tired. Clodomir intended they sleep in his bed upstairs, but Haslar banged his head on a beam attempting to

The centre of St Meme-les-Carrieres where Haslar and Sparks unexpectedly encountered German soldiers.

climb up, so they used Yves' and Marc's bed on the ground floor for the first decent night's sleep in nine days.

Next morning they were up before dawn. Overnight Irene had washed their outer clothes. Clodomir wanted them to stay, but they had to get on. Before leaving they had a wash and shave in hot water and coffee and bread for breakfast. Then they set off back up the muddy track, carrying the remains of the chicken, bread and flasks of red wine. Haslar hoped they would come across more communists.

Yves and Marc went along to ensure they took the right road to cross the River Charente at Vinade. They passed through St Preuil again and a few hours later, having parted company with Yves and Marc, went into St Meme-les-Carrieres. They had a shock as a party of German soldiers appeared to be assembling in the centre of town. They turned down a side street and were beginning to relax again when a young soldier burst out of a gate. He rushed past them with hardly a glance. 'Obviously late for parade', said Haslar. 'Hope the silly ******* gets put in his company commander's report,' replied Sparks.

Despite the shock, their confidence grew as they realised they looked less suspicious to a German than to a Frenchman. They passed through Triac, crossed the Charente and by secondary roads crossed the Route Nationale at Lantin. They ate sparingly

Vinade bridge used by Haslar and Sparks to cross the River Charente.

of the Pasquereau's food to reduce the times they would have to beg for more.

They walked on in the rain through Fleurac and Vaux-Rouillac, mumbling greetings to anyone they passed to avoid suspicion. They covered 15 miles before last light and reached Le Temple, where they found a small hut beside a light railway line and spent a reasonable night on the floor. On the road again early next day they were only 21 miles from Ruffec. After eight

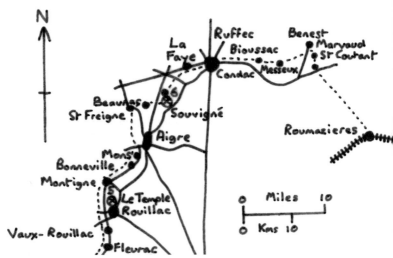

Haslar's and Spark's continued escape route from Vaux-Rouillac to Ruffec. Their subsequent route with the escape line via Marvaud Farm to Roumazieres station is also shown.

miles they finished the last of the food. As they neared Ruffec, Haslar began moving to the west to avoid the main roads and large villages, particularly Aigre. They passed through Montigne, Bonneville and Mons.

As night approached they reached the village of Beaunac, just

Haslar's and Sparks' view of Beaunac as they approached from the south.

The eastern boom at Southsea at low tide with Horse Sand Fort and the Isle of Wight in the distance.

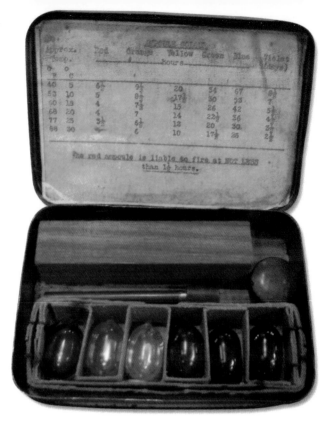

Approx. Temp.		AMPOULE COLOUR					
		Red	Orange	Yellow	Green	Blue	Violet
F	C			hours			(days)
40	5	6½	9½	20	34	67	8½
50	10	5	8¾	17½	30	55	7
60	15	4	7¾	15	26	42	5½
68	20	4	7	14	22½	36	4½
77	25	3½	6½	12	20	30	3½
86	30	—	6	10	17½	25	2⅞

The red ampoule is liable to fire at NOT LESS than 1½ hours.

A Limpet Mine fuse box with time delay chart – the Orange ampoule would give an estimated 9¹/₂ hours delay at 10 degrees centigrade.

From l'Amelie looking north along the Atlantic coastline. Pointe de Grave is around the headland on the right. The distant shore forms the northern entrance to the Gironde.

The American First World War monument at Pointe de Grave – the original was destroyed by German troops during the Second World War.

The original and far more impressive American monument at Pointe de Grave that was destroyed by the Germans.

LYING UP
4TH DAY

CRAYFISH ATTACK

CATFISH
ATTACK

U-boat pens under
construction

Air photographs showing the attack routes. The route for Crayfish is not
depicted accurately as it is known Laver and Mills went some distance
upstream towards Bordeaux before returning to Bassens South. The U-
boat pens under construction are very clear at Bacalan.

Above: Close to the 'Frankton' memorial and American monument, this stone commemorates French parliamentarians who refused to accept the armistice and escaped from here on 21 June 1940 aboard the Massilia to North Africa.

Right: From the upper floor of the former H15 warehouse (now a car park) at Quai Carnot looking north along the Garonne – Haslar and Sparks approached from where the new bridge is being constructed.

Above: From Pointe de Grave lighthouse there are impressive views in all directions. This is looking south down the Gironde towards Bordeaux over the Verdon ferry terminal with the derelict ferry pier in the distance. Fort du Verdon is in the trees on the right.

Below: From the last hide looking across the Garonne to Bassens South, where Laver and Mills attacked Alabama and Portland.

Quai Carnot looking south along the Garonne towards the centre of Bordeaux. It was along this section of the quayside that Haslar and Sparks made their attacks.

Sunset over the Gironde from Blaye Citadelle. *Catfish* and *Crayfish* passed between the island and the far shoreline on their way into and out of Bordeaux. MacKinnon and Conway were seen by French fishermen in the nearest channel.

Above: Memorial and village green at Beaunac.

Above: Dining room of the Hotel l'Angle d'Or (formerly Hotel de la Toque Blanche) at Ruffec, where Haslar and Sparks made first contact with the Resistance and escape organisation.

Inset: The name of Lieutenant John Withers McKinnon commemorated on the Portsmouth Naval Memorial on the seafront at Southsea. The names of the other missing from 'Frankton' are recorded on the similar memorial at Plymouth. Three names above MacKinnon's is that of Lieutenant Colonel Joseph Picton-Phillipps from whom Haslar sought advice while forming the RMBPD.

Right: The Portsmouth Naval Memorial. MacKinnon is commemorated on a panel in the low building to the left rear of the main memorial.

east of St Fraigne and tried to beg food. Having been turned away from three houses they tried a farmhouse. The woman was frightened and called her husband, Andre Latouche. He was unsure and Haslar promised they would be gone before morning. Andre showed them to the loft of a cowshed and they settled into the hay. He came back with bread and told them not to move as it was dangerous in the village. While they were eating they heard raised voices in nearby houses, but being so tired were soon asleep.

In 1960, Royal Marine subalterns following the 'Frankton' route for the first time since 1942, visited Beaunac. They met the wife of Lucien Gody, who told them what happened next. A week or so before Haslar and Sparks turned up, two Germans came to the village dressed as escaping British soldiers. The whole village was consequently on edge, which explains the unwelcoming reception when Haslar and Sparks arrived. News of their arrival spread quickly. Andre Latouche was uncertain about their identity and while they slept decided to seek advice from the Mayor at Ebreon.

Lucien Gody, one of three men from Beaunac arrested and deported to Germany where they died.

At 2300 while Latouche was away, Lucien Gody went to the barn and warned Haslar and Sparks to leave quickly. The Mayor sent for the gendarmes at Aigre to investigate, knowing full well they would not do so until the morning, giving the British time to escape. Haslar and Sparks were moving in two minutes down a track to the east. Sparks recalled this incident differently. He says they found shelter in a barn and were found by a farmer who insisted they went to the house for soup and bread before returning to the barn, but they were woken later and escaped as Haslar described.

Sparks was upset, but Haslar realised their presence made it dangerous for the villagers. It was raining and they splashed along the flooded track; at least it made it difficult for dogs to follow thought Haslar. Their last compass seized up in the wet and they were weary and suffering from dislocated expectations, having expected a good night's rest in the hayloft.

Haslar was correct about the danger to the villagers. The gendarmes submitted a report to the Prefecture in Angouleme, which may have implicated people in Beaunac. On 22 December the German Feldgendarmerie arrested Latouche and two other men, named Bineau and Picot. On 24 December they returned and arrested Maurice Rousseau, Lucien Gody and a man named Souchard. On 26 December they arrested 16 year-old Rene Rousseau, who was not related to Maurice. Most of those arrested were released later, but Lucien Gody died in Germany and the two Rousseau's never came home, so it has to be assumed they also died there. Their names are included on the 'Cockleshell Heroes' memorial at Pointe de Grave.

When just about exhausted they emerged onto a road southeast of Souvigne, burrowed into a haystack and went to sleep. At dawn on 18 December they were moving again. They had no food and were weak, but it had stopped raining. With about nine miles to go, Haslar managed to get one of the damp compasses to work. They passed thorough Raix and hit the main road out of Ruffec leading west at La Faye. As they got closer to the town they began to take interest in passers-by, expecting someone would be looking for them. No-one paid them the slightest notice and they were soon in the middle of Ruffec. About six weeks previously the Germans had arrested and deported 12 members of the Resistance; only one returned after the war, but Haslar and Sparks had no idea about this at the time.

Sparks appears to confuse a number of incidents. He recalls on the night of the 18th they sought refuge and a girl invited them in. Then a 16 year-old lad agreed to take them to someone who could help. After 30 minutes they came to a house in a clearing. The Maquis were meeting there and interrogated Haslar, while he listened to the BBC. Once accepted they were fed and slept in a double bed. Next day the guide took them on and they slept in a barn. The guide stayed with them until La Faye just short of Ruffec. Much of Sparks' version appears to relate to the night spent with Clodomir and his family at Nâpres some days before.

They had travelled 105 miles by canoe and another 100 miles on foot, with only one proper meal and one night under cover in 11 days; it was an incredible feat of endurance and determination. They walked through the town to the east side, taking their time, looking in shop windows and at passers-by in the hope of recognition. They turned back to the west and passed a policeman, but neither he nor anyone else took any notice.

130

Haslar and Sparks were confused and desperate. After everything they had been through, they expected to be met. Haslar checked a few cheap bistros, pretending to study the menus, but was in reality checking out the owners, looking for the one that appeared the least threatening; they had to have food. He selected the Hotel de la Toque Blanche on the corner of Rue de l'Hopital. There were only a few customers and they sat well away from them. The proprietor was a friendly looking woman named Yvonne Mandinaud and her sister Alix was serving. They ordered potage and coffee as it did not require ration cards. Alix took their order without a trace of curiosity; France was full of displaced persons.

Sparks could have eaten a bucketful, but Haslar advised eating slowly to allow the other customers to leave. It was already 1400, but the others made no move. Haslar ordered more bowls of potage and after they had eaten decided to take a risk. He asked for the bill and gave Alix a 500 Franc note with a note inside, "We are two escaping English soldiers. Do you know anyone who can

Hotel de la Toque Blanche on the corner of Rue de l'Hopital in Ruffec. It was the Café des Sports in the 1930s, later Le Baroque and is currently the Hotel l'Angle d'Or. It was close to the German HQ in 1942 and some rooms were used as billets.

A modern view of the inside of the Hotel de la Toque Blanche looking from the dining room towards the entrance. The owner in 2011 had previously played in the English and Scottish Football Leagues.

help us?" She took it to the cash desk and there was not a flicker of interest in her face as she read the note. When she returned with the change she had scribbled on the bottom, "Stay at your table until I have closed the restaurant." Although Alix had shown no interest when they entered the restaurant, she mentioned the odd couple to her siblings in the kitchen, suspecting they were German deserters due to Haslar's accent.

Alix eventually told the customers she was closing. The Frenchmen made their way out still chattering away. She bolted the door and led them into the kitchen where they met her brother, Rene, the chef. Both were friendly, but asked a number of questions, in particular they wanted to know whom they were to contact in Ruffec, which Haslar did not know. The couple said they could stay there while they found someone to help and took them to a guest bedroom. There were two staircases in the hotel, so the Germans staying there never came into contact with them.

Rene Mandinaud.

Alix brought a hipbath, soap, towels and hot water and while they bathed she washed their clothes. Haslar wondered what to do if they were given away? They could not make a run for it stark naked in mid-winter. They had been very lucky; had they asked for help in any other restaurant in Ruffec it is almost certain they would have been betrayed.

They slept and later were brought more food and clean underwear. While asleep, two gendarmes asked if the two men were escaped British soldiers. Yvonne said no and they seemed satisfied. The local gendarmerie was pro-British and it is likely that the Commandant in Ruffec, Lieutenant Henri Peyraud, was part of the escape chain Haslar was trying to contact. It is possible the gendarmes were asking questions because a woman in Souvigne had seen the two climbing out of the haystack that morning and reported it to the Germans.

Yvonne (right) and Alix Mandinaud in 1960.

Then they heard the tread of feet

coming up the stairs. Rene entered with two men who sat on chairs around the bed and questioned them closely. One was Jean Mariaud, the local taxman and organiser of the local Resistance. He would link them with the Resistance escape chain, which was to organise their covert travel through France into Spain. The other was named Paillet, a retired English teacher who had taught French in England and lived in a house named Villa Livingstone. Mariaud was taking a bigger risk than the others as he had been arrested by the Germans only a few weeks before, but had been warned and managed to burn all incriminating papers before they arrived.

Jean Mariaud.

Paillet assured everyone that Sparks' Cockney accent could not be replicated by a German. They told the two to be ready to leave next afternoon. In some ways they were relieved to be in the escape system, but until then they had relied on themselves and were now utterly dependent on others.

At first Mariaud approached Francois Rouillon who owned the nearby Hotel de France in Ruffec. They needed to gain access to the 'Marie-Claire' escape organisation. Rouillon admitted he knew Marie-Claire through the local head of the Red Cross, but had nothing to do with escaped Allied servicemen. It was known he had helped in the past, but he would not be drawn this time. For unrelated reasons, he and his wife were deported in May 1944 and she died in Ravensbruck concentration camp.

Mariaud then went to see Madame Marthe Rullier who had served with Marie-Claire as a nurse in 1915. She lived in a large house, most of which had been requisitioned

Marthe Rullier.

by the Germans. She did not know where Marie-Claire was at the time, but knew she was in contact with Armand Dubreuille on the other side of the Demarcation Line. Mariaud had made

133

Rene Flaud with his baker's van.

the first link in the chain, but needed someone trustworthy to drive the two Marines close to where they could get over the Line. The baker, Rene Flaud, was willing to help.

On the 19th, Haslar and Sparks awoke refreshed with clean dry clothes. Mariaud returned at 1400 and they took their leave of the Mandinauds, who refused to take payment. Outside the baker's van was running and its windows were blacked out. They jumped inside, the doors closed and the van set off immediately. It avoided main routes and travelled via Condac, Bioussac and Messeux. En route Flaud picked up Fernand Dumas near Benest. After about 30 minutes it stopped and they got out on a country road in a wood. The van drove off leaving Haslar and Sparks with Dumas. Flaud returned to Ruffec, signalling to Mariaud with his horn as he passed that the drop off had been accomplished successfully.

Fernand Dumas.

The three moved into the undergrowth and Dumas explained the wood was just southeast of Benest, between there and St Coutant. They were heading for a farm a kilometre away and provided they were careful should get over the patrolled Demarcation Line, despite the dogs. They settled down to wait for nightfall. In another version of the story, when it got dark the guide stood at the side of the road while they remained in cover. He came back with a young lad and it was he who took them over the Demarcation Line.

As soon as it was dark no time was wasted and they moved through the wood, then across fields hugging the hedges for cover. Dumas stopped periodically to listen. About 1930 they reached a long low building, the farm at Marvaud on the far side of the Demarcation Line. Marie-Claire established 'safe' farms

Marvaud Farm.

either side of the Line. Farm A in the occupied zone was owned by Maxim de la Vergne. The intention was for escapers to stay there until conditions were right to cross the Line to Farm B owned by the Dubreuille family.

A dog barked and light could be seen through a shutter. Dumas placed them behind a wall and knocked on the door. It was answered by a man in his early 30s and a few words were exchanged. Dumas came over, took them to the door, shook hands and left immediately. Inside they met Armand Dubreuille, wife Amelie and a few children. There were no questions now they were in the escape chain. Haslar and Sparks were the first 'parcels' the Dubreuilles looked after and due to the circumstances, did not get the agreed two to three days notice of arrival. The Dubreuilles eventually sheltered 40 escaping Allied servicemen and Armand received the Legion d'Honneur for this work.

Armand Dubreuille.

Armand took them to their room where they spent the next three weeks except when using the privy across the yard. Before opening the external door they had to check for strangers outside. As the door had glass panels, they kept it locked and at night the curtains were always drawn.

Better clothes were found, so they did not look like tramps. There were a few ageing English

Amelie Dubreuille.

135

novels and each day they saw the French newspapers, which Haslar translated for Sparks. Although the stories had a Nazi/Vichy slant they were able to read between the lines. Occasionally their hosts brought news from BBC radio bulletins, particularly of the Allied successes in North Africa.

Meals were served in their rooms and hot water was brought for washing and shaving. Armand told them a message had been sent to Marie-Claire, the woman who would arrange their onward journey. Haslar had not heard of her and was surprised to learn she was English. A few days later Armand reported he had been unable to get through to Maire-Claire. After another few days he discovered she was in hospital, which explained why no-one met them at Ruffec. Armand then tried to contact Marie-Claire's son.

For a few days they enjoyed relaxing and recovering from their exertions, but Haslar and Sparks had little in common. The extrovert Sparks needed the company of pubs and cinemas and was not good at amusing himself. Haslar was used to living off his wits, preferred his own company and longed for the coast and his sailing boat. He was also desperate to get back to put into practice all he had learned. Haslar borrowed a knife from Armand and carved some figures. Sparks managed a rudimentary elephant; these carvings were treasured by the Dubreuilles until lost in a house move. Haslar later commented, with tongue in cheek, "The only time I thought of giving myself up while escaping ... was when I realised that I had to shack up with Sparks." Food was another issue. Sparks craved the simplicity of steak and chips, whereas Haslar was completely at home with Amelie's French dishes.

Armand eventually contacted Marie-Claire's son, Maurice, who was studying law at Lyon to escape military service or deportation to work in Germany. He attended the minimum number of lectures while a fellow student submitted papers to allow him to get on with Resistance work. On Christmas Eve, Maurice visited his mother in hospital to let her know that setting up the escape route over the Pyrenees was proving difficult. When he got home there was a letter from Dubreuille saying he had 'two parcels of food'. Maurice went back to the hospital with the news. As a result he was to make arrangements to receive the two escapers in Lyons and arrange with Armand to pick them up on 6 January. She would leave hospital on 26

December to return to Lyons.

For Haslar and Sparks, Christmas Day was the same as any other, except Amelie made some pancakes. They exchanged greetings with the family, similarly on New Year's Day, and had a meal of roast duck. A day or so later news arrived that Maurice would be there on 6 January. Armand asked them to send a message when they made it back to England. Haslar told them to listen for, "Le poulet est bon", the message for Clodomir Pasqueraud's family, but Armand wanted a message just for his family. He asked them to send, "Two chickens have arrived." Haslar agreed and the BBC broadcast both messages in late April.

Amelie later recalled, 'We were asked to keep them for 48 hours and we said yes. Our toddler could not talk properly yet, which meant the secret was safe. We had to be very careful, the Germans were only 700m away from the farm. After the agreed two days, we still had no telegram telling us who and when the two would be fetched. We began to worry. Days passed and still nothing. We established a code for the Marines to venture in the garden: if the lid of my wash boiler was inverted it meant that they had to stay indoors. Eventually we did receive the telegram; instead of a couple of days Hasler and Sparks had stayed with us 41 days!' Amelie was mistaken about the length of the stay, which was 18 days, although in the circumstances it probably felt much longer.

Armand refused payment; they would need their francs later and in any case Marie-Claire recompensed them. Maurice arrived at 1200 on 6 January. He was about 19, slim, good looking and well dressed. Haslar and Sparks had been inactive for over two

Maurice Milleville was arrested and severely beaten, but refused to reveal the whereabouts of Marie-Claire and was eventually released when his sister Barbe bribed a German officer. His brother Oky was also arrested and beaten, but revealed nothing and was deported to a concentration camp, never to be heard of again. After the war Maurice worked for the UN Relief and Rehabilitation Administration in Germany and later as a radio engineer for the US Army. Thereafter he worked in insurance, petroleum, a scuba school, aluminium and was Charge de Mission of the Agence Nationale pour l'Emploi in the Rhone-Alpes. Awarded the Legion d'Honneur, Croix de Guerre, Medaille de la Resistance and Medaille des Evades.

137

weeks and were quite plump and white faced. They hoped they didn't have to walk too far as they had lost the edge on their fitness.

Maurice spoke good English and explained about his mother. Having spent the night at Marthe Rullier's house with one of her helpers, they were run down deliberately on their way to Farm A next morning by a pro-German group. Initially thought to be dead, she was taken to hospital 150 kms away at Loches with serious head, leg and arm wounds, five broken ribs and internal injuries. Ten days later when the Gestapo arrived, she was hidden in the cellar behind some wood. Her husband and the hospital doctor were arrested, but released for lack of evidence.

Maurice told them they were going to Lyons. Haslar was surprised as it was 320 kms away from the Spanish border, but Maurice explained the previous route had been closed down. They would be safe until a new route was opened. They would firstly cycle 11 miles to the station at Roumazieres to board the train to Lyons. The journey would be difficult because they did not have time to produce identity cards. Getting on the train without identity meant avoiding ticket collectors and policemen on the entry barriers. However, the stationmaster at Lyons was in the know. If anyone spoke to them on the train they should reply in a gutteral voice, "Breton", as many people in Brittany did not speak French. He asked if they had anything that might identify them. Both had ID disks and Sparks had his lifejacket; all of which were left with the Dubreuilles. Why Sparks carried his lifejacket all that way is a mystery.

After lunch they bade farewell to their hosts and set off on three rickety bicycles. Sparks embellishes this part of the tale by saying there were only two bicycles and the guide sat on his handlebars, which is highly unlikely. Heading south through Alloue, Maurice chatted away openly in English. He told them his mother was English, married to a Frenchman of position. She had a flat in Lyons, a city in which the Germans had not yet established themselves. Maurice had a good laugh when Haslar asked if they would be pulled up for cycling without lights.

At Roumazieres they dumped the bikes and found an unfenced section of the railway about 50m from the entrance. Maurice went to buy the tickets and told them to wander in casually up the line. On seeing his signal they boarded the third class compartment and wedged themselves in between other

Roumazieres railway station.

Escape organisations in France hid people amongst crowds, such as at a busy railway station.

travelers; many were already sleeping. Haslar and Sparks were not keen on the train and crowds; their instinct was to avoid people, but escape organisations did the opposite and hid people amongst crowds.

The journey seemed to go on forever, with many stops and much shunting. At Limoges they changed to the night train to Lyons. It was impossible to sleep and Maurice took an impish delight in periodically leaning over and making remarks in English.

As daylight came they arrived in Lyons and split up to surrender their tickets. Maurice and Haslar got through the check barrier without incident, but when Sparks tried the gendarme was interested in the parcel he was carrying. This contained spare underwear washed by their previous hosts and the garments bore English labels. The gendarme became increasingly angry that Sparks would not release the parcel. Eventually Sparks let go and disappeared into the crowd. Outside he told Haslar what had happened and they expected pursuit at any moment, but kept walking quickly and followed Maurice onto a tram. Maurice telephoned his mother from a newsagent and they went to her flat.

Marie-Claire was about 45, typically English with blue eyes and she was wearing a Red Cross uniform with two rows of medal ribbons, including two British ones from the First World War. She was very much English despite the time spent in France, including her accent. One of her legs was in plaster from the assassination attempt.

Marie-Claire allowed them to bath and shave, giving Haslar a pair of nail scissors to remove his moustache, before giving them breakfast. While they ate she told them her previous network had folded and she was going to establish a new one over the Pyrenees. In the meantime they would be accommodated in a house in the north of the city. The only rule was no girls, as it always led to trouble; Haslar and Sparks were disappointed.

She took them to a photographer, looking incredibly conspicuous in her uniform on the tram. They were horrified when she shouted in English, 'Here we are', and tried to leave the tram as if they were not with her. Photographs were taken and they received ID cards with false French names, but kept their British ID disks as well, which is contrary to accounts of them leaving their ID disks with the Dubreuilles.

Marie-Claire was going to Switzerland for treatment and would take a short message. Haslar crammed as much about the raid as possible into a few words and encoded it using the No.3 Code. The first stage was to apply the codeword to the message, which he did, but then neither he nor Sparks could remember how to convert the resultant string of letters into innocent looking plain text. So he sent it just as the string of letters and hoped the other end would realise what he had done.

Marie-Claire enjoyed playing a dangerous game and did little to hide her sentiments. She was openly pro-British and Haslar thought it was a hell of a way to run a secret escape organisation, but because she was so eccentric she got away with a great deal.

'Marie-Claire' post-war. Gertrude Mary Lindell was a VAD nurse in WW1 awarded the Russian Order of St Anne and French Croix de Guerre serving with the French Red Cross. She married a Frenchman and became Comtesse de Milleville. Helped by children Maurice, Oky and Barbe, she collected evaders from the summer of 1940 to link into the escape lines. By bluff and boldness she obtained travel permits and fuel coupons, but she was amateurish, the Gestapo arrested her and she spent nine months in solitary confinement.  Using an old passport in her maiden name, she posed as governess to an elderly lady being repatriated to Britain and arrived at Poole by flying boat in July 1942. Having been debriefed by Airey Neave of MI9, she demanded to go back. She was trained in the escape business and landed in France by Lysander on 21 October. In May 1943, information she passed about the movement of blockade runners from Bordeaux resulted in a successful interception, for which she was MID. The Marie-Claire line she set up, collected evaders and sent them in groups over the Pyrenees.

On 24 November 1943, Mary was arrested by the Gestapo at Pau station, having been betrayed by a disaffected member of the escape line, Marie Odile, who ironically died in Ravensbruck. On the way to Paris she threw herself out of the train toilet window, the guards opened fire and she was seriously wounded. A German surgeon saved her and she recovered in Dijon prison until being transferred to Ravensbruck in September 1944. By working in the hospital she narrowly missed the gas chamber and survived to become a key witness in war crimes trials.

Mary's husband was imprisoned for two years due to frustration at not being able to catch her. After the war, she became the RAF Escaping Society's representative in France. A film of her exploits, *One Against the Wind*, was released in 1991. Her story is also told in *No Drums, No Trumpets* by JB Wynne. Haslar helped her obtain compensation from the British government for British women who helped their countrymen. She was awarded the OBE in 1969 – too little and too late. Mary died on 8 January 1987 aged 91.

She had been arrested twice and released. In prison she continued to behave arrogantly. When told to mop out her cell by a warder she refused and appeared before the Commandant, who she told flatly, "I won't take orders from that fellow. I am not accustomed to that kind of thing." The Germans at that time were trying to keep the French sweet and the Commandant was a polite man. He showed her a copy of the prison standing orders and asked for her cooperation. "Oh in that case I will, but remember I don't take orders from that fellow."

That night Maurice took them to a large house on the banks of the Saone in a northern suburb. The owner was a German sympathiser, but had been run over by a tram a few weeks before, losing both legs and was bed ridden. His wife and daughter supported the Allies. One day they had to hide as the Germans conducted house searches. They heard soldiers rummaging about next door, including in the garden. As soon as it went quiet they knew their house was next so hopped over the fence and hid in the garden that had just been searched.

For a month they were moved from place to place within the city. Bad news accompanied Marie-Claire when she returned from Switzerland – she had been unable to establish a new escape line and was going to hand them over to a larger organization run by 'Pat O'Leary'. The news was depressing.

An Englishman collected them and Sparks recalled his name was Carter; he disapproved of Marie-Claire and her methods. Other sources indicate the man was named Martineau and was a French communist. For five or six days the two were separated and during this time Haslar spent one night in the flat of Paul Reynauld and the rest of the time in the flat of another Englishwoman married to a Frenchman. This was the Bonnamour family and the wife was the daughter of Mr Barr who managed Barclay's Bank in Baker Street, London. Sparks' hosts had a daughter who fancied him and he had to be careful not to be alone.

They were then moved together by Carter/Martineau to a large house owned by Mr Barr. Haslar found a piano to play the one tune he knew and Sparks messed about with a music box. They were looked after by a young Frenchwoman.

After six days a man named Fabien arrived. He was a Parisian who spoke a little English and was lively, quick witted and fun. He was to take them to Marseilles by train that night.

On board he sought out a compartment with two German soldiers and sat Haslar next to one of them with an impish grin on his face. During the journey he made remarks in English and Haslar wished the Germans would be swallowed by a huge hole. They didn't seem to notice and the two escapers were glad to see a sunny morning in Marseilles.

Boulevarde Cassini overlooking the observatory gardens in Marseilles.

They went to a block of flats at 12 Boulevarde Cassini overlooking the observatory gardens, where they were admitted by a fierce looking woman, Madame Martin, who turned out to be very generous. She had daughters aged about seven and 11. Inside were two RAF men on the run after their bomber was shot down. They had to keep their voices low as the occupants beyond the walls could not be trusted. The flat was full of beds and mattresses and the turnover of escapers and French guides was constant. Madame Martin fed them all and was out of the flat every morning at 0500, returning with lots of black market food, which was not difficult to find in Marseilles. She cooked wonderful Mediterranean dishes, not much to Sparks' liking, but he struck up a good relationship with the younger daughter, who tried to teach him French and collapsed in gales of laughter at his attempts.

Monsieur Martin worked in the docks and was a communist. His brother, Georges, was a boxer defeated by Bruce Woodcock at King's Hall, Belle Vue, Manchester on 15 November 1946. The escape organisation rented the flat in another name and was headed by a man known only as 'Pat', who visited them on 28 February. Sparks believed he was a French-Canadian mercenary. In reality he was Albert-Marie Edmond Guérisse, an incredibly brave Belgian who ran the 'Pat O'Leary' escape line.

The escape route was broken again and the projected stay of a few days turned into weeks. Haslar fantasised about getting away in a boat. In the third week they were joined by Flying Officer Prince Werner de Merode, Flight Sergeant Jack Dawson and a French girl named Edit on her way to England to join the Free French. Edit and a British radio operator had been captured

'Pat O'Leary' – Albert-Marie Edmond Guérisse qualified in medicine before joining the Belgian Army. He escaped through Dunkirk, was commissioned in the RNVR and joined HMS *Fidelity*, the former French *Le Rhin*, for special operations. He escorted agents ashore in small boats, but on 25 April 1941 while landing SOE agents in southern France, his skiff turned over and he had to swim ashore. To the Vichy coast guards he claimed he was a Canadian airman named Pat O'Leary. He was held at St Hippolyte du Fort near Nîmes until an SOE agent, Ian Garrow, got him released and took him to Marseilles where he joined the escape line. When the Vichy French captured Garrow in October, Guérisse took over the network. He smuggled a German uniform to Garrow in Mauzac concentration camp and he escaped on 6 December to return to London. Guérisse expanded the line, eventually moving over 600 escapees to Spain and back to Britain. In January 1943 the line was infiltrated by French turncoat, Roger le Neveu. Guérisse was arrested in Toulouse in March and sent to a series of concentration camps, the last being Dachau. He survived, rejoined the Belgian Army and served in Korea where he was wounded trying to rescue a wounded soldier. He became head of the Belgian Army medical services and retired in 1970 as a Major General. Guérisse received 35 decorations from a variety of nations, including the George Cross in 1946 and an honorary knighthood. The King of Belgium made him a Comte in 1986.

by the Gestapo; the Briton dived through a window and in the commotion she slipped away. Sparks helped her learn English and Haslar was alarmed at some of the phrases. However, Haslar had his moments too. At one meal he was asked by Edit if he'd had enough to eat. Haslar replied in French that he was 'full', but the word he used had a completely different meaning and had Edit and the Martins rolling on the floor.

Sparks took an instant dislike to Merode whom he regarded as arrogant, smarmy and in need to a good thump. He always had cigarettes when others were short. Edit became quite taken with Sparks, but fortunately for him there was no privacy in the flat and he escaped her closer attentions – he estimated she weighed at least 100 kgs.

Haslar worried about escaping over the Pyrenees. They were getting flabby and soft having had no exercise for weeks. After about a month Haslar, Sparks, Merode and Dawson were warned to be ready to leave at short notice. They were given a small canvas rusksack each and two pairs of rope soled espadrilles.

Early on 1 March a young French guide took them by train to Perpignan along the Mediterranean coast. They waited for an hour in a garden near a street café, until being picked up by a rickety van and squeezed in amongst a pile of crates. A fifth companion joined them, a tall French left wing intellectual carrying a rucksack and a pile of books tied together with string. He was wanted by the Germans and the books were incriminating, so he carried them separately so they could be discarded easily.

Werner de Merode was commissioned in the Belgian Army and transferred to the Aéronautique Militaire. When Belgium capitulated he evaded capture, reached Gibraltar and joined the RAFVR in January 1942. On 12 December he was shot down and evaded capture to be returned to Britain via the 'Pat O'Leary' line on 28 March 1943. He joined the administration of the Belgian Section of the RAF and the Air Ministry Unit in February 1944. Post-war he served in the Belgian Diplomatic Corps and was ambassador to several countries, including the Holy See.

The van travelled through Boulou and westwards. It climbed and the air became chilly as they passed through Ceret and Amelie-les-Bains. The guide told them they were heading for a crossing place over the Pyrenees rough enough to deter the Germans or Spanish from manning it effectively, but low enough that it would not be blocked by snow. The van stopped near Ceret and two tough Catalan guides took over. It was getting dark, but they set off up a rough path and after two miles reached a hut where they lit a fire, ate some food and settled on the earth floor for the night. Sparks' says the hut was occupied by Germans and they skirted round it having crossed a rickety bridge.

They were moving before dawn, climbing on rough paths ever higher. It became colder and Haslar and Sparks suffered

145

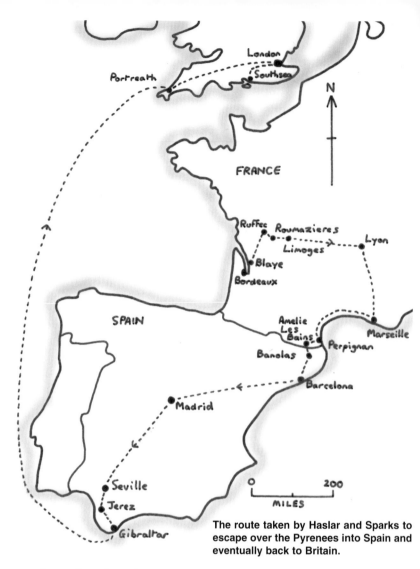

The route taken by Haslar and Sparks to escape over the Pyrenees into Spain and eventually back to Britain.

from altitude sickness – their strength drained, their breath was laboured and they felt constantly dehydrated. The Frenchman, Merode and Dawson had not been immobilized as long as Haslar and Sparks and were able to keep up without difficulty.

Haslar was embarrassed; three months previously he could have run up the mountain. Now he and Sparks were struggling at the back while the others urged them on. Eventually they had to have some liquid and drank some wine, but the tall Frenchman snatched the bottle out of Haslar's hand and threw it away. Haslar kept calm despite being furious. They continued but when they crossed a stream he and Sparks drank deeply. After that they still laboured for breath but could move a little easier.

Up and up they went across a barren wasteland and it became ever colder. On reaching the snow line Haslar, ignoring all he had been taught about eating snow, told Sparks to hold it in his mouth to melt before drinking. Their bodies craved liquid and as they moved along scooping up snow every few yards they slowly gained strength and their pauses for breath became fewer. Soon they were able to keep up. Sparks remembered having to dive for cover when a German ski patrol was sighted, but no other accounts mention this incident.

About midday they were close to the frontier, but visibility was restricted and the guides argued about which way to go. Haslar cursed giving away his compasses as souvenirs to those who had helped them. They were following the course of valleys where the snow was about 2m deep, although there were deeper drifts. Eventually the Frenchman took the lead as he seemed to know the area better than the guides, which seemed odd to Haslar. After a few hours the Frenchman told them they had crossed into Spain and back into France before recrossing the frontier again into Spain. They began to head down from the snow line where another patrol was evaded according to Sparks. Merode's report says their route passed through Las Illas and Massanet-de-Cabrenys.

That night was spent in a cold cave; they had covered only ten miles in 24 hours. They ate a little food and before dawn were moving again. Merode berated Sparks for being slow and Sparks threatened to throw him off the edge. Haslar intervened and suggested Merode get to the front away from Sparks. They had to avoid the police, but Catalonian civilians were anti-Franco and were unlikely to give them away. The route was downhill all day, although they were still not sure where they were. The food was finished and they staggered on into the night, eventually reaching a rough road, which they followed for some distance. The place names were not visible on a 3m high signpost and no-one had a torch. The Frenchman climbed on the back of one of the guides with Merode's cigarette lighter to read it.

The names meant little and the guides argued again until they set off down one of the roads, which ran out into cart tracks.

Signs of cultivation meant there had to be a farm nearby. One of the guides barked out an impression of a guard dog and was answered immediately by two real dogs. They set off towards the closest, with the guide periodically repeating his bark to check they were going in the right direction.

At 2100 they arrived at a small farm; it was locked, shuttered and showed no lights, but a dog was barking inside. The occupants did not stir and they had to knock long and hard before an upstairs window opened and the farmer was persuaded to let them in. The fire was stoked up and the farmer's wife produced food and rough wine that went down like paint stripper. They spent the night on the floor.

Next afternoon, 4 March, they reached a small hotel nine kilometers north of Banolas (Banyoles). They were expected, but had to maintain a low profile to avoid attention from the police. On 7 March a truck arrived to take them the 96 kms to Barcelona. It was full of toilet china protected by piles of straw, under which they concealed themselves to get through a police check post.

In Barcelona a skeptical British Consulate employee questioned them at length, but gave them fresh Spanish clothing. They gladly threw away their stinking escape clothes. The less than welcoming reception was explained by the Vice Consul. The Consulate was inundated with escapees from France, many of whom were French. The French Consulate invariably sent them back, so they came to the British and claimed to be French-Canadians. The Consulate had a transit camp where they were checked out; real British servicemen being sent back to Britain and the rest to a Free French district in North Africa.

They heard some amusing stories, including one about a British private who had evaded capture all the way to Lisbon dressed in uniform. When he reached the Embassy he looked very worried, "I'm afraid I've lost me rifle sir!" Haslar realised they had been lucky not to be picked up by the Spanish police. Anyone of military age coming out of France was imprisoned for a fixed period in appalling conditions. Haslar met a few RAF escapers who had experienced this treatment.

The Consulate kept genuine escapers hidden, including Sparks, but because Haslar was balding and appeared to be over military service age, he persuaded the Spanish police he was a commercial traveller. Haslar stayed at the Hotel Victoria with

Hotel Victoria (now the Hotel NH Duc de la Victoria) on Plaza de Catalunya, where Haslar stayed while in Barcelona.

some of those released from Spanish prisons. On 12 March he wrote to his mother from the hotel assuring her he was well and on his way home. He also mentioned being there for a day in 1936 during the Civil War, while serving aboard HMS *Queen Elizabeth*.

The Consul told them that the mysterious Frenchman (Belgian according to Sparks), who accompanied them over the Pyrenees, had disappeared and had not sought help from the French or British Consulates. He was suspected of being a Gestapo agent. Haslar hoped those who ran the escape chain were safe.

Haslar as a commercial traveler in Barcelona.

Orders came from London for Haslar to be returned by air as soon as possible; Sparks was to follow by sea. It was two weeks before a car was able to take them to the Embassy in Madrid on 22 March. Haslar was looked after by the Naval Attaché and attended a few parties and the Prado art gallery. Sparks was confined to the Embassy, but had the company of a couple of RAF airmen, who taught him bridge.

149

One day he says they learned the German Attaché had died during an appendectomy and they jeered as the funeral procession went by.

A car took Haslar to Gibraltar with an overnight stop in Seville. There he watched flamenco dancing, but was troubled by a party of German officials dining at the next table. Following lunch and a glass of Tio Pepe in Jerez next day, 1 April, he crossed into Gibraltar.

When the Germans heard of the escape, a stiff diplomatic note was sent to the Spanish government about their lax and inefficient border security along the Pyrenees. Franco's response was, 'If you think you can do any better, do it yourself!'

On 2 April, Haslar arrived by air at Portreath in Cornwall. He

was dressed in civilian clothing, but the station commander had been warned off and met him. He travelled to London by train where he met Captain Stewart before going to HQ Combined Operations to start the debrief. One of the first things he did was enquire what had been heard of the others; there was no news from any quarter. Haslar was there for the next five days, during which he was debriefed by MI9, but he took some time out for celebrations.

Haslar returned to Southsea on 8 April. The other RMBPD officers had to scrape together the money to replace his stock of alcohol, which they had consumed when he was posted missing. At breakfast on his first morning Haslar found volunteers to go sailing for a few

Kettner's restaurant in Soho, a favourite of King Edward VII, Lillie Langtry and Oscar Wilde.

hours and was in his office at 1030. By 1700 he had visited Bill Ladbrooke's workshops at HMS *Northney* on Hayling Island, Clogstoun-Willmott of COPP, Courtney of Army SBS and was on the water with an improved Cockle Mk.II. That evening he was at the Sergeant's Mess dance.

On 12 April, Haslar returned to HQ Combined Operations to give a verbal report to the Plans Committee. His full written report included a detailed account of the escape for MI9 and an intelligence summary of everything seen during the mission.

Afterwards he met Dick Raikes and wife Joan for a belated reunion lunch at Kettner's restaurant in Soho. On 16 April, Haslar took four days leave and girlfriend Val arrived at Portsmouth. While sailing they were arrested as Haslar's permit had expired.

Sparks followed later. The Spanish border guards were not interested in him, but when he arrived at the British checkpoint in Gibraltar without identity he was arrested and questioned closely. He was

Sparks' identity card photograph from Barcelona.

kept on the Gibraltar depot ship, HMS *Cormorant*, until being put on a troopship where he was kept in a separate cabin. At Liverpool, military policemen put him in a locked compartment on a train to London, but during the journey Sparks realised the door was not locked. When the train arrived at Euston he evaded two military policemen waiting for him and took the tube to Finsbury Park. He knew he had been posted missing, so his first priority was to put his father's mind at rest.

After a couple of euphoric days at home he reported to the Euston Hotel. A naval intelligence officer suggested that while he checked a filing cabinet, Sparks should slip out of the other door to evade the escort and make his way to HQ Combined Operations. On arrival senior officers congratulated him on his

Sparks was confined aboard HMS *Cormorant* before leaving Gibraltar for Britain. She was launched in 1877, reduced to harbour service in 1889, renamed HMS *Rooke* in 1946 and broken up in 1949.

achievement. He jumped on a train and arrived in Southsea in early May for a reunion with Haslar. Six months after setting out, only two of the ten who started had returned.

Chapter Eleven

RESULTS OF THE RAID

MOUNTBATTEN wrote, 'Of the many brave and daring raids carried out by the men of Combined Operations Command, none was more courageous or more imaginative than Operation Frankton'. *Korvetten Kapitan* Peter Popp went even further. He described it as, 'the outstanding commando raid of the war'. Popp, a mine and explosives expert, cited it in his lectures and reminded the German naval authorities that the Elbe ports were just as vulnerable as Bordeaux.

At 0700 on 12 December the first of the Limpets exploded on *Alabama*, the last went off at 1300, also on *Alabama*. The Germans were shocked. The spread of explosions over time was disconcerting. No sooner had repair parties plugged one hole than another Limpet went off. This was an unintended consequence of the less than perfect fusing system. French fire and salvage teams tried their best to add to the problems by using excessive amounts of water to put out the fires. At times pumps intended to pump water out of the ships were used to pump more into them.

A Frenchman who was in Bordeaux until mid-March 1943 was interviewed by the Naval Intelligence Department on arrival in Britain. He confirmed the blockade-runners were good ships, crewed by men with high morale. As far as he could tell the raid sank three ships, two on an even keel in shallow water, which were patched up fairly quickly. The third heeled over, but by flooding tanks the Germans righted her, allowing temporary repairs to be made prior to taking the ship into dry dock.

The cynical reaction amongst the French was the Italians had carried out the sabotage because they had been denied use of the U-Boat shelters. The truth came out fairly quickly and vigilance was increased.

It is alleged an SOE group was carrying out a reconnaissance of the harbour to attack shipping the following night, only to see their prospective targets sinking before their eyes. In reality the local SOE agent, Claude de Baissac (Scientist), was in the early

MS *Portland* – early in 1941 she was heading for Bordeaux from Chile when she met the raider *Nordmark* and took off her 327 prisoners. These included a number of Royal Navy personnel. AB Arthur Fry assisted by ABs Lynch, Kitson, Merrett and others plotted to take over the ship, but it was leaked to the Germans by another prisoner. Fry set the ship alight to attract the attention of a British ship, but it was brought under control quickly. Next morning the power suddenly failed and a guard opened fire in the hold wounding two prisoners, one fatally. *Portland* arrived at Bordeaux on 14 March. The four prisoners mentioned and twenty-six others were tried at Hamburg with mutiny and arson. Fry was sentenced to death and the others imprisoned for periods of three months to 15 years. Fry survived the war and he and some of the others were awarded the BEM. *Portland* departed Bordeaux 22 October 1941, arrived in Osaka on 1 January 1942, departed Yokohama on 26 February and arrived back in Bordeaux on 10 May. Having been repaired after 'Frankton' she put to sea, the only ship attacked during the 'Frankton' raid to return to blockade running. She was intercepted off Dakar on 13 April 1943 by the Free French cruiser *Georges Leygues* and her crew scuttled her

stages of planning to introduce explosives into the docks. Had he gone ahead there would have been severe reprisals against civilians, so it seems likely the plan would have entailed a delay to ensure the charges went off at sea. De Baissac was a volatile character, known to be miffed at Haslar's attack without his knowledge and may have embellished his preparations to make a point. However, he had only been in France since 30 July and for some of that time he was recovering from an injury sustained in the parachute drop. Some explosives had been dropped to him, but not sufficient to make an impression on the blockade-runners.

Hitler received the news with consternation and demanded to know why it had happened. At first the Germans believed the attacks had been by drifting underwater weapons. The reality became clear from interrogating the prisoners and the discovery of *Crayfish* and *Catfish* near Blaye on 12 December, together with items of equipment – holdfast, hand grenades, charts etc. *Crayfish* and *Catfish* were stored at Bordeaux, their names being identified by removing the camouflage paint on the port bow. The Germans thought the ease with which they had recovered the canoes had been intentional to mask other aids. What became of them subsequently is not known. An unexploded Limpet was discovered on the pier side of MS *Portland* and *Conger* was discovered some time later fifty miles north of the Gironde.

An intercepted signal revealed *Dresden*, *Alabama* and three other ships were damaged by mysterious explosions on 12 December. Later analysis revealed the following details:

SS *Alabama* (5,641 tons) – five Limpets exploded at 0700, 0703, 0800, 1005 and 1305 all 1.5m below the water line. Water penetrated through Hatches 1 and 5. She was subsequently moved to dry dock for repairs.

MS *Portland* (7,132 tons) – a sentry felt slight vibrations on the ship at 0550 and 0630 and a confirmed Limpet exploded at 0955 below Hatch 1. Little water penetrated and the hole was sealed provisionally, but there was some fire damage. She was moved to dry dock for repairs, where an unexploded Limpet was discovered.

MS *Tannenfels* (7,840 tons) – two Limpets exploded at 0830 and 30 seconds later, 2.5m below the water line. Water penetrated through Hatches 2 and 3 into the empty hold. She listed to 24° until counter-flooding prevented her capsizing. Divers sealed the holes and she was refloated on the high tide, but was still listing at 16° when moved to dry dock for repairs.

MS *Dresden* (5,567 tons) – two Limpets exploded on the stern at 0845 and 0855, one damaging the shaft tunnel. Holds 4, 5, 6

MS *Dresden* and MS *Tannenfels* listing heavily soon after the Limpets exploded. *Dresden* had departed Bordeaux 15 April 1942, arrived at Yokohama in June, departed on 20 August and was back in Bordeaux on 3 November. On 6 November 1943 she struck a mine on her way down the Gironde.

The Germans brought in a floating crane to assist in the recovery operation.

and 7 filled with water and the stern sank. Leaks were sealed by 2130 and she refloated on the high tide, but work continued until the following evening. The holds were pumped out by the morning of the 14th.

Python – one Limpet caused a large hole and a fire.

Sperrbrecher 5 (formerly *Schwanheim* 5,339 tons) – one Limpet exploded on the seaward side at 1030. No damage was caused and it was assumed the charge dropped off the ship's side and exploded on the riverbed.

That accounts for 13 of the 16 Limpets (or 15 if the vibrations on *Portland* are included); of the other three nothing is known. The holes were all about 1.25 x 0.7m and all the ships attacked were unloaded at the time. Divers from the Coastal Mine Defence Service were assisted by three Italian divers. They used wooden plugs and bags of quick setting cement to fill the holes temporarily, so the water could be removed and the ships refloated for repairs.

The Germans, not unnaturally, reviewed their security arrangements. The Bordeaux Harbour Master recommended strengthening pickets and patrols in the harbour area. The guard vessel at the harbour entrance was to have more crew and sweep the shore with its searchlight regularly. Ships in harbour were to be illuminated from the shore. In addition he recommended booms to protect vulnerable installations.

Kapitän zur See Max Gebauer ordered a number of counter-measures. Future radar contacts were to be swept by searchlight and fired upon. If an explosion occurred on a ship, its sides were to be probed for more mines with long poles. Ships in harbour were to have two sentries, one on the gangway and the other on the seaward side. The entrance to the estuary was to be patrolled by two vessels between Pointe de Grave and Royan and covered by searchlights at Royan, St Georges and Le Verdon. There were to be increased land patrols.

The raid had a devastating psychological effect. Striking at the heart of German occupied France stunned the German High Command. Nervous sentries shot at driftwood and headquarters became paranoid. Reports were circulated to German and Italian commands so they could take precautions. They concluded erroneously, '…. the enemy knows precisely our coastal and defence installations'.

With hindsight it is clear that 'Frankton' disrupted the

blockade-runners, it did not stop them, but it showed (as did other raids), that nowhere in German occupied territory was safe from attack. The Germans were forced to divert huge numbers of troops from front line service. The raid also raised French morale.

The combination of increasingly effective Allied naval and air patrolling and Ultra decryption of U-boat radio traffic proved battle winning; the blockade-runners had had their day. Of the twenty-three ships involved in 1942-43, six reached the Far East and four returned, fourteen were sunk at sea, one was sunk in port and five more were damaged in port. Another eight departures were cancelled.

In the winter of 1943-44 Operation 'Stonewall' effectively ended the trade and only one blockade-runner, the *Osorno,* made it back to France from Japan. In January 1944 the Germans stopped the surface trade completely and thereafter all movement was by submarine. As a result the quantity of materiel moved was minimal.

SS *Osorno* owned by Hamburg Amerikanische Paket Aktien Gesellschaft (Hapag). She managed to evade interception and got into the Gironde on 25 December 1943, but was bombed there, damaged and forced to anchor in shallow water. Two destroyers were assigned as anti-aircraft protection, but she had to be beached. Captain Hellman was awarded the Knight's Cross to the Iron Cross for saving *Osorno's* valuable war cargo.

Chapter Twelve

THE FATE OF THE OTHERS

O N 28 OCTOBER 1942 the head of the Operations Division of the Naval War Staff promulgated to naval commands Hitler's *Kommandobefehl* (Commando Order), which denied commandos the protection of the Geneva Convention. Commandos were to be shot immediately, whether in uniform, armed or not and regardless of if they had surrendered. Only twelve copies were produced and distributed in great secrecy, indicating it was known to be a deliberate violation of the laws of war.

The first victims were seven officers on Operation Muskatoon, an Anglo-Norwegian raid on the Glomfjord power plant on 23 October 1942. The survivors of Operation Freshman, a glider operation against the Vemork Norsk Hydro heavy water plant in Norway, were shot in November 1942.

Wallace and Ewart

Having become separated in the first tide race, Wallace and Ewart carried on until around 0400, when the surf capsized them near Pointe de Grave lighthouse. In a state of collapse they swam ashore, discarded their waders and lifejackets and may have hidden for a time.

About 0545 they tried a house and were surprised when the door was opened by a German, who was equally shocked. His shout brought a NCO with drawn pistol and the two offered no resistance. They had been captured at the medical room of a *Luftwaffe* flak battery covering the ferry across the Gironde. Wallace claimed they were sailors torpedoed the previous night, but their dress and camouflaged faces indicated otherwise. The German gunners treated them well, their medical officer looked at them and they were given blankets and allowed to sleep.

Pointe de Grave lighthouse, close to where Wallace and Ewart came ashore.

Equipment, including explosives and maps, were recovered, but not the canoe, which was smashed below the low water mark and the surf made it impossible to recover.

News of the capture passed quickly from *Gemischte Flak Abteilung 595* (Mixed Flak Battalion 595) to commander of the *Hafenschutzflotillen* (Harbour Protection Flotilla), *Leutnant* Wild, who telephoned *Kapitän zur See* Gebauer at Royan at 0800. Gebauer told Wild to bring the prisoners before *Admiral* Johannes Bachmann, *Marinebefehlshaber Westfrankreich* (Naval Commander West France), on his arrival at Le Verdon. Gebauer forwarded the information to *Hafenkommandant* (Naval Command) Bordeaux and ordered a search for other raiders. Reports spread up the chain of command to *Oberbefehlshaber West* or OB West (Commander-in-Chief West) in Paris. It ordered the Army to protect the U-boat base at Bordeaux. OB West informed *Wehrmachtführungsstab* (usually shortened to WFSt – Armed Forces Operational Staff) at 1820 and *Marinegruppenkommando* West (Navy Group West) at 1950.

At 0845, Bachmann was informed. He and Gebauer crossed the estuary and inspected the vessels and crews of the Harbour Protection Flotilla at Le Verdon; the ships Haslar and the others had slipped past the previous night. The prisoners were brought before Bachmann on the road near the quarters of the Harbour Protection Flotilla. He said nothing, as he and Gebauer had agreed that interrogation should be left to Counter Intelligence

The road where Admiral Bachmann saw Wallace and Ewart. The Harbour Defence Flotilla at Le Verdon was based in the harbour on the right with the Pointe de Grave lighthouse beyond. On the left are the ramparts of the old French fort.

Section (CIS) Bordeaux. It was clear to Gebauer that the men were in uniform with Royal Marines shoulder titles and rank badges.

Initially CIS Bordeaux refused to be involved, pointing out correctly that the prisoners should be sent to the prison camp at Fallingbostel in Germany. Bachmann told Gebauer he would deal with the matter himself, which was a relief to Gebauer as he had two jobs at the time and it allowed him to get on with the practice firing.

At 1730, Bachmann spoke to *Admiral* Marschall, CinC Navy Group West, to report the situation and backed this up by signal at 2015, including the statement:

I have ordered immediate execution at conclusion of interrogation (if present facts confirmed) on account of attempted sabotage.

Leutnant Helmut Harstick of CIS Bordeaux arrived about 1800 and Bachmann briefed him at Le Verdon, specifying the issues he wanted resolving before they were shot. Bachmann and

Wilhelm Marschall entered the Navy in 1906 and served on SMS *Kronprinz* until becoming a U-boat commander in 1916. He gained a reputation for cruelty and inhumanity. Between the wars he remained in the *Reichsmarine* and at the end of 1934 took command of the pocket battleship *Admiral Scheer*. In 1936 he headed the operations division in *Oberkommando der Kriegsmarine* and commanded German naval forces off the Spanish coast during the Civil War. In contrast to his reputation in the First World War, in 1939-40 while commanding the squadron containing *Scharnhorst* and *Gneisenau* he took considerable risks to pick up survivors. At the time of the 'Frankton Raid he commanded Navy Group West. Its subordinate commands were Channel Coast and Western France, the latter commanded by *Admiral* Bachmann at Nantes. Defence of the Gascony coast was vested in Senior Naval Officer Gascony with HQ at Royan and one of its subordinates was Naval Officer in Charge Bordeaux. On 1 February 1943, Marschall was promoted to *Generaladmiral*, but replaced soon after at Navy Group West and deactivated. He was reactivated as special agent for the Danube and later as commander of *Marinekommando West* shortly before war's end.

Vizeadmiral Meisel had served with distinction on the raider *Moewe* in the First World War and commanded *Hipper* in the Atlantic in First World War, before becoming COS at Navy Group West.

Gebauer then returned to Royan.

Harstick telephoned Bachmann at 2330 stating progress was being made and asked for a postponement of the execution. Bachmann refused to withdraw the order, but after receiving a call from *Kapitän sur Zee* Koenig, liaison officer to OB West, deferred the execution to allow more time for interrogation.

The signal sent by Bachmann at 2015 was seen soon after by *Admiral* Marschall. He called an immediate conference to consider the safety of the blockade-runners, attended by the COS, *Vizeadmiral* Meisel, *Korvettenkapitän* Bernhard Viehweger, *Korvettenkapitän der Reserve* Henno Lucan along with *Korvettenkapitän* Hans Joachim Lange. Marschall was not present throughout, but was kept informed of developments and issued instructions accordingly.

When Viehweger was questioned on 27 March 1948, he said Marschall placed great importance on conducting a thorough interrogation, but tried to protect the prisoners from execution. A series of calls was made between Royan, WFSt in Poland and Navy Group West. Marschall was perturbed by Bachmann's execution order, but could not go against it because of the Commando Order.

When questioned on 6 April 1948, Lange said he suggested to Viehweger calling in a naval interrogation team from Bremen. Viehweger told him there was insufficient time, as the prisoners had to be handed over to the Security Service (*Sicherheitsdienst* or SD – *Gestapo* in occupied countries), within twenty-four hours. Lange suggested Marschall speak to WFSt, but he was not willing to risk unpopularity at the Führer's HQ. Marschall tasked Meisel to make the call late on 8 December. Lange prepared notes for Meisel to try to circumvent the Commando Order because of the necessity of having naval experts carry out the interrogation.

It is clear that Marschall and the staff of Navy Group West

staff were concerned about gleaning all possible information from the prisoners and did nothing to protect them in accordance with the Geneva Convention. They were legitimately concerned for the safety of the blockade-runners, but their lack of consideration for the prisoners was considered criminal.

In his post-war interrogation, Marschall claimed the call to WFSt was to protest about the handover of the prisoners to the SD. He believed that until a trial was held the prisoners should be protected. As far as the Commando Order was concerned, it was passed directly to Bachmann's HQ and he could not be held responsible for it.

The call came through at 2200. Meisel could not speak to *Generalfeldmarschall* Wilhelm Keitel (*Wehrmacht* COS) or *Generaloberst* Alfred Jodl (WFSt Chief of Operations), because they were at the pictures with the Führer. Meisel spoke to *Oberst* Werner von Tippelskirch, who didn't know what the fuss was about. The Führer's order was clear, the men were to be shot at once, but he conceded interrogations should be carried out first 'with no methods barred' to obtain quick results.

Meisel instructed Lange to contact CIS and SD to see if they had 'laughing pills' to induce the prisoners to talk. Lange rang Dr Erich Pfeiffer of CIS Bordeaux. Pfeiffer was interrogated on 21 March 1948. He contacted *Kapitän sur Zee* Otto Schulz of CIS Wilhelmshaven to request an interrogator from Dulag Nord, but Lange told him on orders of Navy Group West the interrogation had to take place that night.

Oberst Werner von Tippelskirch while being investigated for war crimes.

Lange asked if they had special methods to extort confessions such as pills or drugs. Pfeiffer refused to use the term confession, as these were soldiers in uniform and had nothing to confess. They had no drugs and would not use them anyway. They were under strict orders from CIS and Admiral Canaris not to use coercion. According to Pfeiffer, Viehweger had given the orders to Lange that the confession had to be ready by 0600 latest next morning after which the prisoners were to be shot on the Führer's orders. Pfeiffer refused to cooperate and protested about the proposed action, with which Lange agreed.

On the 9th orders were received to delay execution until a specialist interrogator could question the prisoners. *Vizeadmiral* Meisel ordered the specialist be sent from Dulag Nord at Wilhelmshaven. This was *Sonderführer* Heinz Corssen, a tobacconist who had spent time in England. The interrogation was to take place at CIS Bordeaux on 11 December.

Meanwhile Harstick continued to make progress. Wallace crafted a plausible story to explain the equipment found and deflect attention from his comrades; Ewart said nothing. Wallace told Harstick theirs was the only canoe as the second was damaged and could not be launched. Their mission was to attack any ship found in the Gironde with the two Limpets they carried. Wallace revealed some details of their training and that they had embarked on submarine *P49* in Portsmouth two weeks before being launched. Harstick commented in his report that the recovered map showed the British were well informed on German defences. The report was clear that the prisoners were in Royal Marines uniform.

On the morning of 9 December, von Tippelskirch's superior at WFSt, *General* Walter Warlimont, Deputy Chief of Operations, telephoned Meisel to confirm the prisoners were to be shot having first been interrogated 'with no methods barred'. As a result Marschall signaled Bachmann:

'With no methods barred, also using the subterfuge of sparing their lives and the assurance of good treatment, try to obtain before execution the following information...'

The specific information required was – who else was involved, their orders, where they disembarked and from what craft.

Viewweger believed, '...before they are shot...', was not an order, but meant, 'before the execution that has been ordered'. Marschall had not given up hope that the order may be rescinded and tasked Lange to see if the SD would make representations to WFSt to postpone the execution, but they had already been refused.

When Lucan was interrogated on 8 April 1948, he could not recall where the phrase, '...also using the subterfuge of sparing their lives...', came from. He thought it may have been included so the prisoners would not be subjected to physical violence.

The interrogator Corssen was recalled when he was at

Oldenburg station and told to report to Navy Group West in Paris instead of going directly to Bordeaux. This was probably due to the decision to hand over interrogation to the SD.

During the course of 9 December the prisoners were transferred to the Fort at Royan. That afternoon, Gebauer saw a signal from Navy Group West saying Corssen would arrive at CIS Bordeaux on 11 December and the execution was to be postponed until then; Bachmann was informed. That evening a signal from Navy Group West stated the prisoners were to be handed over to the SD in accordance with the Commando Order by 1100 on 10 December.

At 0400 on 10 December, Wallace and Ewart were taken to Bordeaux and handed over to the SD. What happened next is not known, but it is clear they did not reveal any significant information about the raid. Not until the Limpets exploded did the Germans realise there were other parties involved. Wallace and Ewart remained loyal to their comrades and the mission to the end.

At 1015, Dr Schmidt, Adjutant to *Sturmbannführer* Dr Knochen at SD HQ in Paris, rang Bachmann's Flag Lieutenant, *Leutnant* Lell, to request another delay to the execution as interrogation had not been concluded. Although the prisoners had been handed over to the SD for interrogation, it was understood that the execution would be carried out by the Navy. The SD was told they needed to obtain the postponement themselves.

At 1820, SD Bordeaux requested the Security Service authorities at WFSt to postpone the shooting for three days. No-one there was willing to incur Hitler's wrath and the postponement was denied. Meisel was scathing, saying they were hiding behind each other. SD Bordeaux called *Korvettenkapitän* Ernst Kühnemann, Naval Officer in Charge Bordeaux, but he was unable to help. Kühnemann had received orders about the shooting either from Bachmann or directly from WFSt. He told his Adjutant, *Leutnant* Theodor Prahm, he would be uncontactable that evening, probably to avoid any responsibility for the impending execution.

Prahm was interrogated on 29 April 1948. Around 1930, *Chief Petty Officer* Otto Rechstadt of HQ Company telephoned from *Admiral Luetjens* Barracks to say the SD had requested an execution detail. Prahm was aware of Bachmann's order and did

165

Place de Tourny, Bordeaux.

not believe anything was abnormal. At 2200, Prahm received a call from Dr Luther, a former prosecution lawyer from Frankfurt, who commanded SD Bordeaux. He demanded to speak to Kühnemann. When Prahm was unsuccessful in contacting him, Luther asked Prahm to meet him urgently. Prahm said he could as easily come to see him, but Luther said he was in town with a convoy and could not leave it. Luther sent a car to pick him up.

They met at Place de Tourny where a small convoy was drawn up. Luther demanded Prahm witness the execution, which he refused. Luther produced a written execution order to be carried out by the Navy and giving him authority over all armed forces. Because of the order Luther refused to carry out the execution with his own men, but acknowledged he was in charge and bore the responsibility. The firing party was sitting in a truck and the two prisoners were in a large car guarded by SD men. Prahm eventually agreed and travelled with Luther in another car. Luther was under pressure to carry out the execution before midnight.

The convoy went to the U-boat base to pick up the naval surgeon. Luther told Prahm a priest had been with the prisoners all afternoon and the death sentence had been read to them. Prahm recalls the convoy drove 5-10 kms northeast (he probably meant northwest) into a wood at the edge of which, were two coffins. These were loaded into the truck and taken to a sandpit where the SD men dug in two posts and the prisoners were tied to them. The two cars were positioned so their lights illuminated the scene. Prahm lined up the sixteen ratings in two ranks, the front kneeling and at 0030 on 11 December gave the order to fire. The firing party was marched off while the SD fired a few rounds into the necks of the two prisoners and the surgeon declared them dead. The SD loaded the bodies into the coffins and put them on the truck. Prahm and the sailors felt that travelling with the bodies was irreverent and walked to the edge of the wood instead. The coffins were removed to a nearby building and the party drove back to Bordeaux. Next morning Prahm reported his actions to Kühnermann who said he had acted correctly.

At 0945 Kühnemann reported by signal to Navy Group West that the shooting had been carried out at 0030. Gebauer could not recall seeing the Top Secret Officer Only signal from Navy Group West on 9 December, but was clear that the execution order did not come down the naval chain of command as he would have been informed.

The execution site is usually given as Chateau du Dehez at Blanquefort, the German Naval HQ for Bordeaux. However, this does not match Prahm's description, the only known witness. The association of Chateau du Dehez with the executions is at

Château Magnol at Blanquefort, headquarters of the wine company Barton & Guestier. Formerly Chateau du Dehez, the German Naval HQ for Bordeaux. A plaque on the bullet marked wall of a bunker commemorates where Wallace and Ewart were allegedly executed, but there is little evidence to support this. A ceremony is held annually around the anniversary – 11 December. It is sadly ironic that the plaque contains the first lines of Rupert Brooke's poem, 'The Soldier':

> **"If I should die, think only this of me:**
> **That there's some corner of a foreign field**
> **That is for ever England…"**

Wallace and Ewart were Irish and Scottish respectively. In December 1999, Bill Sparks and wife Renie accompanied George Ewart, brother of Robert, to the ceremony. The Château is private and permission needs to be obtained to visit.

best tenuous and there is no hard evidence to support the claim. The bodies were allegedly buried in the POW cemetery in Bordeaux, but no such cemetery existed. They may have been buried in unmarked graves in the German military cemetery, but it is more likely they lie in a wood somewhere to the northwest of Bordeaux.

The shooting was murder. Marschall claimed after the war he was not involved in issuing orders for naval personnel to provide the firing party. He believed WFSt issued orders to the SD for the Navy to carry it out. The British interrogators concluded Marschall was a follower of orders – he picked up survivors in 1939-40 due to *Admiral* Raeder's order to act chivalrously, but willingly followed the Commando Order and allowed prisoners of war to be murdered.

Senior German officers, despite their conscience in some cases, took the easy way out and let the Commando Order take over. Bachmann exceeded his authority in executing the two Marines, as the Commando Order was clear this was a matter for the SD. The war crimes investigators concluded he was a weak character, unable to take decisions unless the answer was in the book. His war diary entries gave the impression he was trying to be noticed in high places.

However, *Korvettenkapitän* Peter Popp had a conflicting view. He was an anti-Nazi freemason forced to rejoin the *Kriegsmarine* in April 1936 or lose his business and had no reason to support Bachmann. His opinion, when questioned on 26 September 1945, was that Bachmann was too much of a proper officer and gentleman to order the execution of Wallace and Ewart and believed it came from above.

Warlimont and von Tippelskirch were instrumental in ensuring the order was carried out. Marschall and members of his staff accepted the order and passed it on to Bachmann to be carried out. Their actions completely disregarded the Geneva Convention. The shooting was the subject of considerable indignation amongst German officers. It had been a legitimate military operation carried out with great bravery.

Sheard and Moffatt
Having been abandoned close to Le Verdon pier, Sheard and Moffatt would have succumbed to hypothermia shortly afterwards. It is highly unlikely they drowned because they

Le Bois-Plage en Re, Ile de Re – Moffatt's body is buried somewhere in these sand dunes.

were wearing lifejackets. At 1600 on 14 December, six days after she had been scuttled, *Conger* drifted ashore south of the Ile de Re, but there was no trace of her crew. An alert was ordered on the Ile de Re and around La Rochelle for British saboteurs.

A routine report on 18 December summarising recent events by OB West, mentions that two 'Englishmen' were washed ashore at Ile de Re and Sables d'Olonne. Another report confirms a body was washed up on 17 December by strong point 'Fanny' near le Bois-Plage en Re. The official German *Totenliste* (casualty list) says the body was buried on the 'ridge of dunes'. It was identified as Moffatt by his ID disks and the fact they spelled his name correctly when others generally omit the last T, proves this. The body would have been in the sea for nine days and decomposition would have

Sables d'Olonne is now a very busy holiday resort.

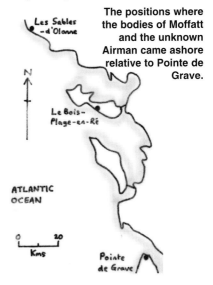

The positions where the bodies of Moffatt and the unknown Airman came ashore relative to Pointe de Grave.

169

advanced quickly as soon as it was out of the water. There is little surprise the Germans buried it quickly, close to where it was found.

It was not unusual for the bodies of Allied servicemen to be washed ashore on the Ile de Re. They were normally from downed aircraft involved in raids on the Atlantic ports. If local civilians spotted them before the Germans, they would try to secrete them for a decent burial.

Locals with knowledge of currents say that objects going into the sea off Pointe de Grave usually wash up at Ile de Re or Sables d'Olonne. It is not known how the Germans identified the body washed up at Sable d'Olonne as British without some form of identity. Either no ID was found or the Germans were content with notification by the French and never saw the body.

The Commonwealth War Graves Commission record the dates of death for both men incorrectly. Illogically Moffatt's is given as 17 December and Sheard's as 7 December. It is known from Haslar's post-operation report they were both alive in the

early hours of 8 December when they were abandoned. There are no German reports of them being seen or captured. Indeed they disappear until 17 December, which is the date given for the death of Moffatt, i.e. the date his decomposing body was washed ashore. It is inconceivable he could have survived in the North Atlantic in mid-winter for nine days to die as he came ashore on 17 December. It is almost certain the two died a few hours or even minutes after being left by Haslar around 0300 on 8 December 1942.

The grave of neither has ever been

The grave of the unknown Airman in Les Sables-d'Olonne (La Foire-Aux Chats) New Communal Cemetery, that may be that of Corporal Sheard. The cemetery is on the northeast side of the town on Rue du Docteur Laennec, about 500m north of the D36 road running east to Château d'Olonne. The grave is 30m northeast of the large Cross in the centre of the cemetery.

identified. However, in Les Sables d'Olonne cemetery there is a War Grave of an unknown Airman whose date of death is given as 17 December 1942. Given the information about currents in the area and Moffatt washing up the same day not far up the coast, this seems to be an incredible coincidence. The identification as an Airman was made by a Graves Concentration Unit in 1947, five years after the death. The 'Frankton' raiders wore some items of clothing similar to aircrew, for example thick pullovers and lifejackets. There is at least strong circumstantial evidence that the unknown body at Sables d'Olonne is that of Corporal Sheard.

McKinnon and Conway

It is not known why MacKinnon and Conway became detached from the other canoes at Le Verdon. About 2200 on 8 December, Jean Raymond was net fishing illegally with his father in a small boat just north of Blaye. A noise was heard approaching and low voices that were not French. The two dropped down in the boat thinking it was a

Corporal Sheard's family suffered another loss when his wife, Mabel aged 26, died in an air raid on Plymouth in mid-1943.

German patrol. A single canoe passed 20m away without seeing them. Given the position this could only be *Cuttlefish* as it is known where the other two canoes were at the time.

What happened to them subsequently comes from the German interrogation report for Conway conducted by Dulag Nord Wilhelmshaven and from Frenchmen who helped them. MacKinnon refused to cooperate with the interrogators.

They spent 10 December on the east side of Ile de Cazeau only a few miles from the others. At 2100 they hit a submerged object opposite Bec d'Ambres, the point of land where the Garonne and Dordogne join. The canoe was sunk and Conway only got out with some difficulty. They swam back to the island having just managed to recover their escape bags. Next day they

171

managed to contact some French fishermen who deposited them on the mainland. Conway said they found help in Margeaux and the SD was directed to investigate. The Germans believed Conway was obscuring the real village, but decided not to press him on this to ensure he carried on talking. He said they walked for three days, sleeping in the open the first night and in a barn on the second.

The German interrogators concluded they had travelled by train or car as the light canvas shoes worn by Conway showed little sign of wear. Given the distance they covered in three days it does seem likely they were transported for at least some of it. It is also likely they travelled separately for some of the time. Late on 13 December, MacKinnon was sitting on a pile of rubble at the side of the road near Saint-Medard-d'Eyrans. He spoke to

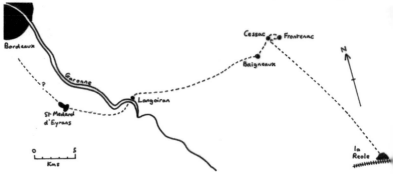

MacKinnon's and Conway's attempted escape route. It is not known how they reached St Medard d'Eyrans, but it is likely they had help and were transported some of the way.

Anne-Marie Bernadet, a young girl herding cows, who took him to the farm, where he was fed and the blisters and wounds on his legs treated. He was allowed to sleep in the barn. MacKinnon asked about crossing the Gironde at Langoiran and showed them his escape map. He said he had a contact on the other side of the river, which indicates he had been in touch with others previously to gain this information.

It isn't clear why MacKinnon chose this route as their instructions were to head for Ruffec. It may be because they were taken to the west bank of the Gironde by the fishermen instead of the east.

Conway was seen wandering through the village early the next day and his naval blue pullover linked him with

172

MacKinnon; the two were reunited. They then headed for Langoiran and that evening they were in Baigneaux. As the river crossing at Langoiran would have been guarded it is possible they got over by boat.

French sources tell us Edouard Pariente, a quarry labourer, was on his way home in the gathering darkness when he came across Conway. They met close to the church and school. Pariente had the impression Conway had just got off the bus and he appeared neatly dressed but anxious. It was clear Conway was an escaped British serviceman. Pariente was married with two children and lived in a very small abode. He had nothing to give Conway, but took him to a neighbour who spoke English. Unfortunately Monsieur Guilhon, a lawyer, was not at home and his pregnant wife, who already had three children, was not inclined to risk having the fugitive in her house and declined to help.

Pariente took Conway to Robert Pouget

Edouard Pariente was of Spanish origin and came to live in Baigneaux in 1926.

Baigneaux centre below the school with the Frankton Trail plaque on the wall of the house to the right.

The disused railway line near Cessac.

The tenanted property at Seguin where the Jauberts lived. In the foreground is the plinth for the missing (October 2011) Frankton Trail plaque at the side of the disused railway.

who lived in a three-bedroom house, Chez Loulou. Pouget was just back from two years in a German jail, possibly for black marketeering, but agreed to take Conway in. Pariente never saw MacKinnon, but Pouget did later, so Conway must have gone to recover him. Pouget noted that MacKinnon was dragging a leg. They stayed with Pouget overnight.

Late on the 15th another volunteer, Monsieur Cheyreau, took them to other people who would help. He led them along a disused railway line to a tenanted property at Seguin near Cessac. Shepherd Louis Jaubert who lived near the railway line, looked outside to see his neighbour, Cheyreau, walking along the track with two strangers carrying sacks. Cheyreau told him they were English coming from Bordeaux. Jaubert invited them all in to share a bottle of wine and was anxious to help. His son, evacuated from Dunkirk, had been well treated in Britain, but on his return to France the Germans had imprisoned him. Jaubert first satisfied himself they were not German agents. Once content he agreed to take them in for dinner, bed and breakfast if Cheyreau provided lunch.

Madame Louise Jaubert dressed a boil on MacKinnon's knee. He was finding it difficult walking. Jaubert noted MacKinnon was dressed in a blue serge suit. That night when she washed their clothes, Madame Jaubert checked the labels were British.

MacKinnon, despite his painful leg, wanted to keep moving,

Louis and Louise Jaubert.

partly to avoid risk to his hosts. Jaubert, Cheyreau and the two Marines went to Frontenac to see if anyone in the cafes could get them into the escape organization. In spite of taking this terrible risk, they found no-one to help. MacKinnon told Jaubert they were heading for Bilbao in northern Spain and asked him to find out the fare from Toulouse as they only had 1000 francs. Jaubert confirmed it was sufficient.

To get to Toulouse they had to get a train from La Reole, twenty-five miles southeast. After three days they took their leave of the Jauberts who were tearful to see such nice boys leave. Both promised to write and visit one day; a promise they would be unable to keep. A guide offered to take them over the Demarcation Line and may have been paid as MacKinnon was 400F short of the original 1,000F when arrested. Jaubert believed they spent the next night near Sauveterre and crossed the Line there.

The circumstances of their arrest are not entirely clear. One version says the wife of Captain Olivier, gendarme commander in La Reole, saw two suspicious men through the window of the office and warned her husband, who sent gendarmes to check their identity. Police reports by Adjutant-Chef Jean Bernard Barbance and Gendarme Pierre Hennequin state they arrested the British at 1000 on 18 December as they had no papers. Another version is they were arrested as they waited for a train near La Reole.

A deposition by Gendarme Hennequin dated 3 November 1945 says the British said they had parachuted from a crashed aircraft and Olivier arrested them. Hennequin mistranslated the interrogation results to save the situation for the two and Olivier threatened to punish Hennequin when told by another gendarme. Despite this, Hennequin believed that Olivier did not betray the British.

Hennequin spoke English and questioned the two separately. MacKinnon said they had landed at Dieppe in the raid in September (actually 19 August) with the mission of destroying some factories. They had been cut off and, having dumped their explosives and uniforms, split into small parties. He and Conway had made their way from farm to farm intending to get to Spain. When MacKinnon was searched they found his Army pattern knife, a small saw, compass, watch, Michelin map and 600F. His rucksack contained a pair of shoes, a sweater, stockings and a few rations. He was wearing black trousers, grey overcoat, blue naval sweater, beret and shoes with yellow socks. He had no passport or authorisation to be in France.

Conway was dressed similarly in grey trousers and sandals. He was carrying similar items to MacKinnon and in addition had 1,700F, a torch, some meat, bread and a pot of jam. When questioned by Barbance he also gave the Dieppe story. They were arrested for being in contravention of Article 2 of the Decree dated 2 May 1938, to appear before the public prosecutor at La Reole, to whom the records of the arrest were sent, as well as the Regional Prefect at Toulouse and the Prefect of Lot and Garonne Department. Barbance and Hennequin wanted to help the Marines. Captain Olivier telephoned the Colonel at Montauban who told him to 'fix it for the Englishmen'. Hennequin believed this meant hushing up the affair.

MacKinnon's knee was in need of medical attention and he was admitted to the local hospital late that night or early on the 19th. About 24 December, Marcel Galibert, a local lawyer, was instructed to defend the two. He visited Conway in the police cells and MacKinnon in the hospital, telling them he believed it was possible they had been placed in close arrest to avoid handing them over to the Germans; they should ultimately be freed and he was prepared to take them to the Spanish border. Local people were very kind to MacKinnon, providing reading material, cigarettes and fruit and Galibert provided Conway with the same. About 26 December, Marcel Galibert and Louis Jaubert wrote to the parents of the Marines through the Red Cross and these reports eventually got through to Britain.

The front of the Old Hospital in La Reole. The new hospital is out of shot to the right.

The rear of the Old Hospital with the Frankton Trail plaque on the wall extreme left. The prison is down the hill to the left.

The disused prison in La Reole where it is believed Conway was held. The Old Hospital where MacKinnon was treated is 150m up the hill to the left.

On 29 December, two German NCOs from SD Bordeaux arrived at the police station to question the two Britons. It was suspected, that Olivier had informed them, but just about the whole town knew about it and anyone could have passed on the information. Olivier's sons at college gave the matter a lot of publicity. Too many people had seen the two and had access to them, particularly MacKinnon in hospital. It is likely the Germans got to know of their presence by loose talk.

Gendarme Marcel Drouillard was on desk duty and refused to allow the Germans access. He consulted Adjutant Espace, who told the Germans the British were detained for unlawful presence in France. If they wanted to see the Marines, they would have to apply to the judge, who refused their demands politely. They left in a temper vowing to be back that evening. Their superiors contacted the Vichy Ministry of the Interior, who in turn contacted the judge at 2245 and gave the order to hand over the Marines.

At 2300, about fifty Germans led by a *Leutnant* surrounded

the prison and hospital and took the two Marines. In accordance with the Geneva Convention, MacKinnon and Conway supplied their basic military details. It was noted that MacKinnon wore a Spanish 20 centavos coin dated 1937 on a chain together with his ID disks. The SD concluded it was used as a recognition sign. Details gleaned from Conway gave the Germans the bare outline of the raid and the names of the participants, but almost nothing else they did not already know.

Laver and Mills

Having separated from Haslar and Sparks after the raid, Laver and Mills landed near some fishing cabins perched over the river. They scuttled *Catfish* and made their way inland towards Ruffac as instructed. They crossed the D255 and found shelter in a small toolshed as daylight was approaching.

Soon after a young man, Olivier Bernard, out hunting rabbits with a catapult, found them. The Marines indicated they meant no harm and asked for food. Bernard went back to the village of Fours and told Pierre Gacis. He went home and without his wife Solange knowing, took a rabbit pie to the two fugitives. Pierre did not mention this to his family in order to protect them. Solange was furious when she discovered the pie had gone; it was meant to feed the whole family. She accused the children and scolded them accordingly. It wasn't until 2002 she was able to tell them the truth and apologise.

That night, very well fed, the two set off again passing through a wooded area between Reignac and St Savin. Having rested through the next day they continued, keeping the N10 to their left. They came to a deserted farm named Chez Ouvrard, near Clerac. Inside they devoured some stale food and wine and rested before setting off to find somewhere else to lie up for the day. Unknown to them they were seen by two farm workers.

Raymond Furet's parents owned the farm. He worked it although he was only 14, because he refused to stay at school. He went to the farm every morning at 0800 and that morning realised someone had been there. Laver had left a note in English thanking him for the food. Raymond's father burned it as soon as he was shown it.

About 1700 on 14 December, Gendarme Warrant Officer Georges Rieupeyrout, commanding the Montlieu la Garde brigade, was approached by Monsieur Gagnerot, a resident of

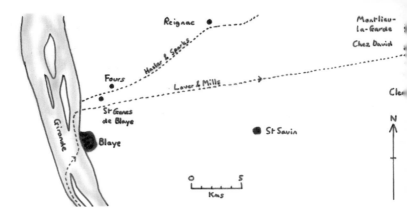

Laver's and Mills' attempted escape route. Their precise route to Chez Ouvrard is not known.

Chez David and a well-connected collaborator. He had met two British parachutists on the road near his home and directed them to an abandoned house for shelter. Gagnerot said they should be arrested immediately. Rieupeyrout placated Gagnerot that he would do what was necessary when his men returned from other jobs.

As soon as Gagnerot left, Rieupeyrout got hold of Monsieur Gaujean and asked him to cycle to the house and warn the soldiers to leave. Gaujean didn't find them as they had hidden under a heap of hay in a barn and fallen asleep. When Rieupeyrout went to Chez David it was clear Gagnerot was watching the gendarmes. He asked Gagnerot where the men were and was shown the house. Laver and Mills did not resist. On the way to the police station Rieupeyrout suggested they ditch any papers they had. At Montlieu they were fed and allowed to wash. While being searched Laver's escape map was discovered. Rieupeyrout thought it would be compromising if the Germans turned up and took it away, keeping it in his family thereafter. After the liberation it is understood that Gagnerot was taken to the Maquis command post at Reignac and shot.

Chez Ouvrard.

Rieupeyrout was in an impossible position. Because Gagnerot knew of the Marines, he had to inform higher authority. At 2230 he telephoned Captain Borie at Jonzac, who in turn informed the German Field Security Police. Borie accompanied the Germans to Montlieu at midnight and later boasted that he personally disarmed the two 'English' soldiers. In accordance with Vichy orders they were handed over to the German Field Security Police who took them to the police prison in Bordeaux. They were still in uniform.

In Bordeaux they were handed over to the SD. In his deposition to war crimes investigators on 23 April 1948, *Leutnant* Franz Drey, head of the port guard post of Bordeaux, says he was requested to translate and took *Leutnant* Gautier, also an English speaker, with him to the Army prison. He saw two prisoners and confirmed they were in a combination uniform with rank badges. They were questioned initially by *Leutnant* Harstick. Drey believed they were also interrogated by *Korvettenkapitän* Dr Krantz and Leutnant Corssen a few days later. Drey refused to question the prisoners until the SD released their bound hands. He learned from the Sergeant (Corporal Laver) that they were from a special unit trained in the Scottish fjords, but he refused to give the location so it could not be bombed by the *Luftwaffe*; Drey acknowledged he would have done the same. The two were concerned whether or not they would be treated as soldiers or saboteurs. Drey said he regarded them as soldiers as they were in uniform. Thereafter they were kept in separate cells awaiting further questioning.

Subsequent Treatment of MacKinnon, Conway, Laver and Mills

Heinz Corssen was questioned on 19 February 1948. He told how he had arrived in Paris on 26 December to meet

Korvettenkapitän Dr Krantz, who had returned from Christmas leave. They were informed by Lange that four prisoners were to be interrogated at Bordeaux; two others had already been killed. Corssen saw the interrogation reports and concluded they had been conducted ineptly. Krantz wanted the four transferred to Dulag Nord, but Lange refused, so Krantz asked to see the Commando Order. They were taken to see *Vizeadmiral* Meisel, who said the order had been destroyed according to orders. Meisel asked Krantz to find out from the prisoners about their tactical employment, training, strength and if other operations were planned. Krantz and Corssen then drove to OB West to see the Commando Order, but it had apparently been destroyed there too. They drove to SD HQ in Paris where *Sturmbannführer* Dr Knochen also told them the Order had been destroyed.

The next night Krantz and Corssen travelled to Bordeaux where the prisoners were held by the SD in the municipal police prison. Krantz and Corssen were briefed on events by the harbour control unit commander (either Drey or Kühnemann), various people in CIS Bordeaux and the local SD. Some reports claim the interrogation would have been severe, but as it was mainly conducted by CIS officers, this seems unlikely as they were bound by Admiral Canaris' orders not to use coercion.

Sturmbannführer Dr Knochen.

The Germans were determined to learn what had happened. On 17 December, they believed eight or nine men were still on the run. There was some disquiet that despite having captured two men on the 8th, some of the other raiders had reached Bordeaux unobserved.

Eventually the Germans got all they needed to know. By 3 January 1943 the interrogators had produced two detailed reports on their findings. They had a fairly accurate picture of the team, their intentions, equipment and training. They were aware in outline of the escape route, but apart from getting descriptions of those unaccounted for, the prisoners did not reveal their home base or anything else that would help the Germans. By then the Germans had accounted for all ten raiders except Haslar, Sparks and Sheard. Detailed descriptions were circulated and an alert issued that they intended crossing the Demarcation Line.

The fact that the Germans managed to learn so much should not be regarded as a weakness on the part of the captured Marines. They obscured and delayed giving information for as long as possible and we can only imagine what pressures they were subjected to; everyone talks eventually. Certainly they gave away the names of the other raiders, including Colley the reserve, and No.2 Section in Britain, plus details of their training and previous service, but well after this information could have compromised the mission. They did not give away the names or locations of any of the brave French people who helped them.

On 1 January, Kühnemann, or one of his officers, was accused of passing secret information to the British or Resistance, as the captured maps showed so much detail. He was adamant that such material was properly secured. Although ordered to secretly watch over his officers, he heard nothing more about it.

The Dulag Nord team returned to Paris on 6 or 7 January. Krantz verbally briefed *Vizeadmiral* Meisel, *Korvettenkapitän* Lange and Dr Pfeiffer of Counter Intelligence HQ in Paris. Pfeiffer wanted more personal particulars, but Krantz had other urgent work and left for Wilhelmshaven next day. Corssen went back to Bordeaux, but learned nothing new and returned to Paris on 10 or 11 January. He left the same evening having briefed Pfeiffer.

Corssen was certain that the prisoners were not transferred to Dulag Nord. It is often claimed they were transferred to Paris for more interrogation by the SD, but this does not make sense. It is usually quoted that McKinnon, Conway, Laver and Mills were shot in Paris about 23 March and their bodies buried in Bagneux Cemetery. However, the Germans faked burial cards giving the dates of death of all as 12 December caused by drowning in Bordeaux harbour, except Wallace and Ewart whose date was given as 8 December. It is known from other German records that four of the prisoners were certainly alive in early January, which discredits 12 December as the date of their deaths.

Pfeiffer prepared a detailed report on the raid critical of the Commando Order. When it arrived in the Counter Intelligence HQ of *Oberkommando der Wehrmacht* (High Command of the Armed Forces) in Berlin, *Oberst* von Bentivegni telephoned to say it could not be presented or Pfeiffer would be tried for undermining *Wehrmacht* morale. Pfeiffer refused to change the report, but believed it was edited in Berlin. He was critical at CIS meetings of the actions taken against the Marines in relation to International Law and military honour.

A German report by *Major* Reichal, dated 12 January 1944, catalogued the actions taken against Allied servicemen captured in various raids. The section on 'Frankton' states that the special uniforms worn by the raiders bore no badges to identify them, which was untrue; even German witnesses admit they were clearly identifiable. The report stated no punishable offences had been committed by the men, but they were shot on 23 March 1943. This was clearly inaccurate, as it is known Wallace and Ewart were shot the previous December. Once the interrogations of the other four were completed in early January, why keep them alive any longer and risk the wrath of the high command for not complying with the Commando Order? It is much more likely that McKinnon, Conway, Laver and Mills were shot soon after the completion of the interrogations in January in or around Bordeaux and were buried nearby in unmarked graves.

As soon as the war in Europe ended in 1945, investigations commenced into war crimes, including the missing Marines from 'Frankton'. War crimes investigations were mainly carried out by Major EA Barkworth of the SAS War Crimes Investigation Team. The team interviewed a large number of the Germans and French involved.

By October 1945 prosecutors in the Judge Advocate General's Office concluded they had a strong case against Bachmann, as he had exceeded his authority in ordering the execution of Wallace and Ewart. On 5 September 1945 the Admiralty ordered the military authorities in Germany to keep him under surveillance.

Bachmann retired from the Navy in February 1943 and on 1 August became *Landrat* (head of local administration) of Kreis Warburg in Westphalia. It was known the family left Wilhelmshaven on 22 April 1944. In March 1945 he had been ordered to command a *Volksturm* artillery formation. It was surrounded on 1 April and he was last seen on 3 April in a car with a corporal and a driver heading north on the Willibadessen – Dringerberg – Altenheeren road, away from the advancing Allies. A shell hit the car and two men got out, but it was not known if Bachmann survived or not.

On 7 November 1945, Captain GM Heard saw Bachmann's wife, Gertrud, at their farm, where she lived with her three daughters, single sister and a son-in-law. She had not seen the *Admiral* since March and feared he was dead. A local informant confirmed Bachmann had not been seen and no mail had been sent to his wife. The investigators turned their attention to his subordinates to see if they could be implicated. Another check made for Bachmann in 1948 also drew a blank and a death certificate was obtained dated 13 March 1948, stating he died on 2 (sic) April 1945 at Willibadessen.

While searches were being made for Bachmann in Germany, another investigator went to France to interview people who had seen the escapers. On 2 November 1945, Captain RA Nightingale of the Intelligence Corps obtained statements from Louis Jaubert, who helped MacKinnon and Conway, Marcel Drouillard of the La Reole Gendarmerie concerning how they passed into German hands and Marcel Galibert, who was their defence lawyer.

On 5 November, Nightingale contacted Gendarme Gibaud, a member of the resistance deported to Germany. He was secretary to Captain Borie who had taken the German Field Security Police to arrest Laver and Mills. Gibaud made a report against Borie on his return from Germany, accusing him of collaboration. Borie was known to have transferred to a motorized platoon at Courbevoie and was later in Rheims.

The same day Nightingale took a statement from Georges Rieupeyrout, the Gendarme Warrant Officer forced to arrest Laver and Mills by the collaborator Gagnerot. He confirmed the details already known, but added that Laver and Mills told him they had been dropped by parachute four days previously to find a group of comrades at Chez David. Next day Rieupeyrout discovered there was an officer and three men with wireless and explosives in the woods, where they stayed for four or five days. Who they were remains a mystery.

A report by No.2 War Crimes Investigation Team on 27 December 1945 states that four unknown graves in Bagneux Cemetery, Paris (111th Division, 1st Line, Grave 50), were exhumed, but the remains had been cremated and could not be identified. However, it makes no sense to take the bodies of the Marines allegedly recovered on 12 December 1942 from Bordeaux harbour all the way to Paris for burial over three months later. In a letter to Mrs Helen MacKinnon in October 1947 the Admiralty concluded that the German records quoting burial at Bagneux were false. The most likely resting place for MacKinnon, Conway, Laver, Mills, Wallace and Ewart is an unmarked grave in a wood somewhere outside Bordeaux.

By March 1946 it was concluded there was no case against a number of the Germans involved, including *Korvettenkapitän* Kühnemann. In June 1948, after considerable deliberation, it was also concluded that although a case could be made against *Admiral* Marschall, it would not stand up in court.

More information came to light from the war diaries of *Admirals* Bachmann and Marschall in the war crimes trial of *Oberst* Werner von Tippelskirch in Hamburg August-October 1948. The Court President was Colonel EA Howard and the Judge Advocate was Mr CL Stirling. Von Tippelskirch was accused of being involved in the killings, but the evidence was insufficient. Many witnesses were cagey about giving evidence as they might also have found themselves in the dock. Bachmann was dismissed as a bloodthirsty ruffian by Stirling. Prahm, who commanded the execution party for Wallace and Ewart, could quote no documentary order except a verbal late night request by the SD. Stirling told him, 'You brought the German Navy into complete and everlasting disrepute by this monstrous thing'. Despite Sparks testifying that von Tippelskirch had lied about the uniform worn by the raiders, he was acquitted.

No-one living was ever brought to account for the 'Frankton' murders.

Chapter Thirteen

EVENTS IN BRITAIN

IN LONDON THERE WAS CONCERN following a German radio announcement on 11 December about the destruction of a sabotage squad, but hope remained that some canoes had got through. When the news was received in Southsea, Captain Stewart gave orders that it was not to be discussed. Heather Powell and her mother saw it in the papers and, although Heather had nothing to link it to Haslar's Party except her intuition, she fell ill.

HMS *Tuna* adopted a normal patrol profile and arrived at Plymouth on 13 December. She became the first submarine to be fitted with the 267W radar, able to show coastlines like a chart. While it was being fitted, Raikes took leave with his wife at the Moorlands Hotel, Yelverton.

Colley had been entrusted with six letters to post. After two weeks aboard *Tuna* he was dirty, smelly and grease covered. At the gate of Stonehouse Barracks he was viewed with suspicion until called to the Adjutant's office where he delivered a letter from Haslar requesting his men be accommodated, fed and given new uniforms. All three were well looked after until being picked up in a lorry by Marine Phelps and returned to Southsea next day along with the damaged *Cachalot*.

Fisher, Colley and Ellery returned on 14 December. Initially they were kept separate from No.2 Section and forbidden to talk about what they knew. A few weeks later they rejoined training with the rest. They didn't stay at 'White Heather' at first and when they were eventually allowed back, all the spirit and fun had gone. Mrs Powell wasn't keen to have them back and some time later they went to live elsewhere. *Cachalot* was put in one of the RMBPD Nissen huts until being returned to Saros for repair. She remained there until the 1980s and can be seen in the Combined Military Services Museum, Chelmsford, Essex.

On 15 December, Captain Stewart and one rank who returned from 'Frankton' went to HQ Combined Operations to see Lt Cdr L'Estrange. It seems likely this was Ellery as the most senior of the three.

Sufficient information trickled through by 16 December for

Mountbatten to report the apparent success of the raid to the COS and Churchill, who added his appreciation for an extremely gallant and enterprising operation. Mountbatten's report put the German broadcast down to the capture of only one section and the likelihood that this had not compromised the others. When Mountbatten was told a month later that no survivors had emerged, he glowered at Neville and said, "I was persuaded against my better judgement to let Major Haslar go on the raid and now we have lost him."

On 25 January 1943, Captain Stewart initiated the necessary action to list all 10 men 'Missing'. The families received telegrams, experienced all the distress they entailed. Haslar's mother had received one before when her husband was lost in 1917.

'Blondie' Haslar's father, Lieutenant (Quartermaster) Arthur Thomas Haslar MC RAMC who was lost when the troopship *Transylvania* was torpedoed in the Bay of Genoa on 3 May 1917.

Late in January, Mrs Powell received a letter from Mrs Ewart in Glasgow telling her she had received the 'Missing' telegram. Mrs Ewart visited the Powells later. Heather's health worsened and the doctors sent her to St Mary's Hospital.

On 23 February 1943, Haslar's coded message sent via Marie-Claire from Switzerland, was received by HQ Combined Operations. The duty intelligence staff was unable to decipher it, but knew it was from Haslar. Ronnie Sillars was on duty and asked Wren 2nd Officer Marie Hamilton to try. Sillars assumed it was in the No.3 Code superimposed on some bogus cipher used by Haslar.

Marie Hamilton set to work and having created a pile of cigarette butts suddenly leapt to her feet, "It's coming out, it's coming out!" There was sufficient detail to know what happened in outline. Haslar and Sparks were mentioned so it was known they were in the hands of the Resistance, but there was no mention of any of the others. Haslar's message read verbatim:

COHQ. Tuna *launched five cockles seven Dec. Cachalot torn in hatch. Pad hatches. In bad tide race SW Pte de Grave Coalfish lost formation fate unknown. Conger capsized crew may have swum ashore. Cuttlefish lost formation nr Le Verdon fate unknown. Catfish Crayfish lay up in bushes Pte aux Oiseaux. Found by French but not* *betrayed. Ninth in hedges five miles north of Blaye. Tenth in field south end Cazeau. Eleventh in reeds thirty yds south of pontoons opp Bassens South. Attack eleventh. Catfish Bordeaux West three on cargo ship two on engines of sperrbrecher two on stern of cargo ship and one stern of small tanker. Crayfish Bassens South five on large cargo ship three on smaller liner. <u>Back together</u> same night. Separate and scuttle cockles one mile north of Blaye. Sparks with me. Fate of Crayfish crew unknown. Haslar.*

The only puzzling part was due to misreading 'back together' (underlined above), which came out as 'back to get her', which of course made no sense.

On 13 April, Mrs MA Conway, mother of Marine Conway wrote to the RMBPD to say she had received news from France via the Red Cross dated 29 December that her son was a prisoner. The words she received were, 'Have seen James last week, he is healthy and conveys New Years greeting to you, don't worry'. This was the message sent by Louis Jaubert. She sent a standard 25 word reply, but received no further news. It later transpired the Red Cross had also forwarded a message from Marcel Galibert of La Reole, 'Dear Mrs MacKinnon I expect that you and the whole family are rather well. Seen last week John who was healthy and well, sincerely yours'.

On 16 April, Mrs Moffatt wrote to say she had been informed that her son's body had been recovered and buried in France. The news came from a German casualty list via OC Plymouth Division. Mountbatten wrote to her expressing his sympathies on 12 May, but was unable to say what Moffatt had been engaged in, save that it was very hazardous and successful. Haslar wrote to the next of kin of all those missing.

When Sparks returned he went to see Mrs Powell at 'White Heather'. She was pleased to see him, but he looked older and was upset about something. He could say little about what they had been up to and when she asked about the rest he just said, "they will be along." He went to see Heather in hospital next day, but could give her no news of Ewart and the others. Heather was allowed home some time later and broke down again when she noticed the men's wardrobes had been cleared. She declined further and tuberculosis was diagnosed. Her father came home from sea and she told him she had dreamed they were all dead. Heather gradually lost the will to live and died a month before her 17th birthday in the middle of 1944.

Distinguished Service Order.

Mountbatten recommended Haslar for the highest possible decoration on 7 May 1943. In the same recommendation to the COS he passed on Haslar's recommendations:

Corporal Laver for his skilful boat handling, initiative and coolness in making his independent attack.

Marines Sparks and Mills for coolness, efficiency and eagerness to engage the enemy.

Lieutenant RP Raikes RN for his acceptance of serious risks to fix his position accurately and launch the canoes in a favourable position.

Lieutenant Commander GP L'Estrange for carrying out most of the detailed planning and personally preparing the charts and tide tables carried by the attacking force.

Despite Mountbatten's recommendation, Haslar was ineligible for the Victoria Cross, because his actions had not been in contact with the enemy. The *London Gazette* Supplement of 29 June 1943 confirmed the award of the DSO to Haslar and Distinguished Service Medal (DSM) to Marine Sparks. Because of the need to preserve security, the citations merely stated the awards were, 'For courage and enterprise'. Corporal Laver and Marine Mills were recommended for the DSM, which at the time could not be awarded posthumously, so instead they were Mentioned in Despatches. Sparks wasn't able to tell his comrades much about it, but they nevertheless had a good celebration in town that night. He received a congratulatory letter from Mountbatten.

Distinguished Service Medal.

Transcript of Marcel Galibert's letter to Mrs MacKinnon. Unfortunately Mrs Conway was so elated at receiving news that her son was alive, she forgot to retain Louis Jaubert's letter.

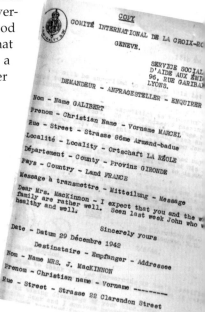

Chapter Fourteen

AFTERMATH

HASLAR RESUMED command of RMBPD and went on to develop different canoes, the MSC and underwater swimming for covert operations. He met Canadian, Sub Lieutenant Bruce Wright who was another advocate of underwater swimmers for reconnaissance and sabotage. Mountbatten saw the potential and placed development under RMBPD. It was known as the Amphibious Recce Party, later changed to the Sea Reconnaissance Section. Endurance was the key and development involved many lengthy swims.

On 19 August 1943, Haslar sat in on the Combined Operations Plans Committee's deliberations on repeating the 'Frankton' operation. Haslar advised against it for a number of reasons. His party had launched in almost flat calm and lost two canoes in the tide races. Conditions would be almost certainly worse in a repeat attempt. As the nights lengthened the Germans would increase surveillance and security measures around the harbour. Successful attacks with Limpets had resulted in the targets settling on the shallow bottom and were therefore relatively easy to refloat. A Limpet that did not explode until the ship was moving in deep water was required.

On 12 December, Haslar was promoted to Lieutenant Colonel and ordered to Ceylon to join Detachment 385/Special Operations Group. Stewart was promoted Major and took over RMBPD. With the loss of No.1 Section, the few survivors joined No.2 Section, which was renamed Earthworm Detachment for deployment to the eastern Mediterranean. No.3 Section became Detachment Celtic dealing with BPB and MSC.

On 16-18 June 1944, Lieutenant JF Richards led a raid by elements of Earthworm Detachment against enemy shipping in Portolago Bay, Leros in the Aegean Sea (Operation Sunbeam A). Three Mk 2** canoes were involved – *Shark* with Lieutenant Richards and Marine Stevens, Salmon with Sergeant King and Marine Ruff and Shrimp with Corporal Horner and Marine Fisher. The third seat in each canoe was unfilled. Richards' No.2, Marine Stevens, was urinated on by a German sentry as they attached Limpets to the bow of a destroyer. Richards was

The later three seat Cockle Mk.II** seen here with the central position unoccupied.

awarded the Distinguished Service Cross. Sergeant King and Marine Ruff's canoe was holed and sinking before they reached their hideout; they were awarded the DSM. Horner was MID. Two Italian destroyers crewed by Germans were badly damaged and later sunk by the RAF as they were being towed for repairs, together with three escort vessels.

Major William Herbert Alexander Pritchard-Gordon, who became great friends with MacKinnon as they went through officer training. He commanded No.2 Section, later Earthworm Detachment in the Mediterranean, and when 'Jock' Stewart departed, took command of RMBPD.

In 1944 RMBPD moved to the shore based HMS *Mount Stewart* at Teignmouth and Earthworm Detachment returned to join the other sections there in October. Stewart was invalided out late in 1944 or early 1945 and the unit was commanded by Major Pritchard-Gordon thereafter. In September 1947 RMBPD became part of the Amphibious School Royal Marines and moved to Portsmouth. It eventually became Special Boat Section Royal Marines, which carried on the expertise of the numerous canoe borne units disbanded after the war. Eventually the Special Boat Section became the Special Boat Squadron and later still the Special Boat Service that it is today.

In 1955 a fictionalised version of the 'Frankton' story was told in the film *The Cockleshell Heroes* made by Warwick Films and released by Columbia. It starred Anthony Newley, Trevor Howard, David Lodge and Jose Ferrer, who also directed. Haslar was chief technical director, but was embarrassed by the title and the script. He suggested 38 alternative titles, none of which was accepted. He regarded the raid as a rather insignificant incident in the war, but acknowledged the techniques developed were invaluable in later operations. Bryan Forbes' original screenplay, written with Haslar's assistance, did not find favour in Hollywood and was jazzed up with extraneous and fictitious material. Haslar even wrote a spoof ending for the film as a parody.

Despite his issues with the film, Haslar formed a life long friendship with Jose Ferrer. When it was premiered at the Empire, Leicester Square on 16 November 1955, Haslar decided he would not attend and shortly before wrote to say that he needed to be in France. His mother fully intended to attend and told him forcefully if he said he was going to be out of the country he better had be. Accordingly he slipped over to France and sat out the premiere drinking wine in a French café.

Poster for 'Cockleshell Heroes' - Haslar sat out the premiere drinking wine in a French bar.

The premiere was attended by Prince Philip, Mountbatten, Clement Attlee, Elizabeth Taylor and Douglas Fairbanks Jr. It was also the first time the 'Cockleshell Heroes' march was played publicly. Afterwards Prince Philip pointed out to Cubby Broccoli the real reason for the raid was not made clear, which resulted in a hasty and obvious 30 second insert into the final version of a German officer explaining why.

Before the film was made, Broccoli called Bill Sparks to ask if he'd be an adviser on a film about the raid. Sparks thought it was a joke and put the phone down. A letter followed explaining the venture and he agreed to help with the production. Following the premiere in London he attended the French premiere in Bordeaux and afterwards on stage Armand Dubreuille presented him with the ID disk he took off him during the escape. Sparks was critical of

Sparks' ID disk, returned to him after the French premiere of *Cockleshell Heroes*.

193

Haslar's part in promoting the film; he took the money as an adviser, but then walked away from it in Spark's view.

The Royal Navy cooperated closely in the production providing a submarine, drill instructors, numerous Royal Marines as extras and SBS canoeists. The latter were Captain RM 'Dickie' Brounger, Colour Sergeant FW Evans, Sergeants E Moorhouse, R Adamson, EN Bailey and D McKerracher, Corporals C Close, E Richens and JF Walters and Marines N Phillips, R Evans, Lonergan and Howells. They were paid 10 guineas a week on top of their normal pay, which was about £5 per week for a Corporal at the time.

Filming took place in Eastney Barracks, Shepperton Studios, London docks and the River Tagus in Portugal. It was fortunate that experienced canoeists were on hand as Trevor Howard and David Lodge were saved from drowning by Corporals Richens and Close when their canoe capsized. Not unexpectedly for fit and adventurous young men, the Royal Marines burned the candle at both ends, working up to 12 hours each day and then partying all night in Lisbon.

Bill Sparks in Baltimore on the USA promotional tour for 'Cockleshell Heroes'.

Despite input from all the advisers there were numerous inaccuracies such as using the Mk.1** Cockle which was not in service until mid-1943 and positioning Limpets by frogmen. Dick Raikes, the submarine adviser, said, "the script was a mass of ballocks and omitted many incidents, hazardous, amusing or merely commonplace because they aren't good box office".

The Portuguese authorities granted permission to make the film if a documentary promoting the country was shown with it. Trevor Howard provided the narration. When 'The Cockleshell Heroes' was premiered in the USA and Canada, Bill Sparks went with it on a six-month promotional tour.

In August 1960 four Royal Marines Probationary Second Lieutenants (Jake Hensman, Peter Cameron, Michael Hodder and Brian Mollan), set off to trace the 'Frankton' route. In two canoes they left Royan, paddled across the Gironde estuary and then along it following Haslar's route. As they were struggling ashore at Pointe aux Oiseaux they met a young girl who rushed off and returned with her father. It was Yves Ardouin, who had helped the raiders in their first lying up place. Wine was drunk and the Marines missed the next tide. They went on to trace the rest of the route, meeting many people who helped Haslar and Sparks in particular.

In 1961, Mary Lindell traced the French people who had helped the escapers and the Royal Marines invited them to London. Each was presented with a gilt Royal Marines badge. On 3 April 1966 many of those involved met again at Bordeaux when the first 'Frankton' memorial was dedicated at St Nicholas' Church. The wooden plaque was unveiled by Haslar in what was then the English church. HMS *Londonderry* ferried over a Royal Marines party. The relatives of those who died and Haslar and Sparks flew out on a plane chartered by the *Daily Express*. Relatives of Wallace (two sisters), MacKinnon (mother, brother and two sisters) and Sheard (eight members of his family) attended. A number of those who helped the escapers were also there – Mary Lindell, Marthe Rullier, Rene Flaud, Armand and Amelie Dubreuille, Jean Mariaud, Alix, Rene and Yvonne Mandinaud and Irene Pasqueraud and son Robert. The church was sold in 1990 and the plaque can now be seen in the Centre Jean Moulin in its 'Frankton' Exhibition. A list of 'Frankton' memorials appears in Appendix 4.

On 27 September 1969, Haslar and Sparks again flew courtesy

Haslar and Sparks meeting up with many of those who helped them at the dedication of the first 'Frankton' memorial at St Nicholas' Church, Bordeaux on 3 April 1966.

of the *Daily Express* to meet with the French people who helped them. Haslar carried a brass engraved plaque with his and Sparks names, plus the names of those who helped them and presented it to the Mayor of Ruffec. It is not known why Rene Mandinaud's name is missing, unless it was a genuine mistake or Mary Lindell, who gave Haslar the names, believed he was not involved.

They met the Mandinauds in the Hotel and later Haslar drove Sparks, Mary Lindell and the Daily Express reporter and photographer to the Dubreuille's farm. There was a very jovial reunion. Sparks wore the lifejacket he left there, which was still in use by Arman's eldest son, Maurice, for waterskiing. The whole party then moved to the Moulin Enchante restaurant in Condac where they met with other resistance workers. On return to England, Haslar ensured Royal Marines gilt badges were sent to Rene Mandinaud and Fernard Dumas, as they had missed out in 1961, plus a replacement for Mary Lindell who had lost hers.

Sparks was troubled the others had not been properly

recognized, particularly Laver and Mills, who did exactly the same as him and Haslar. He wrote to MPs, the Queen and the French government until Sir Bernard Braine MP suggested a monument to them all. An appeal by the Daily Telegraph raised the money and a memorial was dedicated on 11 January 1983 at Royal Marines Poole, home of the SBS, with Haslar and Sparks in attendance.

Bill Sparks returned to canoeing on a number of occasions after the war. In June 1983 aged 60, he paddled from Royan to Bordeaux in four days with Gerry Lockyer of the Imperial War Museum. Each evening they met up with Sparks' daughter Gillian and son-in-law in their motorised caravan. Stepping onto the quay at Bordeaux he was met by Mayor Jacques Chaban-Delmas, a former resistance fighter. Sparks remarked, 'Although it was much more dangerous during those nights we paddled 40 years ago, we at least got the tides right and were not nearly so weary as we were this time'.

1969 reunion with the Dubreuilles at Marvaud farm, with Sparks making everyone laugh.

Haslar enjoyed a very varied and interesting life after his time in the Royal Marines. He married late but happily and settled in Scotland where he died on 5 May 1987 aged 73.

In France an Anglo-French organization was formed to keep alive the story of the raid, led by Francois Boisnier a former paratrooper. He researched what happened to those who died and the routes they took. Fifteen plaques recording the routes and fate of the escapers and their French helpers were erected. The 100 mile 'Frankton Trail' following Haslar's and Sparks' escape route was inaugurated on 12 June 2002 when 150 British-French walkers in six groups, including 80 year old Bill Sparks and Brigadier Nick Pounds, Commandant Commando Training Centre Royal Marines, walked different sections. On the wall of Chateau de Segonzac north of Blaye, a plaque marks the start of the Trail, although it actually starts on the river a little to the west.

Despite his sprightly performance that June, the years finally took their toll and Bill Sparks died on 30 November 2002 aged 80; the last of the 'Cockleshell Heroes'.

Chapter Fifteen

'FRANKTON' BATTLEFIELD TOUR

General – A visit to the main sites in the 'Frankton' story can be completed in two days and may be fitted into a longer holiday in the area, which has much else to offer. The beaches are extensive and the wine and food of the region are outstanding.

Rather than outline a formal tour this guide gives directions to each site in a logical sequence, but the visitor is free to omit sites and go on to the next. Good maps of the area are essential – see Useful Information. Except for Pointe de Grave, Bordeaux and in a few small towns, there are few facilities and the coastal areas in particular can be windswept and forlorn in poor weather. Visitors should be prepared and take a few drinks and snacks and sensible clothing and footwear. Once off the main routes, roads are narrow and it is not advisable to take large vehicles.

Figures in brackets refer to positions on the maps.

Royan Ferry

Excellent views across the mouth of the Gironde, over Pointe de Grave and out to Cordouan lighthouse. The first ferry in the morning (recommended) is around 0745, but times vary a little by season so it is best to check the timetable – http://www.montalivet-info.com/verdon-royan-ferry.htm. It can be very busy in summer, but it leaves on time and takes cars to the last minute before departure. It isn't cheap (25.90 Euros for a car and passenger in 2011), but it is well worth it for the view and it saves hours motoring around through Bordeaux.

Le Verdon

Once off the ferry **(1)** turn right (north) on the D1215 and stop after 500m at the end of the breakwater **(2)** for views of Royan, west over the 3rd tide race and south to the old jetty at le Verdon. Return towards the ferry and after 400m park in the large car park **(3)** on the right. Cross the road to see the 'Frankton' memorial and US WW1 memorial repaired after WW2 **(4)**.

There are plenty of cafes and restaurants around the port in le Verdon, but if on the early ferry note they do not open much

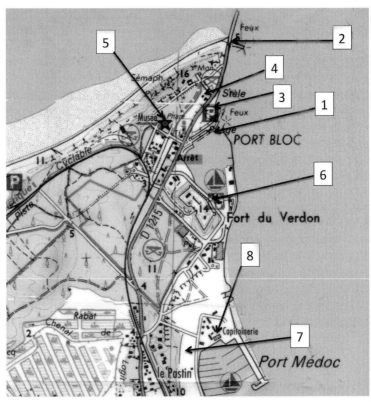

This and the next three maps are extracts from IGN Série Bleue (1:25,000) Sheet 1433 OT - the full map is available from www.ign.fr. This one shows locations 1-8 around Pointe de Grave.

before 0900.

Pointe de Grave Lighthouse (Phare de Grave) **(5)** is well worth the climb for the views of the canoeist's route, Cordouan, Royan, le Verdon, old jetty, Plage de la Chambrette etc. Entry is ?2.50 (September 2011). However, the lighthouse is only open May – October and opening days and times vary:

May	Fri-Mon 1400-1800
Jun	Fri-Mon 1400-1800
Jul	Daily 1100-1900
Aug	Daily 1100-1900
Sep	Fri-Mon 1400-1800
Oct	Fri-Mon 1400-1800

Return to your car, leave the car park, turn left onto the D1215 and take the first turning left along the southwest side of the port. At the southern end of the small port **(6)** is where the German flotilla was based. On the other side of the road, where

Wallace and Ewart were brought before Admiral Bachmann, are the ramparts of Fort de Verdon. The Fort is now a French Army leave centre and cannot be entered.

Port Medoc

Continue south from Fort de Verdon. The road bends sharp right and after 600m turn left to the large marina. There is a huge car park **(7)**. At the northern end of the marina is the Capitainerie (shown on IGN map Serie Bleue Sheet 1433 OT) with a memorial plaque on the wall to Sheard and Moffatt (8). There are a number of cafes here. Drive to the southern end of the marina right up to the sea wall **(9)** for views over Plage de la Chambrette where Sheard and Moffatt were abandoned and the old ferry jetty beyond.

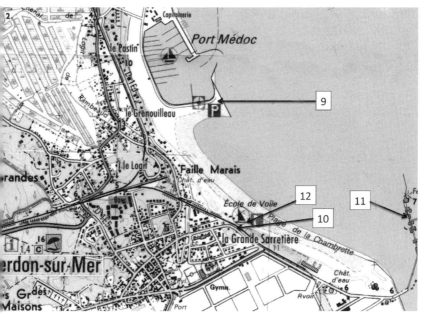

Locations 9-12 around Verdon-sur-Mer. The start of the route to l'Amelie is along the prominent road running west just above 'Verdon-sur-Mer'.

Old Jetty

Return to the road from the marina, turn left and 100m on turn left again on the D1E1. Continue south over the disused railway for 1250m to a T-junction. Turn left and after 300m the road bends right just before the locked gates to the old jetty. Park on the right **(10)** under the trees and walk over the disused railway line to the dunes for views over Plage de la Chambrette and the old jetty **(11)**. If you have time the beach **(12)** is ideal for a picnic and a swim in mid-summer, but spare a thought for Sheard and Moffatt who almost certainly perished here.

L'Amelie

Return to the D1215 and follow signs for Soulac-sur-Mer. Pass through the town and head south on the D101E1 **(13)** coast road

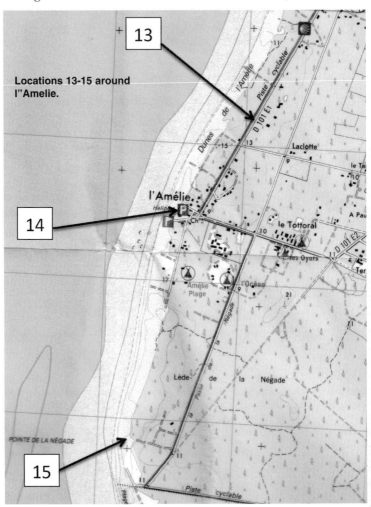

Locations 13-15 around l''Amelie.

to l'Amelie and park **(14)**. There is no vehicular access to Pointe de la Negade, but you can cycle or walk the 2 kms on tracks to get there if you have the time. If not stand on the beach at l'Amelie and look south over Pointe de la Negade **(15)** towards the submarine drop off point beyond. Look north towards Pointe de Grave and imagine the canoeists battling through the tide races offshore.

St Vivien

Follow the road north from Port de St Vivien **(16)** for 500m then turn right for 2.1 kms to the site of the first day's hide. Often described as being at Pointe aux Oiseaux **(17)**, it is actually

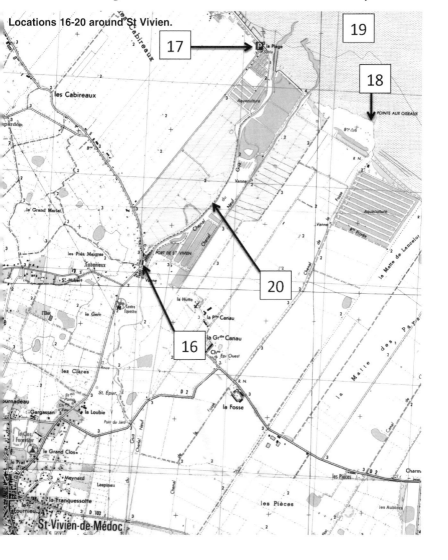

Locations 16-20 around St Vivien.

1400m northwest of it. Park in the car park **(18)** on the right and climb to the top of the seawall for views over the Gironde **(19)** and left to le Verdon and Pointe de Grave. If the tide is low (it can go out up to 1,800m here) you will see the vast expanse of smelly mud encountered by the raiders.

Port de St Vivien

Head back from the car park. At the T-junction turn left and the village is about 500m on the left for views down the creek (Chenal du Gua) **(20)** used by the fishermen.

2nd Day Hide

Now under the nuclear power station. There is no point crossing the Gironde to see it, as it can be viewed from numerous locations on the road hugging the shoreline south of St Estephe and north of Paulliac. With outstretched arm measure three fist widths left of the left hand end of the power station to find Port des Callonges.

Ile de Patiras (inter-tidal break) and 3rd Day Hide

Both are island sites and unless you have a boat there is little to see, but both can be glimpsed travelling south on the D2 road running close to the shore.

Château Magnol (Chateau du Dehez)

Marked as 'le Déhès' **(21)** on IGN map Serie Bleue Sheet 1536 OT. (Appx 6/5 map) It can best be seen from the side road to the west **(22)**, rather than from the front gate. Formerly the German Naval HQ for Bordeaux, there is a plaque on a bullet marked wall of a bunker commemorating where Wallace and Ewart were allegedly executed, but there is little evidence to support this. The Château is private and permission needs to be obtained to visit – Tel 0033 (0) 5 56 95 48 60.

4th Day Hide

From the Château Magnol **(23)** gates head north for 250m to the roundabout and turn right (east) for 3.4 kms. Turn right at the last roundabout **(24)** and head south on the D209 **(25)** parallel with the Garonne **(26)**. After 2.8 kms enter 'Zone d'Entrepots Bordeaux Nord' **(27)** by the first road on the left. Go to the end,

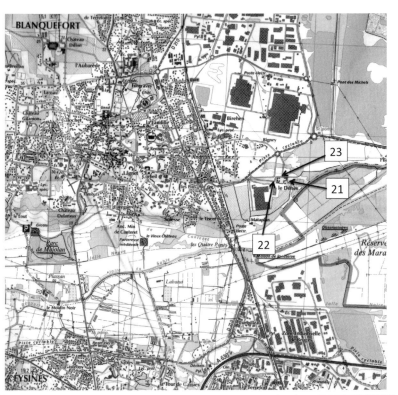

These two maps are extracts from IGN Série Bleue (1:25,000) Sheet 1536 OT – the full map is available from www.ign.fr. Above shows locations 21-23 around Blanquefort. Right shows locations 24-37 in the north and east of Bordeaux

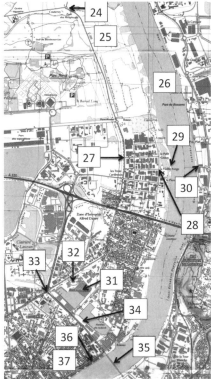

turn right and park on the left opposite the next junction **(28)**. Keeping a large storage tank to your left and allotments to your right, walk on top of a dyke towards the river. The dyke swings right after 100m to run parallel with the river. There are numerous private wooden walkways to fishing huts and the ground between is marshy, thickly vegetated and infested with mosquitoes in summer. However, for the intrepid it is possible to get to the river bank about 100m after the right turn in the dyke to the raiders' last hide **(29)** before the attack. It's up to you! Opposite is Bassens South where Laver and Mills attacked *Alabama* and *Portland* **(30)**.

U-Boat pens

Although not part of the 'Frankton' story, they are worth a visit on the way into Bordeaux. Return to the D209, turn left and head towards Bordeaux. After 2 kms you will see the massive concrete structure on the left **(31)**. The pens are only open when events are staged, but the view from the outside is impressive. Turn into the huge car park on the left **(32)**. Alternatively continue past the U-boat pens southwest to the major roundabout junction **(33)**. Turn left (southeast) with the quays on your left. About halfway to the river, about 1 km, there is free parking on the left **(34)** with good views into the front of the pens.

Quai Carnot

Continue southeast towards the river where a new bridge (2012) **(35)** crosses the Garonne. Do not go onto the bridge, but turn right, parallel with the river heading southwest and immediately get over into the left lane. There are a series of former warehouses on the left **(36)**, two of which are now car parks. Park in H19 or H15 (best option). Obey traffic lights to get into the car park. If possible park upstairs near to the river for views over the quayside **(37)** where Haslar and Sparks made their attacks. Take the ticket and pay on return – the first hour is 2 Euros, but gets pricey after that; 6 Euros for 2-3 hrs (September 2011). There is a Frankton Memorial on the ground outside the H14 Exhibition Centre. There are lots of cafes along the Quai and it is worth sitting a while and contemplating the scene on that bitterly cold December night in 1942.

Place de Tourny

Return to your car and continue southwest along the quayside. After about 1,800m turn right into Allee de Bristol **(38)** just before the gardens (Esplanade des Quinconces) **(39)**. At the end, the road curves to the left. Follow it to the apex and turn right onto Cours de Tournon, which leads into Place de Tourny **(40)**. This is where the execution party for Wallace and Ewart formed up.

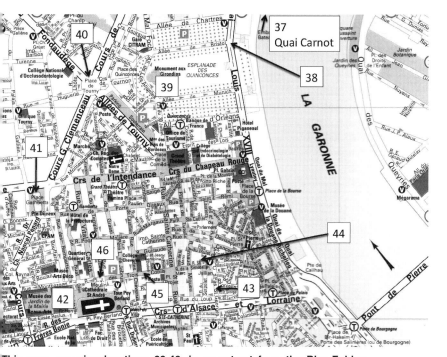

This map, covering locations 38-46, is an extract from the Blay-Foldex 1:17,000 Bordeaux Agglomeration Plan de Ville - the full map is available from www.blayfoldex.com.

Centre Jean Moulin

Take the left exit off Place de Tourny down Cours Georges Clemenceau. Turn right and left around Place Gambetta **(41)**. Go left and immediately right into Rue Dr Charles Nancel Penard. Go half left into Cours d'Albret. After Musee des Beaux Arts **(42)** turn left into Rue Elisee Recluse, then half right behind the Cathedral into Place Pey-Berland, which runs into Cours d'Alsace et Lorraine. Turn left into Rue du Pas St Georges (43). Park at Camille Jullian Car Park **(44)** – access is on the left on entering Place Camille Jullian. Come out of the car park and walk west along Rue de la Simeon Maucoudinat, which runs into Rue des Trois Conils **(45)**. In Place Jean Moulin **(46)** is Centre Jean Moulin – document centre of resistance, deportation and FFF, with a small 'Frankton' section. It opens 1400-1800 Tuesday-Sundays. Closed Mondays and Holidays. Admission is free.

Cathedral St Andre

Although nothing to do with the 'Frankton' story, while in Bordeaux the cathedral is worth a visit. It is just south of Place Jean Moulin.

207

Opening times:

	1 June – 30 September	1 October – 31 May
Monday	1500-1930	1400-1800
Tue-Fri	1000-1300 & 1500-1930	1000-1200 & 1400-1800
Saturday	1000-1300 & 1500-1930	1000-1200 & 1400-1900
Sunday	0930-1300 & 1500-1930	0930-1200 & 1400-1800
	(2030 Jul-Aug)	

There are lots of shops, old streets and cafes in this area.

La Reole

Leave Bordeaux southeast along the D113/D10 **(47)** to Langon (45 kms) **(48)**. Avoid Langon town centre and head east on the D1113 **(49)** to La Reole (17 kms) **(50)**. Entering the town from the west go up the hill to where the road widens into Place Georges Chaigne (large war memorial on the right next to the church), turn left uphill. 100m in front is the old prison where Conway was held. Go round it to the left and park (this is Place de Verdun, but there are no signs). The prison is open Mon-Fri 0900-1200 & 1330-1700. Look up the hill. The building with the tower and cock weather vane is the old hospital where MacKinnon was treated and arrested. On the left side is an extension with a large green door and the memorial is to the left of it.

If cafes etc are required, return to the bottom of the hill from the prison, turn left into the town centre. At the bottom of the hill in Place de la Liberation join the one-way system on the right and follow around the contours of the town, bending slowly to the left. Follow signs for Monsegur, Libourne and Centre Ville, until at a Stop sign there is a left turn to a free car park. Take it and park in the car park on the right above the road. Place de la Liberation is down the hill from the car park, which has a basic public toilet.

Baigneaux

From la Reole head north on the D670 (51) to Sauveterre-de-Guyenne (14 kms) **(52)** and then west on the D671 **(53)** to Baigneaux (11 kms) **(54)**. Take the first left on entering the village and park on the right outside the Mairie. The house with the memorial is on the left.

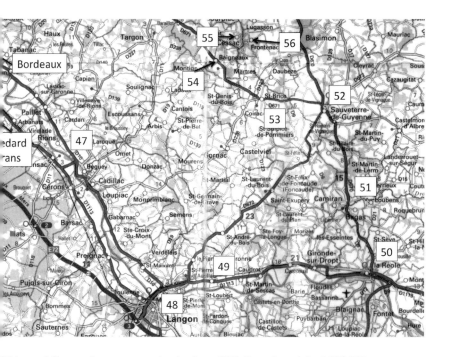

This and the next map are extracts from IGN Departmentale 1:200,000 Sheet D33 - the full map is available from www.ign.fr. This one shows locations 47-56 southeast of Bordeaux.

Frontenac

From the Mairie turn round and go straight over the D671 into Rue de Frontenac. Follow towards Cessac **(55)** for 3.5 kms. At a prominent junction, the road to Cessac goes straight on and Frontenac **(56)** is right over the cycle track/old railway line. Park here. Walk 300m north along the line to the memorial below the house where MacKinnon and Conway sheltered (the plaque was missing in September 2011).

Château de Segonzac

Head north out of Blaye on the, which runs 500m east of and parallel with the Gironde. About 2.5 kms out of town, Château Segonzac **(58)** is on the right up the hill. When the road forks after 200m keep left to the memorial, which is right of the gate. Return to the main road, go right and immediately left onto a track. There is a gate after 100m, turn round and park on the grass verge. Walk through the gate for 450m to the river bank where Haslar and Sparks came ashore (59).

Chez Ouvrard

From Blaye make your way inland 20 kms to the east and pick up the E606/N10 road (60) heading northeast towards Angoulême. After about 14 kms leave on the Montlieu exit on the D730 (61) heading southeast. Ignore the first few turnings. After 400m turn right onto the D258 (62). After 1.3kms pass a US Flying Fortress memorial on the left. After 600m note the turning

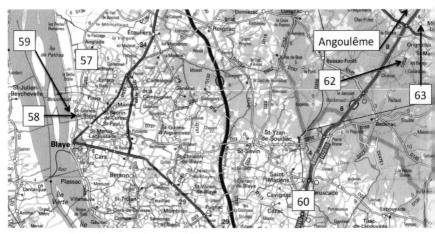

Locations 57-63 around Blaye.

on the left to Chez David where the informant Gagnerot lived. Go on 200m and turn left onto the D259. Go on 1 km and turn right signed La Jourdaine and Chez Ouvrard. After 350m turn left at the Chez Ouvrard sign. The farm is 100m along the track with the memorial to Laver and Mills on the facing wall.

Montlieu La Garde

Retrace the route just taken to the D730 and turn left back towards the N10, but before it take the right into the centre of town (63). Pass the first war memorial (it is for La Garde). After 600m the war memorial for Montlieu is on the left with parking in front; Laver's and Mills' names have been added to it. There is a café across the road.

Opposite: This and the next map are extracts from IGN Department 1:200,000 Sheet D16 – the full map is available from www.ign.fr. This shows locations 64-71 around St Preuil.

Chez Coutin

Continue north through Montlieu into Pouillac and rejoin the N10 north of it. Follow the N10 beyond Barbazieux. Come off signed Barbazieux Nord **(64)** and go left back over the N10 towards St Medard **(65)**. After a few kms at a T-junction, St Medard is signed right, but turn left and after a few kms turn right onto the D1 heading north towards Touzac **(66)**. Go through it down a hill and Chez Coutin is on the right **(67)**. This is where Haslar and Sparks begged food from the woman feeding her chickens.

Nâpres

Continue north on the D1 and follow signs right to St Preuil **(68)**. About 800m before entering St Preuil go right signed Nâpres (if you pass a large walled cemetery on the left you have gone too far – note there is no sign for Nâpres off this road heading south). After 100m take the right fork. Nâpres is 500m on at the

bottom of a hill **(69)**. The memorial is on the left of the main building.

Vinade Bridge over Charente

Return to the road and turn right into St Preuil. The first house on the left may be Maine-Laurier farm where Haslar asked for help, but there are no signs. Go through the village and follow signs for Ste Meme les Carrieres **(70)**. In the village go over the crossroads and stop momentarily in the car park on the right. This is where Haslar and Sparks ran into German soldiers dashing to get on parade. Continue downhill past a large cemetery on the left. Pass some large ponds on the left, go over the railway and cross the Charente at Vinade Bridge **(71)**. Park 100m beyond on the right and walk back.

Beaunac (shown as Baunac on some maps)

From Vinade bridge navigate northeast using the Department map to Aigre **(72)**. Head north from it on the D737 **(73)** and approach St Fraigne **(74)** from the south. Enter the village and just before the bridge turn right on the D182 **(75)**. At the cemetery stay right and 2kms on enter Beaunac **(76)** and stop at the Calvary on the green. The memorial is just behind it. Signs for German fortifications in the area are not worth the diversion.

Ruffec

Navigate east from Beaunac to get on the main N10 road **(77)** running north from Angoulême. Approach Ruffec **(78)** from the south coming off the N10 onto the D911 **(79)**. Go along Rue General Leclerc over the top of a low hill, passing the semi-derelict Hotel de France on the left (owned by Francois Rouillon at the time). 100m beyond on the left at a crossroads is Hotel L'Angle d'Or, where Haslar and Sparks contacted the escape chain. Turn left and park in Rue de l'Hopital. If you have time go into the Hotel and have a drink. You may consider staying in one of its 16 rooms, perhaps the very one used by Haslar and Sparks. In September 2011 the Hotel was run by Ivan Mballa, a French Cameroonian and former player with Aldershot and Raith Rovers.

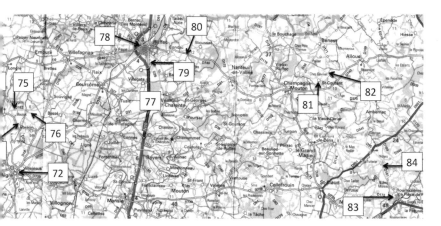

Locations 72-84 around Ruffec.

Marvaud Farm

Described as being at St Coutant, but it is actually well to the north of it. Leave Ruffec on the D740 **(80)** heading east. After about 20 kms go through St Coutant **(81)** and continue after the end of the village sign. Go to the bottom of the hill, cross a bridge and ignore the D311 turning to St Coutant Cemetery. 150m on turn left (there is a prominent cream house on the right). If coming from the east the farm is signed here, but not from the west. Go through the hamlet for 400m. At the last house the road swings right. Continue for 1.1 kms to Marvaud Farm **(82)** where Haslar and Sparks spent Christmas and New Year 1942. The memorial is on the facing wall as you approach.

Roumazieres-Lambert Station

From Marvaud Farm return to the D740 and cross it heading south. Navigate to Roumazieres-Lambert **(83)**. Approach the village on the D161 **(84)** from the north. In the village turn right on seeing the Gendarmerie Station on the left. Park in the village hall car park and the station is opposite. This is where Haslar, Sparks and Maurice Milleville cycled from Marvaud Farm to catch the train to Lyons.

Chapter Sixteen

USEFUL INFORMATION

ACCOMMODATION – there is a wide variety of accommodation available in the area, with the greatest concentration being in Bordeaux. As availability etc changes so quickly it is best to search on-line for your requirements. There are also numerous campsites, but many close for the winter from late September.

CLOTHING AND KIT – even in summer it may be cool on the coast. Consider taking:

> Waterproofs.
> Headwear and gloves.
> Walking shoes/boots.
> Shades and sunscreen.
> Binoculars and camera.
> Snacks and drinks.

CUSTOMS/BEHAVIOUR – local people are generally tolerant of visitors but please respect their property and address others respectfully – Monsieur, Madame or Mademoiselle. It is rude not to give a general greeting when entering a shop, 'Bonjour Messieurs Dames'. The French are less inclined to switch to English than other Europeans. If you try some basic French it will be appreciated.

DRIVING IN FRANCE – rules of the road are similar to UK, apart from having to drive on the right of course! If in doubt about priorities, give way to the right (*serrez à droite*). The minimum age to drive is 18 with a full driving licence. Obey laws and road signs – police impose harsh on-the-spot fines. Penalties for drinking and driving are heavy and the legal limit is lower than UK (50mg rather than 80mg). Stop signs mean it.

> **Fuel** – petrol stations are only open 24 hours on major routes. Some accept credit cards in automatic tellers. The cheapest fuel is at hypermarkets.

> **Mandatory Requirements** – if taking your own car you need:
> Full driving licence.

Vehicle registration document.
Comprehensive motor insurance valid in France (Green Card).
European breakdown and recovery cover.
Letter of authorisation from the owner if the vehicle is not yours.
Spare set of bulbs, headlight beam adjusters, warning triangle, GB sticker, high visibility vest and breathalyzer.

EMERGENCY DETAILS – keep details required in an emergency separate from your wallet or handbag:
Photocopy passport, insurance documents and EHIC (see Health below).
Mobile phone details.
Credit/debit card numbers and cancellation telephone contacts.
Travel insurance company contact number.

FERRIES – the closest ports are Cherbourg and Ouistrehem with Le Havre and Dieppe close by. Less expensive crossings are to Dunkirk, Calais and Boulogne, but entail a longer drive and, depending upon your chosen route, Autoroute tolls.

HEALTH

European Health Insurance Card – entitles the holder to medical treatment at local rates. Obtained by forms from Post Offices, online at www.ehic.org.uk/Internet/home.do or call 0845 6062030. Issued free and valid for five years. You are only covered if you have the EHIC with you when you go for treatment.

Travel Insurance – you are strongly advised to have travel insurance. If you receive treatment get a statement by the doctor (*feuille de soins*) and a receipt to make a claim on return.

Personal Medical Kit – treat minor ailments yourself to save time and money. Pack sufficient prescription medicine for the full trip.

Chemist (*Pharmacie*) – look for the green cross. They provide some treatment and if unable to help will direct you to a doctor. Most open 0900-1900 except Sun. Out of hours services (pharmacie de garde) are advertised in Pharmacie windows.

Doctor and Dentist – hotel receptions have details of local practices. Beware private doctors/hospitals, as extra charges cannot be reclaimed – the French national health service is known as *conventionné*.

Rabies – contact with infected animals is very rare, but if bitten by any animal, get the wound examined professionally immediately.

MAPS – produced by Institut Géographique National (IGN) are available on-line at www.ign.fr or www.mapsworldwide.com. Department maps (1:200,000) Sheets D16 Charente and D33 Gironde give a general overview of the area and are detailed enough to navigate between sites while motoring. Série Bleue (1:25,000) Sheets 1433 OT, 1534 O, 1535 O and 1536 OT cover the 'Frankton' sites in detail. However, if you don't want to purchase so many Série Bleue maps, 1433 OT and 1536 OT are the most important.

MONEY

ATMs – at most banks and post offices with instructions in English. Check your card can be used in France and what charges apply. Some banks limit how much can be withdrawn. Let your bank know you will be away, as some block cards if transactions take place unexpectedly.

Banks – generally open 1000-1200 & 1400-1700 weekdays. Some open all day in towns, some close on Mon and some open Sat a.m.

Credit/Debit Cards – major cards are usually accepted, but some have different names - Visa is Carte Bleue and Mastercard is Eurocard.

Exchange – beware 0% commission, as the rate may be poor. The Post Office takes back unused currency at the same rate, which may or may not be advantageous.

Since the Euro, currency exchange facilities are scarcer.

Local Taxes – if you buy high value items you can reclaim tax. Get the forms completed by the shop, when leaving France have them stamped by Customs, post them to the shop and they will refund about 12%.

PASSPORT – a valid passport is required with a few months remaining.

POST – Post Offices (la Poste) open 0800-1700 weekdays and 0800-1200 Sat. Postcard stamps are more readily available from vendors, newsagents and tabacs. Postboxes are yellow.

PUBLIC HOLIDAYS – just about everything closes on public holidays and banks close early the day before. Transport may be affected, but tourist attractions in high season are unlikely to be. The following dates/days are public holidays:

1 January
Easter Monday
1 and 8 May
Ascension Day
Whit Monday
14 July
15 August
1 and 11 November
25 December

Many businesses close for the majority of August.

RADIO – If you want to pick up the news from home try:
BBC Radio 4 - 198 kHz long wave.
BBC Five Live - 909 kHz medium wave.
BBC World Service - 648 kHz medium-wave.

SHOPS – generally open 0900-1200 and 1400-1900 Mon-Sat. In large towns and tourist areas shops tend to open all day, some on Sun. Some bakers open Sun a.m. and during the week take later lunch breaks.

TELEPHONE

France to UK - 0044, delete initial 0 then dial the rest of the number.
In France – dial the full 10-digit number even if within the same zone.

Payphones – cards purchased from post offices, tabacs and newsagents.

Mobiles – check yours will work in France and the charges.

Emergencies

Ambulance	- 15)
Fire	- 18) 112 from a mobile
Police	- 17)

British Embassy (Paris) – 01 44 51 31 00

TIME ZONE – one hour ahead of UK.

TIPPING – a small tip is expected by cloakroom and lavatory attendants and porters. Not required in restaurants, as a service charge is always included.

TOILETS – the best are in museums and the main tourist attractions. Towns usually have public toilets where markets are held; some are coin operated.

Appendix I

COCKLE MK.II

RMBPD was not unique in using canoes. Other units included the Special Operations Group in South East Asia, the Combined Operations Pilotage Parties, Detachment 385, Special Boat Sections of the Commandos, Force 136 (SOE in Asia), Small Scale Raiding Force (62 Commando) and SOE. Upwards of 4,800 canoes (Cockles) were produced during the war, of which at least 1,127 were Mk.IIs.

There were very few canoe manufacturers in Britain in 1939.

A comparison of the Cockle Mk.I and Mk.II.

e Fred
patley
signed
ckle Mk.II, as
ed on the
rankton' Raid
ewed from
e stern. Note
e hatches for
ecting the
w and stern
ays, the open
aterproof
nvas spray
vers, rigid
ywood deck,
eakwater and
ooden seats.

One was Folbot Folding Boats Ltd of London, but in July 1942 there were only 20 Folbots in Britain and they were in poor condition. At that time a requirement existed for at least 100 two-man canoes. The original Cockle Mk.I, produced by Cavender and Clark in Cambridge, was an improvement, but had a number of limitations, including being fragile and prone to leaking. Although the Cockle Mk.I had limitations in 1942, it developed alongside the Mk.II and there were ultimately seven separate versions; it was in service until the

219

early 1960s. When the staff requirement was produced for a new canoe, it coincided with Fred Goatley supplying drawings incorporating most of the specifications. Goatley's design, with input from Haslar, ultimately became the canoe selected for the 'Frankton' raid, the two-man Cockle Mk.II.

The final version was semi rigid with sides of canvas or rubberised fabric. It weighed 40 kgs and was able to carry 220 kgs (two men plus 68 kgs of equipment). It was 4.5m long, beam 72 cms, depth 32 cms and collapsed depth 16.5 cms. The dimensions given for the Mk.II vary between sources – these are from *Cockleshell Canoes* by Quentin Rees as the depth of his research indicates they are the most reliable.

The Cockle Mk.II was decked with one-eighth ply, as was the base, which also had runners to allow it to be dragged over sand or shingle. The deck was held up by eight internal hinged stays at the bow, stern and three on each side. The cockpit had a waterproof canvas cover held together along the centre line with spring clips, which disengaged if the crew had to get out quickly. The crew's jackets were elasticated to fit around the circular cockpit cover, making it almost watertight. A folding breakwater on the foredeck helped to deflect waves.

The crew sat on wooden seats an inch above the base, with a wooden backrest. A compass was mounted on the foredeck inside the breakwater. The No.1 sat forward and the No.2 copied what he did. The paddles were double, but could be divided into two singles when there was danger of being seen. This reduced the silhouette and made less noise. When doubled the paddle blades were offset by 90° to present a smaller silhouette and reduce wind resistance.

The pilot Mk.II was inspected by Haslar on 30 April and underwent a brief test from Saro's Folly Works at Whippingham into the River Medina on 13 May. Having been delivered to CODC at Eastney, Haslar tested it alone next day, loaded with 68 kgs ballast and raced it against the Mk.I in the afternoon. In the evening he tried the Mk.II with 227 kgs ballast for a full load test. On 15 May the Experimental Party tested the Mk.II by flooding it and giving it some rough treatment, managing to break the forward deck beam before it was returned to Saro for modifications. Haslar asked for a small bilge pump, operated by the No.2's knee, to be fitted and designed a sailing rig. However, neither was ready in time for the 'Frankton' raid.

On 19 June, a comparison of relative merits was made with the Mk.I. The Mk.II was 4.5 kgs lighter, assembly was much more rapid, it was more robust and could be picked up by the ends loaded. However, it was less comfortable, less stable, slower and more difficult to stow in a submarine. These negative points were addressed in the next version. Trials with the submarine HMS *Unbeaten*, showed that the Mk.II could be widened by 4 cms to increase stability.

The later versions of the Mk.II were very stable, but in rough water had to be kept head to the waves. Unlike an Eskimo kayak it was not possible to roll it back once capsized. The crew had to swim alongside, try to flip it over, bale it out and then climb in over bow or stern. There were buoyancy bags at the bow and stern to keep it afloat even when swamped. There was a shelf forward on which to stow items that needed to remain dry. Canvas pockets were provided inside to keep maps and charts handy. It was standard practice to rest for five minutes in the hour, during which they would bale out and make any adjustments necessary. In company with other canoes, they would raft up during these breaks and the leader would issue instructions for the next hour.

Despite Saro carrying out the development work, the majority of Cockle Mk.II production was sub-contracted to Parkstone Joinery (750) and Messrs Tyler of Griffin's Mill, Stroud (100). The Cockles used on 'Frankton' were six of the 26 produced by Saro at the Folly Works at Whippingham, East Cowes; they cost £160 each. In 1951, Captain Bruce and Corporal Johnny Litherland used a Mk.II Cockle in the Devizes-Westminster canoe race; they were the first to finish in thirty-four hours, the next team taking six hours longer. The Mk.II was superceded by the Mk.II** three-man canoe, which was also designed by Fred Goatley.

Appendix II

EQUIPMENT AND CLOTHING

Each canoe carried:
Three sets of paddles.
Bailer and sponge.
Buoyancy bags fore and aft.
Depth sounding line.
Repair bags.
Charts, P8 Compass, monocular (one per two canoes), protractor.
Dim red torches (Note 1).

Camouflage net and cream.
Waterproof watch.
Wire cutters.
Matches.
Silent Sten – one each with Haslar and Mackinnon plus four magazines.
Two x 69 grenades (Note 2).
Eight Limpets, fuses, placing rods (58.75" extended, 15.5" folded), spanner.
Holdfast.
Cable cutter and wire cutter charges (Note 3) – one each per Division.
Ten day's compact rations (Note 4), five hexamine cookers, 5 pint cooking pot.
2.5 gallons water, water-sterilizing tablets.
Benzedrine, field dressings, iodine, morphia, foot powder, cough lozenges, laxatives.

Silent Sten Gun developed by Royal Small Arms Factory was in use by special forces for decades after WW2.

No.69 Grenade made of Bakerlite was less hazardous to the thrower than the No.36 Mills Grenade.

Bags containing personal items:

Toothbrush and paste, towel, seawater soap, razor and a shaving brush per canoe.

Felt soled boots – to replace gym shoes and waders on land.

Change of socks and pants, spare laces.

Roll neck sweater.

Spare gloves.

Cigarettes and matches.

Each man had escape bags containing:

Binoculars, torch, watch.

V-Victory match books – a means of persuading locals of their identity, but also known to the Germans to ensure proper treatment.

Escape kits (15 cms x 5 cms plastic box) containing escape compasses, rubber water bottle, Horlicks tablets, condensed milk, chewing gum, chocolate, tape, matches, water purification tablets.

Silk escape map.

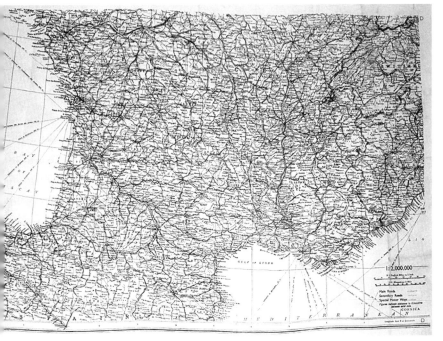

Silk escape map of Southern France.

223

Miniature escape compass.

Luminous miniature compasses – including one in a collar stud and another in a trouser fly button, but they had to be removed or cut off before they could be used and were susceptible to damp.

Spare compact rations.

1st field dressing, iodine, Benzedrine, morphia, foot powder.

Tin of water and water-sterilizing kit.

Camouflage cream.

String, needle and thread.

Toilet paper.

Each man wore or carried:

Gym shoes under thigh length waders with light weight soles.

Long woolen pants and sea boot socks under denim trousers.

Woolen vest, shirt, roll neck pullover and blue scarf.

Camouflaged olive green/black Cockle top with hood - (Note 5).

Life jacket - under Cockle top.

Silk gloves under blue woollen gloves.

Blue Balaklava.

Colt .45 pistol, three magazines, fighting knife (right leg), clasp knife.

Bird call.

ID disks (Note 6).

Notes:

1. Developed by Major Sir Malcolm Campbell of CODC, one time world water speed record holder.

2. They had a smaller destructive radius than the 36 Mills Grenade and were better suited for use where there was little cover. The shell was of Bakelite with metal fragmenting sleeves inside. The screw-off cap was discarded and when the grenade was thrown a linen tape with a lead weight unwrapped in flight, freeing a ball-bearing to arm the fuse and it exploded on impact.

3. Designed by Haslar and CODC to cut mooring lines and add to the chaos after a Limpet attack.

4. Experimental rations consisting of three waxed cardboard boxes per man per day. Each included a small tin of tea leaves mixed with powdered milk and sugar for an instant cuppa. There were tins of cheese, spam, biscuits, oatmeal block, sweets, chewing gum, cigarettes and fuzee matches.

5. Specially designed for the mission – hardwearing and waterproof with an elastic skirt to fit over the cockpit cover.

6. In a letter to war crimes investigators, Haslar specified their dress was as shown, except they wore rope soled shoes or felt soled boots and Battledress trousers. He emphasised their jackets carried RM and Combined Operations badges.

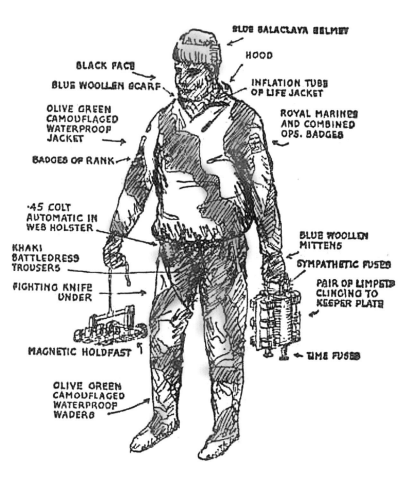

Haslar's sketch of a 'Limpeteer' from *Cockleshell Heroes* by Lucas Phillips.

RAIDING FORCE BIOGRAPHIES

Colley, Ply X/108877 Marine Norman A

Born 22 Nov 1920 at Leeds. Educated at Love Lane School, Pontefract. Delivered groceries in Featherstone by bike. Called up to Plymouth 16 April 1941. Posted to Orkney and was in an honour guard for King George VI's visit. He would have volunteered for the Girl Guides to get away from Orkney. Broke a metatarsal playing bare foot rugby near Eastney Barracks on 31 July 1942 and refused to take sick leave, but Conway replaced him as MacKinnon's No.2. Reserve for 'Frankton' left behind on HMS *Tuna*. Transferred to No.2 Section after 'Frankton' and went with Earthworm Detachment. On VE Day 1945 he proposed by telephone to Alma Warrington, who worked for the same grocery company and they married on 23 June 1945. Discharged March 1946. Turned down a trial with Plymouth Albion as he wanted to go home. Worked in engineering until setting up a baking and confectionery business in Pontefract. He was also a sub-postmaster.

Conway, PLY/X 105763 Marine James

Born 28 August 1922 at Stockport. Strongly built, fresh faced, rather quiet but quick witted. Elder brother was also a Marine. Keen swimmer and cyclist. Milk roundsman with the Coop and loved working with horses. Commemorated on the Plymouth Naval Memorial, Panel 102, Column 3.

Ellery, Ply/X 108875 Marine William A

Born in London early 1915. The only canoe commander with no rank. A fine surface swimmer who hated being underwater. Later Corporal. Went absent without leave mid-February 1943 to sort out a domestic problem. Sparks took his place on a draft abroad.

Ewart, PLY/X 108350 Marine Robert

Born 4 December 1921 in Glasgow. Worked in a textile factory. Member of the Boys' Brigade. When war broke out he was offered work in a munitions factory, but enlisted instead. Served in the Orkneys and volunteered immediately he heard about the RMBPD. A trier, who often got it wrong but took the reprimand in good part and stuck with it. Commemorated on the Plymouth Naval Memorial, Panel 103, Column 1.

Fisher, PLY/X108151 Marine Eric

Born in Birmingham to an Ulster family. Lived at West Bromwich. A little older than the others. Worked as a print machinist. Stout, keen and full of guts. Didn't smoke or drink. Non-swimmer to start with and weak on the surface, but became a very competent frogman. After 'Frankton' he transferred to No.2 Section and later Earthworm Detachment. Took part in the raid on Leros 16-18 June 1944.

Haslar, Major Herbert G 'Blondie' DSO OBE

Born Dublin 27 February 1914. Hated his first name and was known as George in the family and 'Blondie' in the military. Son of Lieutenant (Quartermaster) Arthur Thomas Haslar MC RAMC, who was lost when the troopship *Transylvania* was torpedoed in the Bay of Genoa on 3 May 1917. Educated at Wellington – captain of swimming 1932 and 1st team cross-country and rugby. Probationary Royal Marines 2nd Lieutenant 1 September 1932; trained at Plymouth, Eastney and Deal passing out top on the Military Course in May 1934. Sent to Alexandria during the Abyssinia crisis 1935. Joined HMS *Queen Elizabeth* in May 1936 in the Mediterranean. Fleet Landing Officer in the Mobile Naval Base Defence Organisation (MNBDO) December 1937. Captain 23 May 1939. Joined the Royal Marines Fortress Unit at Scapa Flow September 1939. Acting Major 18 March 1941 to command Landing Company. Commanded landing craft at Narvik 28 May 1940, landing French infantry and tanks under fire. A

Norwegian vessel he was on was strafed by Bf 110s; he got the wounded off before it blew up. Made more trips in landing craft to land troops and re-embark tanks. In the evacuation he took off the rear guard – OBE, MID, Croix de Guerre. Posted to MNBDO Base Depot. After RMBPD he commanded Detachment 385 in Southeast Asia. Went to Italy briefly in January 1944 to report on captured equipment and techniques. In Ceylon he organised the Special Operations Group (SOG) with administrative, intelligence, planning, training and development sections plus operational sub-units – COPPs, Special Recce, SBS and Detachment 385. He commanded until Colonel HT Tollemache RM took over in June 1944, then concentrated on planning, training and development. SOG conducted 154 operations. In October 1945 he joined the Combined Operations Experimental Establishment at Fremington, Barnstaple. 1946 he was adviser to the School of Combined Operations Beach and Boat Section, training men for Combined Operations Small Raiding Organisation. Medical discharge 16 June 1948.

Haslar had a lifelong interest in small boats. He built a canvas canoe with a friend aged 12, paddling it around Langstone Harbour and Hayling Island. At 14 he built a sailing boat and used it all over the Solent, spending nights on the beach. He bought various sailing boats, sometimes with friends, but preferred to be his own master. Elected to the Royal Ocean Racing Club (RORC). After the war he bought the yacht *Tre Sang*, but she was not deemed suitable for ocean racing; Blondie entered six RORC races in the small class and won three to prove his point. In 1947 he joined John Illingworth's *Myth of Malham* in the Channel, Fastnet and Bermuda races. 1948 elected to the Royal Cruising Club. 1951 wrote *Harbours and Anchorages of the North Brittany Coast*, for amateur yachtsman. 1954 worked briefly for SD6, a left over from SOE, developing the rubber assault boat. Designed his own yacht, *Jester*, incorporating innovative ideas such as all lines leading to the cockpit, a roller reefing sail and self steering, to allow her to be sailed by two people over long distances. From 1956 he wrote occasional articles on boating and seamanship for the *Observer*. He initiated and participated in the first east to west Observer Single-Handed Transatlantic Race (OSHTR) in 1960 from Plymouth to New York; *Jester* finished 2nd. In the second OSHTR in 1964, he finished 5th out of fifteen starters. He set up the Observer Round

Britain Race in 1966 and entered with his wife, but in a Force 8 the rudder broke and they had to pull out. 1970 awarded the Royal Cruising Club's Medal for Services to Cruising.

He had numerous inventive ideas, some of which came to fruition, but others did not as he had limited business acumen. In Ceylon he developed what decades later became the windsurfer, but without the universal joint it was not a success. He invented self-steering gear for yachts, used by Francis Chichester and Alec Rose during their round the world trips in 1966-67 and 1967-68. He patented the rope winch for yachting in 1958 and plasticised sails years before it became standard. With the Dracone company he developed huge rubber sausages to transport liquids at sea. He designed a floating breakwater to break up waves and proposed using the damped energy to generate electricity; he was years ahead of his time.

He had many other talents. He wrote a play, *Tulip Major*, a lighthearted love story involving a Royal Marines Major and a girl, in collaboration with Rosamund Pilcher. It opened at the Repertory Theatre in Dundee in June 1957 and reviews were good, but Pilcher was not willing to sell it on. He also had some success with portrait painting. In 1962 he set up the Loch Ness Project sponsored by the *Observer* and during it met Bridget Fisher, who he married on 30 October 1965. She was 25 years his junior, but they were made for each other. Children – Dinah born 1967 and Thomas 1969. In 1975 they bought a farm on Loch Fyne and quickly became part of the local community. 'Blondie' died there on 5 May 1987 and his funeral was held in the village, followed by cremation in Glasgow; his ashes were scattered over his favourite anchorage. A thanksgiving service was held in Portsmouth Cathedral on 19 June 1987.

Laver, PLY/X3091 Corporal Albert Frederick

Born 29 September 1920 at Birkenhead. The family moved to Friern Barnet when he was 14. He worked as a butcher's assistant until joining the Royal Marines as a regular pre-war. Quiet, intelligent, stocky, with great physical stamina and utterly dependable. Served on HMS *Rodney* when *Bismark* was sunk in May 1941, as an ammunition handler in the port forward secondary armament turret. By April 1942 he was at the Royal Marines Military School, Thurlstone, near Kingsbridge, Devon. Not a great drinker or merry maker. MID. Commemorated on the Plymouth Naval Memorial, Panel 102, Column 3.

McKinnon, 2nd Lieutenant John Withers

Born 15 July 1921 at Oban. His family moved to Glasgow. Father was an Argyll & Sutherland Highlander piper in WW1. Sisters Margaret served in WRNS and Isabella worked for Barr & Stroud engraving gun sights in the Second World War. Educated at Napier's Hall and Woodside Senior Secondary School. Worked in a coal merchant's office. Scoutmaster in the Maryhill Road Boy Scouts. Good swimmer and ballroom dancer. Enlisted 7 April 1941 as Marine PO/X 105495. On 26 January 1942 he joined HMS *Atherstone* and was involved in shooting down a Ju88; she was part of the escort for the Raid on St Nazaire on 27/28 March, but he left her on 10 February. Underwent officer training at Thurlstone, passing out almost top on 15 May 1942. Royal Marines Platoon Weapons Course at Browndown 25 May – 27 June. He had initiative, imagination and intelligence. 'Mac' drank little and didn't smoke, but played jazz drums, was sociable, kind and thoughtful. Commemorated on the Portsmouth Naval Memorial, Panel 93.

Mills, PLY/X108159 Marine William 'Bill' Henry

Born Kettering 12 December 1921. Fun loving and high spirited. Worked at Kettering Sports and Rubber Stores and was in Civil Defence before enlisting. MID. Commemorated on the Plymouth Naval Memorial, Panel 103, Column 1.

Moffatt, PLY/X 108881 Marine David Gabriel

Born in Belfast 20 November 1920. Family moved to Halifax, Yorkshire. Boy Scout. A big strong trier, full of life. Rarely drank and known as the Preacher, because he was good at impersonating clergy. Commemorated on the Plymouth Naval Memorial, Panel 103, Column 1.

Sheard, PLY/X 1369 Corporal George Jellicoe

Born 2 May 1915 at Devonport. Father was Royal Navy. Suffered poor health as a youngster. Small, tough, witty and lively. Married Mabelle Irene 'Renee' Bates in Plymouth in the middle of 1942. She was expecting their first child when both were killed in an air raid at her parents' home (21a Sussex Road, Ford, Devonport) on 13 June 1943. Commemorated on the Plymouth Naval Memorial, Panel 74, Column 3.

Sparks, PLY/X3664 Marine William 'Bill' Edward DSM

Born 5 September 1922 in London. Father was a Royal Navy Stoker. Left school at 14 to became a cobbler. Father separated from his original wife and remarried. Volunteered for the Royal Marines in 1939 aged 17 and trained at Deal. Served on HMS *Renown* protecting convoys while she was Admiral Somerville's flagship and during the search for *Bismarck*. *Renown* went to Iceland in case *Tirpitz* broke into the Atlantic. Mooring in Reykjavik, Sparks fell into the icy sea while hoisting out the Admiral's gangway. He developed a fever and was sent to hospital at Aberdeen. Brother Benny (William Benjamin Dean) was killed when HMS *Naiad* was sunk in March 1942 – he is commemorated on the Chatham Naval Memorial. Sparks volunteered for RMBPD as a way of avenging his brother. A cool, competent, wiry Cockney, always grumbling when it was going well, but just the man in a tight corner when he was full of humour. DSM.

After 'Frankton' he trained as a paratrooper at Ringway. In February 1944 as a Corporal he was to train new canoeists when his mate Corporal Ellery went absent without leave. Sparks took his place in Earthworm Detachment when it was sent to the Middle East. Took part in the liberation of Naxos. Discharged March 1946. Worked as a London trolleybus conductor and later as a driver. He married Violet E Honour early in 1947 and had three sons and a daughter. Joined the Malaysian Police Force as a Lieutenant in the Emergency in 1952.

After a number of incidents, including the death of an Army Sergeant Major in the car he was driving, Sparks resigned. He then worked as a building labourer, Post Office sorter, shoe repairer, milk roundsman and in a plastic factory. On his return from promoting the film *Cockleshell Heroes* in the USA, he was employed as an insurance agent and ice cream vendor before returning to bus driving. He later became an inspector and, when his bronchitis became too acute, a garage inspector to keep him indoors. Wife died 1982. 1986 married Rene on a trip to the Isle of Wight.

In 1995 he was forced to sell his medals because of a drop in his pension as a result of new tax rules. Despite bronchitis caused by war service he did not qualify for a war pension. The medals were bought for £31,000 by Michael Ashcroft; £1,000 more than the Royal Marines Museum was prepared to pay. Ashcroft made the medals available to Sparks whenever he needed them. In June 2002 with a support party of Royal Marines he made a 60th anniversary pilgrimage to France to revisit places on the escape route (Frankton Trail). He died on 30 November 2002.

Wallace, PLY/X665 Sergeant Samuel

Born 24 September 13 in Dublin. Boy's Brigade. Worked for a builder's merchants. Enlisted 1931. Gunlayer on HMS *Queen Elizabeth* and *Rodney*. Boxer. Single, tall, dark, good looking, well built and hard. A thorough professional, engaging and cheerful with a good sense of humour. He set an excellent example, but was apt to be impetuous. Commemorated on the Plymouth Naval Memorial, Panel 102, Column 2.

Appendix IV

'FRANKTON' MEMORIALS

In addition to the formal Commonwealth War Graves Commission commemorations, there are a number of other memorials to the raiders and those who helped them.

BRITAIN

Hero's Stone, North Corner, Devonport – commemorates George Sheard and four others, including three other members of the Sheard family:
Sister Mabel – ARP warden awarded the BEM for pulling bodies from wrecked homes and running through fires to get help.
Brother William – awarded the DSM.
Brother-in-law Harold Siddall – POW for four years.
Mabel unveiled the Stone on 17 September 2002.

Lump's Fort, Southsea – plaque on the site of the RMBPD training base.

Hamworthy, Poole, Dorset – memorial at Royal Marines Poole, home of the SBS, dedicated on 11 January 1983 with Haslar and Sparks in attendance.

The landward entrance to Lump's Fort with a commemorative plaque to the right of the gate.

Haslar and Sparks at the dedication of the 'Frankton" memorial at Royal Marines Poole on 11 January 1983.

233

St Nicholas Church in Bordeaux.

Centre Jean Moulin at 48 Rue Vital-Caries, 33000 Bordeaux is open 1400-1800 Tuesday to Sunday.

FRANCE

Bordeaux

Centre Jean Moulin – on 3 April 1966 a wooden plaque was unveiled by Haslar in the Church of St Nicholas. The church was sold in 1990 and the plaque lodged with the British Consulate in Bordeaux. It can now be seen in the Centre Jean Moulin.

Quai des Chartrons – plaque on the ground in front of Hangar 14 (exhibition centre) unveiled by the Duke of Kent and Mayor of Bordeaux in December 2002. The German ships attacked by Haslar and Sparks were at the quay nearby.

Chateau Magnol, Blanquefort – a plaque on the bullet marked wall of a bunker commemorates where Wallace and Ewart were allegedly executed.

Pointe de Grave

Two memorials erected in 2003 where Wallace and Ewart were captured; a plaque on the lighthouse and a monument near where they came ashore 200m away (face the lighthouse door and take the path to the right).

Memorial plaque to Wallace and Ewart beside the entrance to the Pointe de Grave lighthouse.

Monument near where Wallace and Ewart came ashore 200m from Pointe Grave lighthouse.

Frankton Memorial dedicated on 31 March 2011.

Frankton Souvenir – fifteen plaques record the routes and fate of the escapers and their French helpers. The 100 mile Frankton Trail following Haslar's and Sparks' route was inaugurated on 12 June 2002. On the wall of Chateau de Segonzac north of Blaye is a plaque unveiled on 10 June 2008 to mark the start of the Trail, although it actually starts on the river bank to the west.

The impressive **Frankton Memorial** at Pointe de Grave dedicated on 31 March 2011.

A plaque dedicated to Sheard and Moffatt at the marina at Verdon sur Mer (Port Medoc) in December 2005, can be seen on the outside wall of the Capitainerie (Harbour Master's Office), the building on the left.

Verdon sur Mer – plaque to Sheard and Moffatt outside the Capitainerie (Harbour Master's Office) unveiled in December 2005.

Plaque on the wall of Chateau de Segonzac north of Blaye unveiled on 10 June 2008 to mark the start of the Frankton Trail.

St Georges de Didonne (near Royan) – memorial adjacent to the lighthouse on the headland, overlooking the mouth of the Gironde.

From the St Georges de Didonne memorial looking over the mouth of the Gironde.

Bois Plage en Re Cemetery, Ile de Re – plaque to Sheard and Moffat unveiled on 1 November 2007. David Moffatt (nephew) and Peter Siddall and Ian Taylor (Sheard's nephews) attended. The Cemetery is on the market square.

Nâpres - La Maison de Clodomir is private property, but a plaque unveiled in June 2002 can be viewed on the outside wall.

A plaque unveiled in June 2002 at Nâpres Farm is on the left of the end wall.

Plaque to the left of the entrance to the Hotel l'Angle d'Or in Ruffec, unveiled in December 2002.

The names of Laver and Mills were added to the Montlieu la Garde war memorial on 10 June 2004.

The plaque (left) at Marvaud farm where Hasler and Sparks were sheltered by the Dubreilles.

Ruffec – the former Cafe des Sports has a plaque to the left of the door unveiled in December 2002. It is now the Hotel l'Angle d'Or.

St Vivien du Medoc – memorial erected in 2003 in the car park close to the beach, site of the first hide.

Montlieu la Garde – in a touching gesture, the names of Laver and Mills were added to the town's war memorial on 10 June 2004.

Chez Ouvrard – where Laver and Mills spent their last night before being arrested in Montlieu. A plaque (behind the left hand car) was unveiled on 10 June 2004 by Laver's sisters and Mills' brother.

Cessac – plaque unveiled in December 2005 beside the old railway line, below the farmhouse where the Jauberts sheltered MacKinnon and Conway.

Baigneaux – plaque unveiled in December 2005 to MacKinnon and Conway on the house where they were sheltered by the Pouget family.

St Coutant – plaque (left) on Marvaud Farm where Hasler and Sparks were sheltered after meeting the Resistance at Ruffec. It was unveiled in December 2006 by the British Naval Attache and Amélie Dubreuille.

Memorial erected in 2003 close to the first hide at St Vivien du Medoc.

Plaque unveiled 10 June 2004 by Laver's sisters and Mills' brother at Chez Ouvrard near Montlieu.

Plaque to MacKinnon and Conway in Baigneaux.

La Reole – plaque on the Ancien Hospital where MacKinnon was seized by the Germans. Down the hill (left) is the old women's prison on the east side of Place de Verdun, where it is believed Conway was held.

The Ancien Hospital at La Reole where MacKinnon was seized by the Germans. The plaque beside the door was unveiled on 13 December 2007.

Beaunac – immediately south of the crossroads north of the hamlet is a green with a memorial dedicated to the three inhabitants who were the only French civilians to lose their lives as a result of 'Frankton'.

Memorial dedicated to the three inhabitants of Beaunac who were the only French civilians to lose their lives as a result of 'Frankton'.

Appendix V

SOURCES

Cockleshell Heroes. CR Lucas Phillips 1956.
Winston Churchill's Toyshop. Stuart Macrae 1971.
Axis Blockade Runners of World War II. Martin Brice 1981.
Blondie. SE Southby-Tailyour 1998.
Last of the Cockleshell Heroes. Bill Sparks with Michael Munn 1998.
Cockleshell Commando. Bill Sparks 2002.
The Cockleshell Canoes. Quentin Rees 2008.
The Cockleshell Raid – Bordeaux 1942. Ken Ford 2010.
Cockleshell Heroes. Quentin Rees 2010.

National Archives:
Combined Operations, Admiralty and Cabinet Office files relating to Operation 'Frankton'.
RMBPD War Diary - ADM 202/310.

Websites:
War crimes - http://www.jewishvirtuallibrary.org/jsource/Holocaust/Raeder.html
Blockade runners - http://www.ibiblio.org/hyperwar/ETO/Ultra/SRH-008/SRH008-3.html

INDEX